BARTÓK REMEMBERED

in the same series

RAVEL REMEMBERED
by Roger Nichols
MAHLER REMEMBERED
by Norman Lebrecht

Bartók
Remembered

MALCOLM GILLIES

ISBN 0-393-30744-1

W.W.Norton & Company, Inc.
500 Fifth Avenue, New York, N Y 10110
W.W.Norton & Company, Ltd.
10 Coptic Street, London WC1A 1PU

Printed in Great Britain

1 2 3 4 5 6 7 8 9 0

Contents

List of illustrations

Introduction

Béla Bartók was small and tall, chubby and frail. He possessed a good sense of humour, was dour, polite and cutting. In his musical endeavours he was clear-thinking, misguided, radical and boring. Despite these obvious contradictions, those who knew Bartók have remembered him so. Given differing circumstances, time periods and levels of acquaintance, it is not surprising that this variety of perceptions has emerged of his intellectual, emotional and even physical attributes. Indeed, the degree of consensus of opinion about him is, perhaps, more cause for surprise, especially in light of the individual foibles of his several hundred recollectors and the inevitable games which time plays upon memory.

What was Bartók really like? On one score nearly everybody agrees: he had integrity. Power, love, money or social status could not corrupt him. For forty years, for example, he devoted himself to ethnomusicology, collecting and analysing thousands of folksongs and preparing comprehensive studies of half a dozen national folk musics without serious prospect of financial reward, academic recognition, or, in most instances, even publication. In 1940, when his personal circumstance was so grim, he would not accept a lucrative post as a composition professor in America on the ground that to teach composition was to imperil his own composing – a line of argument he had already upheld for over thirty years. On another score there is widespread agreement: he was a hard person to be with. Few could feel really comfortable in his presence. Those penetrating Magyar eyes radiated the same intensity as his clipped multi-lingual tongue. He knew well his own mind and self-appointed mission, and saw no virtue in circumlocution or in furthering the polite banalities of social intercourse. His piano students were sometimes driven to distraction over his uncompromising insistence on exactly the right turn of phrase or rhythmic realization. Although a dutiful and loving family man, he could not completely accommodate domestic demands, which habitually had to take second place to the latest musical task at hand.

In combination, this integrity and personal inflexibility caused Bartók's life to be more fraught and less immediately rewarding than it might have been. As some writers have suggested, his external brittleness functioned like a mask, which with only limited success shielded a naturally shy, super-sensitive yet determined individual from the hurly-burly of the world. His chronic hostility to the promotion of his own endeavours was in stark contrast to the slick PR of such consequentially better-known contemporaries as Stravinsky or Richard Strauss. Even his students were actively discouraged by him from learning his own works. Were they, perhaps, threatening this sanctum of his inner sound world by attempting to do so? Not unexpectedly, at the time of his death in 1945 recognition of the consistently high quality of his compositions was only starting to seep beyond the fringes of specialist contemporary music groups into the wider listening public, where it is now belatedly – sometimes still grudgingly – recognized amid the first tier of twentieth-century composition.

Bartók Remembered presents nearly one hundred recollections of Bartók, from his mother's tale of his earliest years in provincial Hungary of the 1880s, to assorted reminiscences of his lingering illness and death in New York. These recollections have been selected from a large, sometimes obscure literature, with the intention of providing a broad-canvassed collage of the man in private and in public. Aspects of his austere private life are depicted by his two sons, two wives, mother, and a few close friends. His public life was, however, much more varied than is generally recognized. As a musician Bartók was engaged in performance, teaching, musicology and composition, and he gained an international reputation in all four areas. He travelled widely, performing most in Hungary, the United States, Britain and Germany. He spoke and wrote fluently in Hungarian, German, English and French, and knew half a dozen other languages reasonably well. This volume tries to capture something of that range of achievement and contact. It was, of course, inevitable that a majority of the reminiscences would come from Hungarians or Hungarian émigrés, but this selection also seeks to set Bartók against the wider international backdrop of his career. His fitful advancement and recognition owed more to his reception outside Hungary than within, where he was often snubbed and came to behave as a disgruntled internal exile. German, Austrian, British, French, Swiss, Spanish, Belgian, Dutch, Romanian, Australian, Turkish, Russian and American recollections of this volume recall a variety of the impressions he created when away from home. This plurality of sources also serves to allay the simplistic stereotypes of Bartók which have resulted from the application of 'cold war' ideologies to music scholarship. The latter-day Hungarian national hero portrayed on the 1,000-forint banknote and elaborated in some older East European writing is a hagiographic manufacture devoid of the needed warts of humanity. So, too, the visions of the downtrodden, sick and penniless Bartók negotiating the uncaring canyons of capitalist New York, or of the vigorous anti-Communist of those same years, are popular blends of fact and fiction now deserving closer scrutiny. The nearest one can come to the reality of his personality and activity is probably in a comparison of the lines of these varied recollections and, equally importantly, in sustained reading between those lines. When asked for recollections most people are afraid 'to speak ill of the dead', but they frequently betray their true feelings in particular turns of phrase, a heightened rhetorical temperature or some fancy footwork around sensitive areas, all of which should be discernible to the vigilant reader. And a few of those represented felt no inhibitions whatsoever when speaking of the departed.

As Bartók was an aloof and abstemious character – in 1910 he wrote to Delius that Kodály was his only friend in Budapest, and he had 'nobody to talk to' – there are fewer, genuine 'good stories' about him in circulation than for the majority of leading artistic figures. (His compatriot Liszt was more of a bon vivant and has suffered from no such problem.) As a result, many of his acquaintances have had to dine out on narrowly based, even prosaic, experiences of the man. Over the years some have allowed trivial incidents or comments to assume a greater importance than we know to have been the case. (Bartók's personal correspondence provides a healthy antidote to the claims of several posthumously aspiring 'close friends'.) Others have, perhaps innocently, conflated events scattered in time or place into one distilled impression. In compiling this volume, then, I have preferred earlier to later recollections – those from the 1940s and 1950s are often the most accurate and unsensational – and have included a small number of diary and Press recollections written during Bartók's lifetime, as something of a counter-balance to the occasional blurring of focus of the ageing. Where important errors of fact or interpretation have occurred, a comment appears either in the introductory paragraphs or in square brackets within the text. *Bartók Remembered* is, however, a book of memories, not expurgated facts, and the veracity of its contributors' claims should not always be assumed.

Through its very process of selection and presentation of material this book presents a personal image, crafted by the author using the words of others. Let me, then, pre-empt would-be critics by making the following points. This volume, while attempting to be broad in scope, is compiled on the basis of contribution to a constantly developing image rather than any ranking of importance among contributors. The recollections of certain important figures in Bartók's life – Ernő Dohnányi, André Gertler, his sister Elza, to name a few – do not even appear, while many based on only casual acquaintance are included. The reasons for the omission of these 'greats' are several: pen was never put to paper; a recollection could not be accessed; copyright permission could not be secured or its terms were unfavourable; the recollection was simply too repetitive of images already expounded, too contaminated by the recollections of others, or just too pedestrian. A second point concerns the division of material into broad periods or activity groupings, a process which, given the free-wheeling nature of many of the recollections, is crude, but allows for a roughly chronological progression through the volume. This division results in nearly half the volume ending up under the chapter for the years 1920 to 1940, but something of this sort was inevitable as it was in those two decades that Bartók was most prominent in all of his musical activities. Lastly, the horrors of East European place-names are compounded in this volume by the frequent inclusion of present-day alternatives. This is not some pedantic form of punishment dreamed up for the reader but a necessity because of the massive changes over the last century in the political geography of what was the Austro-Hungarian Empire. Most of these changes were caused by the Treaty of Trianon in 1920 whereby Hungary lost well over half its land area. Not one of the provincial towns in which Bartók lived during the 1880s and 1890s remained in Hungary, and all assumed new names – in three different countries. Pozsony, where Bartók had spent his teenage years, ceased officially to exist. It became Bratislava in the new country of Czechoslovakia.

Acknowledgements

To the following I am grateful for permission to reproduce extracts (full references to sources are provided at the end of each passage): Béla Bartók Jun. for his own recollections, and those of his mother (Márta Ziegler) and grandmother (Paula Voit); Edmée Arma (for the recollection of Arma); Käte Roth (Roth); Vicky Bijur (Reis); Jean and Julianne Székely (Székely); Clara Waters (Hatvany); the Artisjus Agency, Budapest (Molnár, Balázs, Vámos, Hernádi, Antal, Gergely, Rácz, Britten); the Estate of Cecil Gray; Lillias M. Forbes (Erik and Diana Chisholm); the heirs of Randall Thompson; Jill Lockhart (Buesst); David Clegg (Buesst); David Dalton (Primrose, Serly); Annette von Wangenheim (Szenkár); Reginald R. Gerig (Sándor, first recollection); the Archives of the Peabody Institute of the Johns Hopkins University (Veress); Nationale Schweizerische UNESCO-Kommission (Ansermet); Grainger Museum, Melbourne (Grainger); BBC Written Archives Centre, Reading (Whitaker, second recollection); Paul Sacher; Péter Bartók; Tibor Polgár; Hans W. Heinsheimer; Sir Georg Solti; György Sándor; Storm Bull; Sándor Veress; Sir Yehudi Menuhin; Alfred A. Knopf, Inc., New York (Leichtentritt, Rothe and Szigeti, second recollection); Boosey & Hawkes Music Publishers Ltd, London (Szabolcsi, Péter Bartók, Hawkes, Dille and Kodály); Oxford University Press, Inc., New York (Sacher, Saygun, Gombosi and Lang); John Calder (Publishers) Ltd, London (Krenek); Faber and Faber Ltd, London (Cohen, Tippett, Klemperer, Bartók and Stravinsky, second recollection); Leykam Buchverlag, Graz (Jemnitz); the State University of New York Press, Albany (Herzog); Occidental Press, Washington DC (Domonkos, Holló); Methuen & Co. Ltd, London (Goossens); J.M. Dent and Sons, London (Weissmann); Houghton Mifflin Co., Boston, for the recollection of Agatha Fassett (© 1958, renewed 1986 by Agatha Fassett); Theodore Presser Company, Bryn Mawr, for the recollections of Földes (© 1955, *The Etude Magazine*) and Balogh (© 1956, *The Etude Magazine*); the editors of the following journals: *Music and Letters* (Gerson-Kiwi, Serly, Primrose); *Muzsika* (Albrecht, Martinov, Copland, Lajtha, Lopes Graça); *Studia Musicologica* (Pávai

Vajna, Béla Bartók Jun., second recollection); *The New Hungarian Quarterly* (Lukács-Popper, Hatvany); *Oesterreichische Musikzeitschrift* (Ditta Pásztory); *The Musical Times* (Whitaker, first recollection); *Tempo*, on behalf of Boosey & Hawkes Music Publishers Ltd (Doráti, second recollections of Földes and Balogh).

To the following I am grateful for permission to reproduce illustrations: György Sándor (p. 189), Hans W. Heinsheimer (p. 191), Käte Roth (p. 120), Jean Székely (p. 126), Tibor Polgár (p. 98), Jill Lockhart (p. 76). All other photographs are reproduced courtesy of Béla Bartók Jun. and the Budapest Bartók Archive.

While every reasonable effort has been made to secure permissions, it may be that in a small number of cases the relevant copyright holder has not been traced. Any such holders who have not received proper acknowledgement are requested to notify the publisher so that the matter can be rectified in subsequent editions.

I acknowledge the assistance of Adrienne Gombocz, Judit Rácz, Hilde Schmidt and Kerry Murphy in the revision of translations, and David Pear for the initial translation of the recollection of Milhaud. To the following I am indebted for their considerable, practical assistance in the compilation of this book: Béla Bartók Jun., Péter Bartók, László Somfai, Adrienne Gombocz, András Wilheim, Tibor Tallián, Helen Kasztelan, the Hungarian Academy of Sciences' Institute of Musicology, the Oesterreichische Nationalbibliothek, the British Library, the New York Public Library, the State Library of Victoria and the University of Melbourne. I also express my gratitude to János Demény, Ferenc Bónis and Denijs Dille, whose studies of the last forty years have proven invaluable to the writing of this volume, and to Patrick Carnegy, Helen Sprott, Helen Gray and Mavis Pindard at Faber and Faber who bore with my tardy fulfilment of their commission.

Chronology

BARTÓK'S LIFE AND WORKS

1881 25 Mar. Béla Viktor János Bartók is born in Nagyszentmiklós,
Hungary (now Sînnicolau Mare, Romania), son of Béla
Bartók (1855–88) and Paula Bartók (née Voit, 1857–
1939), both teachers and amateur musicians

      June Vaccination for smallpox induces skin rash which lasts for five
years

1882 June Already distinguishes between different dance pieces

1883 Summer Begins to speak in sentences

1884 Mar. Receives first musical instrument, a drum

1885 June Birth of sister, Erzsébet (Elza)

1886 Mar. Begins piano lessons with mother

1887 Decline in father's health

1888 Aug. Father dies of Addison's disease in Nagyszentmiklós

1889 Sept. Family moves to Nagyszőllős (now Vinogradov, Ukraine),
where mother teaches in the local primary school, and
Bartók repeats fourth class

1890 July Gains school report with eight excellent and two very good
grades (gymnastics and singing)

      Starts first opus numbering of compositions, with Waltz, Op. 1

1891 Mar. In Budapest Károly Aggházy tests and confirms Bartók's
musical talents, and offers to take him as a pupil. Offer
declined

      Aug. Enters grammar school at Nagyvárad (now Oradea,
Romania). Boards with aunt and takes professional piano
lessons

1892 Apr. Returns to Nagyszőllős

      May First public performance, in Nagyszőllős, including his own
piano piece *The Course of the Danube*

      Summer Family moves to Pozsony (now Bratislava, Czechoslovakia),
where he enrols in the second form of the Catholic grammar
school, and takes piano lessons with László Erkel

1893 July Gains school report with two very good, five good and one
satisfactory grade (gymnastics)

	Sept.	Family moves to Beszterce (now Bistriţa, Romania), where he enrols in third form of the local German-language grammar school
	Oct.	Birth of Márta Ziegler, Bartók's first wife
1894	Apr.	Family moves back to Pozsony, where Bartók's mother works in a teacher-training college. He returns to the grammar school and to piano lessons with László Erkel
		Starts second opus numbering of compositions, with Sonata No. 1 in G minor, Op. 1
1895	June	Gains school report with six very good and two good grades
	Sept.	Succeeds Ernő (Ernst von) Dohnányi as organist at school services
1896	Dec.	László Erkel dies; new piano teacher is Anton Hyrtl
1897	June	Gains school report with five very good, two good (German, mathematics) and one satisfactory (Latin) grade
	Nov.	Performs Liszt's *Spanish Rhapsody* in a school concert
1898	Mar.	Performs his own Piano Sonata (DD51) in Pozsony
	Nov.	Performs movements from his own Piano Quartet (DD52) in Pozsony
	Dec.	Visits Vienna, where he is offered a place and scholarship at the Conservatory. Decides, following Dohnányi's example, to study in Budapest
1899	Jan.	Visits the Budapest Academy of Music, where he is warmly received by István Thomán (piano), who recommends him to János Koessler (composition)
	Feb.	Suddenly falls seriously ill with suspected tuberculosis; continues school studies at home
	June	Gains final school matriculation report with three very good grades (probably in mathematics, physics, religion), and four good grades (Hungarian, Latin, Greek, German)
	Sept.	Admitted to Budapest Academy of Music. Second-year studies in piano (under Thomán); second/third-year in composition (Koessler). Attends many concerts and operas in his first year in Budapest
	Oct.	Relapse in health, causing absence during much of first term

1900 June   Gains fine results in all Academy subjects

     Aug.   Falls ill with pneumonia, and is unable to return to Academy.
                 Later goes to south Tyrol to recuperate

1901 Apr.   Returns to Academy, undertaking third-year piano and
                 fourth-year composition studies. Does not take examinations
                 in June, but starts to repeat these subjects in September

     Oct.   Gains huge success playing Liszt's B minor Sonata at an
                 Academy student concert. Interest in the works of Liszt and
                 Wagner strengthens

1902 Feb.   Attends Budapest première of Strauss's *Also sprach Zarathustra*
                 and is encouraged to resume serious composition under its
                 influence

     June   Gains excellent or very good grades in all Academy subjects
                 and a special commendation from the Director

1903 Jan.   Performs to considerable acclaim his own transcription of
                 Strauss's *Ein Heldenleben* in Budapest and Vienna (his first
                 public appearance outside Hungary)

     Apr.   Presents first public solo recital, at Nagyszentmiklós

     June   Completion of Academy studies and meeting with Hans
                 (János) Richter, who agrees to perform his symphonic poem
                 Kossuth in Manchester

     Summer   Receives piano lessons from Dohnányi

     Oct.   Birth of Edith (Ditta) Pásztory, Bartók's second wife

     Dec.   Public recital in Berlin, which Godowsky and Busoni attend

1904 Jan.–   Performances of *Kossuth* in Budapest, then Manchester,
     Feb.   followed by visits to London and Berlin

     Summer   Spends several months in Gerlicepuszta, Slovakia, where his
                 interest in folk music is aroused

                 Completes Piano Quintet
                 First printed scores issued by Bárd (*Pósa songs* and Four Piano
                 Pieces)
                 Start of third opus numbering of compositions, with piano
                 Rhapsody, Op. 1, and Scherzo for piano and orchestra,
                 Op. 2

1905 Mar.   Performs Liszt's *Totentanz* in Budapest to critical acclaim

Aug.	Takes part in the Rubinstein Competition in Paris, both as pianist and composer. Is unsuccessful in both categories but stays on in Paris for several weeks
	Starts to collaborate with Zoltán Kodály in collecting, transcribing and arranging folk music (to 1940) Composes First Suite, for full orchestra, Op.3, and first three movements of Second Suite, for small orchestra, Op.4
1906 Mar.– Apr.	Tours Spain and Portugal with the violinst Ferenc Vecsey Publication of Bartók–Kodály (Twenty) Hungarian Folksongs Start of annual folk collecting expeditions using Edison phonograph. Collecting tour to Slovakia
1907 Jan.	Appointed to piano staff of Budapest Academy of Music, as successor to his own teacher István Thomán
July– Aug.	Collecting tour in Transylvania, where he discovers the pentatonic basis to much Hungarian folk music
	Growing interest in the music of Debussy and Reger Completes Second Suite, Op.4, incorporating folk melody into final movement, and arrangements of Three Hungarian Folksongs from the Csík district, for piano, and Four Slovak Folksongs
1908 Jan., Mar.	First article about folk music published, in Budapest
June	Meeting with Busoni in Vienna, who recommends his 14 Bagatelles, Op.6, for publication
Oct.	First experiences with Romanian folk music
	Issue by the Budapest publishers Rozsnyai of Bartók's first instructive edition, of Bach's *Das Wohltemperierte Klavier* Completes First Violin Concerto; composes many piano pieces, including 14 Bagatelles, Ten Easy Pieces, and a number of the Op.8, Op.9 and *For Children* pieces
1909 Jan.	Conducts the Berlin Philharmonic Orchestra in a performance of the Scherzo from his Second Suite
Nov.	Marries Márta Ziegler in Budapest
	Commences work on an instructive edition of 25 Beethoven piano sonatas (to 1912) Completes First String Quartet, Op.7, and a variety of piano pieces

1910 Mar.   His works feature in 'Festival Hongrois', Paris; First String
                Quartet premièred in Budapest by Waldbauer–Kerpely
                Quartet

     Aug.   Birth of a son, Béla

                Commences work on an instructive edition of 20 Mozart
                piano sonatas (to 1912)
                Composes *Two Pictures* for orchestra, Op. 10

1911 Apr.   Kodály, Bartók and friends found the New Hungarian
                Musical Society, but the enterprise soon fails

                First String Quartet performed in numerous European
                centres.
                Commences work on an instructive edition of 17 Haydn piano
                sonatas (to 1913); works on editions of Schumann and
                Schubert piano pieces; commences editorial work for the
                Liszt critical edition (to 1917)
                Completes *Two Portraits*, Op. 5; composes the opera
                Duke Bluebeard's Castle, Op. 11, and *Allegro barbaro*

1912 June–   Holidays with his wife in Scandinavia
     Aug.

     Oct.   Draws up plans for a folk music collecting expedition to
                Russia, eventually not undertaken

                Folk music collecting tours continue within Hungary
                Withdraws from Budapest concert life, although continues to
                teach at the Academy of Music
                Composes Four Orchestral Pieces, Op. 12 (orchestration,
                1921)

1913 June–   Travels with his wife to north Africa, where he collects folk
     July   music

                His first book about folk music, *Chansons populaires roumaines
                du département Bihar (Hongrie)*, appears in Romanian and
                French in Bucharest
                Composes simple pieces for Bartók–Reschofsky piano method,
                issued separately as *First Term at the Piano*

1914 June–   Travels in France, returning home just before war is declared
     July

     Nov.   Rejected for military service

                Starts to compose the ballet *The Wooden Prince*, Op. 13

1915   Several folk music collecting trips to Slovakia
               Composes piano works including Sonatina, Romanian Folk
               Dances, Romanian Christmas Songs; starts to compose
               Second String Quartet, Op. 17, and Five Songs, Op. 15

1916 Aug.   Romania enters the war, on Allied side. The threat of
               Romanian advances into Transylvania causes Bartók
               domestic anxieties and further restricts his expeditions

               Further collecting trips to Slovakia
               Completes instructive edition of Bach's 'Anna Magdalena'
               pieces
               Composes piano Suite, Op. 14, Five 'Ady' Songs, Op. 16;
               completes *The Wooden Prince* (except for some
               orchestration)

1917 May   Première of the ballet *The Wooden Prince* in Budapest,
               conducted by Egisto Tango

     July   Takes Tango on a folk music collecting tour in central
               Hungary

     Sept.   Article on north African folk music is published in Budapest

               Commences work on a series of instructive editions of piano
               studies by Duvernoy, Köhler and Heller
               Completes Eight Hungarian Folksongs, Second String
               Quartet, Slovak Folksongs, Four Slovak Folksongs

1918 May   Première of the opera *Duke Bluebeard's Castle*, Op. 11, in
               Budapest, conducted by Egisto Tango

     July–   Final folk music collecting expeditions in Hungary
     Aug.

     Oct.   Contracts Spanish influenza and is confined to bed for 23 days

               Universal Edition, Vienna, starts to publish his compositions
               Completes Fifteen Hungarian Peasant Songs; composes Three
               Studies, Op. 18, for piano; starts to compose pantomime
               The Miraculous Mandarin, Op. 19

1919 Apr.   Joins Kodály, Dohnányi and Reinitz, on the Music
               Directorate of the Communist Republic of Councils.
               Re-emerges into Budapest concert life

     Aug.   Romanian soldiers occupy Bartók's home near Budapest.
               He collects folksongs from them

	Sept.	Takes short-term leave from his teaching at the Academy of Music
		Growing sense of depression at political, military and civil strife
		Completes *The Miraculous Mandarin* (except for orchestration)
1920	Feb.–Mar.	Visits Berlin for concerts and re-establishment of contacts
	May	Attacked in the Hungarian Press for writing 'Romanian propaganda' in his newly published study of Romanian music of the Hunyad county
		Considers emigration to various European countries or to the US, but finally decides to stay in Hungary
		Instructive editions of two Haydn sonatas, as well as Chopin and Beethoven compositions, are published in Budapest; commences work on editions of Scarlatti sonatas
		Feels he is approaching a 'twelve-tone' goal in his composition; composes Improvisations, Op. 20, for piano
1921	Mar.	Special Bartók issue of *Musikblätter des Anbruch* (Vienna), in celebration of his fortieth birthday
		Plans for international concert tours and writes many articles about Hungarian music for foreign journals
		Completes his joint study with Kodály of 150 (Hungarian) Transylvanian folksongs; reaches agreement, never implemented, for publication of his Slovak folk music collection with a Slovak publisher
		Composes First Violin Sonata for violinist Jelly d'Arányi
1922	Mar.–May	Highly successful concert tours of Transylvania, Britain, France and Germany. Makes valuable contacts with many leading personalities, resulting in numerous concert and lecture tours over the following two decades
	Aug.	Takes part in a concert series in Salzburg, at which the International Society for Contemporary Music (ISCM) is founded
		Composes Second Violin Sonata
1923	July–Aug.	Divorces his first wife, Márta Ziegler; marries Ditta Pásztory
		Tours frequently in many European countries
		His volume *Volksmusik der Rumänen von Maramureş* is published in Munich

Composes the Dance Suite, in celebration of the fiftieth anniversary of the union of Buda and Pest

1924 July   Birth of a son, Péter

A magyar népdal (The Hungarian folksong) is published in Budapest (also Berlin, 1925; London, 1931)
Edition of eighteen pieces by Couperin is published in Budapest
Composes *Village Scenes* for voice and piano

1925   Continues European concert tours, including visits to Czechoslovakia, Italy, Holland
Dance Suite gains increasing popularity internationally
Composes nothing in this year, and claims he is an 'ex-composer'; spends much of the year working on his lengthy study of Romanian Christmas songs (colinde)

1926 Mar.   Makes first radio appearance, in Budapest, playing compositions of Beethoven, Scarlatti, Debussy and Bartók

Apr.   Completes his study of Romanian Christmas songs

Nov.   Controversial première of the pantomime *The Miraculous Mandarin* takes place in Cologne

Bartók's 'piano year', in which he composes Sonata, *Out of Doors* suite, Nine Little Piano Pieces, First Piano Concerto, and the first of what would become the *Mikrokosmos* collection. These works evidence a heightened concern for counterpoint, reflecting his renewed interest in Bach's music

1927 July   Premières his First Piano Concerto in Frankfurt am Main under Wilhelm Furtwängler

Dec.   Coast-to-coast concert tour of the US (to Feb. 1928) with mixed receptions from audiences

Completes Three Rondos on Folk Tunes, for piano; composes Third String Quartet

1928 Oct.   Lectures at a world congress on folk music in Prague; awarded joint first prize, with Alfredo Casella, in the Musical Fund Society of Philadelphia's string quartet competition for his Third String Quartet

Dec.   Makes first gramophone recordings of his own works, in Budapest

		Composes First and Second Violin Rhapsodies, and Fourth String Quartet
1929	Jan.–Apr.	Intensive concert activity at home and abroad, performing in the Soviet Union, Switzerland, Denmark, Germany, Britain, Holland, France, Italy
		Works on transcription of two Purcell preludes (published posthumously)
		Composes Twenty Hungarian Folksongs
1930		Publication of piano transcriptions of Baroque Italian keyboard music and a Bach organ sonata
		Publication, in German, of the first full-length study of Bartók's works, by Edwin von der Nüll
		Composes *Cantata Profana*
1931	Mar.	Awarded the Corvin Medal by the Hungarian Government but does not attend the ceremony
	July	Attends his first meeting, in Geneva, as a member of the Permanent Committee for Literature and the Arts of the League of Nations' Commission for Intellectual Cooperation. Fellow delegates include Mann, Valéry, Čapek and Gilbert Murray
	July–Aug.	Teaches piano, composition and theory at an Austro-American summer school
		Completes Second Piano Concerto; composes 44 Duos for violin
1932	Mar.	Attends conference on Arabic music in Cairo, along with Hindemith and Wellesz
	Apr.	Moves to his final home in Budapest, 27 (later 29) Csalán út
	Sept.	Confined to bed for the entire month with influenza
		Composes *Székely Songs*, for male chorus
1933	Jan.	Premières his Second Piano Concerto in Frankfurt am Main under Hans Rosbaud (his last appearance in Germany)
	Apr.	Attends ISCM Congress in Florence, along with Strauss, Berg, Wellesz, Roussel and Kodály
1934	May	Première of *Cantata Profana* in London, conducted by Aylmer Buesst

July–Sept.	Negotiates release from the Budapest Academy of Music and attachment to the folk music section of the Hungarian Academy of Sciences

Composes Fifth String Quartet

1935 Dec. Awarded the Greguss Prize for his First Suite of 1905. He refuses to accept the prize

Publication, in Vienna, at Bartók's own expense, of *Melodien der rumänischen Colinde (Weihnachtslieder)*
First post-war revival of the ballet *The Wooden Prince* in Budapest; first South American performance of this ballet, in Buenos Aires
Composes *From Olden Times*

1936 Feb. Presents his inaugural address as a member of the Hungarian Academy of Sciences on the subject 'Liszt problems'

Nov. Lecture, concert and folk collecting tour of Turkey

Completes *27 Choruses*; composes Music for Strings, Percussion and Celesta
First post-war revival of the opera *Duke Bluebeard's Castle* in Budapest

1937 Jan. Première of Music for Strings, Percussion and Celesta in Basle, conducted by Paul Sacher

Sept. Forbids relay broadcasts of his concerts to German or Italian radio stations

Composes Sonata for Two Pianos and Percussion

1938 Jan. Première in Basle of Sonata for Two Pianos and Percussion, with Bartók and his wife as the pianists (Ditta's concert début)

Mar. With Germany's annexation of Austria, he seeks to break his publishing and copyright links with Vienna; enters into negotiations with Boosey & Hawkes (London), who start to publish his works in the following year

Apr. Starts to send his most valuable manuscripts out of Hungary, initially to Switzerland, and then via Britain to the US, where they remain today

June Takes part in ISCM London Festival (his last appearance in Britain)

		Composes *Contrasts*, to a commission from Benny Goodman; completes Second Violin Concerto
1939	Feb.– Mar.	Final concert tour, with his wife, of Switzerland and France
	Sept.	Initially cancels concert engagements on the outbreak of war
	Dec.	Final Italian concert tour, with his wife. His mother dies. He is too ill and depressed to attend the funeral
		Completes *Mikrokosmos* collection of 153 progressive piano pieces and associated exercises; composes Divertimento, Sixth String Quartet
1940	Apr.– May	Visits the US for concerts, lectures; makes preparations for emigration before returning home
	Oct.	The Bartóks give a farewell concert in Budapest before leaving for the US, via Portugal
	Nov.	Awarded an honorary doctorate at Columbia University and settles in New York
		Arranges the Sonata for Two Pianos and Percussion as a concerto
1941	Feb.– Mar.	Undertakes a coast-to-coast concert tour with his wife.
	Mar.	Takes up position as a short-term research fellow working on Serbo-Croatian folk music at Columbia University (later extended to the end of 1942)
	July– Sept.	Holidays with his wife at the home of Agatha Fassett in Vermont
	Nov.– Dec.	Undertakes concert and lecture tour to the west coast
		Arranges the Second Suite, Op.4, for two pianos
1942	Apr.	His son Péter arrives in New York, after a four-month journey from Hungary. His own health begins to decline
		Dwindling concert, lecturing and publishing opportunities
1943	Jan.	Final concert appearance, with his wife, at the American première of his Concerto for Two Pianos, Percussion and Orchestra in New York
	Feb.	Delivers series of lectures at Harvard University

	May	American Society of Composers, Authors and Publishers takes on responsibility for his medical treatment
	June	Completes the manuscript of his study of Turkish folk music (published in 1976)
	July–Oct.	Spends the summer at Saranac Lake, New York, where he composes the Concerto for Orchestra
	Dec.	Winters at Asheville, North Carolina (to Apr. 1944)
1944	Feb.–Mar.	Composes Sonata for Solo Violin in Asheville
	July–Oct.	Again spends the summer at Saranac Lake
	Oct.	Moves to final New York apartment at 309 West 57th Street
	Dec.	Completes the manuscript of his study of Serbo-Croatian folksongs (published in 1951)
1945	Mar.	Completes final revision of his monumental study of Romanian folk music (published in 1967–75)
	June	Finalizes plans for lecturing at Harvard University in 1946
	July–Aug.	Vacations, with his wife, at Saranac Lake, where he composes most of the Third Piano Concerto and drafts the Viola Concerto. Starts to sketch his Seventh String Quartet. Returns to New York as health fails
	26 Sept.	Around noon, dies of leukaemia in West Side Hospital, New York, five days after admission
	28 Sept.	Is buried in Ferncliff Cemetery, Westchester County, New York. In 1988 his remains are returned to Hungary for reburial

CONTEMPORARY PERSONALITIES AND EVENTS

1881	Myaskovsky born
	Mussorgsky, Vieuxtemps die
	Brahms, Tragic Overture; Bruckner, Sixth Symphony
	Picasso, Pope John XXIII, Alexander Fleming born
	Assassinations of President Garfield (US) and Alexander II (Russia)
	Pasteur demonstrates virtues of vaccination against anthrax
	First electric trams, in Berlin
	Henry James, *Portrait of a Lady*

1882 Stravinsky, Kodály, Szymanowski, Grainger born
Première of Wagner's *Parsifal* (Bayreuth)
Berlin Philharmonic Orchestra founded
Triple Alliance formed between Germany, Austria–Hungary
 and Italy

1883 Casella, Webern born
Wagner dies
Brahms, Third Symphony; Delibes, *Lakmé*
Mussolini born
Marx dies
Secret alliance formed between Austria–Hungary and
 Romania
First run of the Orient Express
Stevenson, *Treasure Island*

1884 Smetana dies
Bruckner, *Te Deum*
Opening of the Budapest Opera House
Formalization of African and Pacific territories by European
 powers
Greenwich meridian established internationally as prime
 meridian
Twain, *Adventures of Huckleberry Finn*

1885 Berg, Klemperer born
Franck, *Symphonic Variations*; Sullivan, *The Mikado*
D. H. Lawrence born
Serbian invasion of Bulgaria, leading to Peace of Bucharest
 (1886)
Galton proves individuality of fingerprints
Nietzsche, *Also sprach Zarathustra*

1886 Liszt dies
Saint-Saëns, *Carnival of the Animals*
Kokoschka born
Manufacture of first motor car by Daimler
Krafft-Ebing, *Psychopathia Sexualis*
Dicey, *The Law of the Constitution*

1887 Nadia Boulanger born
Borodin dies
Verdi, *Otello*
Chagall, Chiang Kai-shek born
First Colonial Conference, London
Hertz produces radio waves
Sardou, *La Tosca*

1888	Alkan dies Mahler, First Symphony; R. Strauss, *Don Juan*, Tchaikovsky, Fifth Symphony T. S. Eliot, T. E. Lawrence born William II becomes German Kaiser Suez Canal declared open to all nations Dunlop invents pneumatic tyre; box camera invented Van Gogh, *Sunflowers*
1889	Sullivan, *The Gondoliers*; R. Strauss, *Tod und Verklärung* Hitler, Cocteau, Chaplin born Paris International Exhibition; Eiffel Tower completed Crown Prince Rudolf (Austria–Hungary) commits suicide

1890	Franck dies
	Mascagni, *Cavalleria Rusticana*; Satie, *Trois Gnossiènnes*
	Ho Chi Minh, Eisenhower, de Gaulle born
	Van Gogh dies
	Bismarck dismissed as German Chancellor
	Start of period of rapid industrial expansion in Hungary
	    (to 1906)
	Population of Hungary 13.7 million, of which 47 per cent are
	    native Hungarian speakers (18 per cent Romanian, 14 per
	    cent German, 14 per cent Slovak)

1891	Bliss, Prokofiev born Delibes dies Brahms, Clarinet Quintet Trans-Siberian railway started Pan-German League founded Pope Leo XIII's encyclical *Rerum novarum* on working conditions
1892	Honegger, Milhaud born Leoncavallo, *I Pagliacci* Nijinsky, Tito born Tennyson, Whitman die Major earthquake in California Toulouse-Lautrec, *At the Moulin Rouge*

1893	Tchaikovsky, Gounod, Ferenc Erkel die
	Tchaikovsky, Sixth Symphony ('Pathétique'); Puccini, *Manon
	    Lescaut*; Dvořák, Ninth Symphony ('New World'); Verdi,
	    Falstaff
	Göring, Mao Tse-tung born
	Judson invents zip fastener
	Wilde, *Salome*

1894   Debussy, *Prélude à l'après-midi d'un faune*; Mahler, Second
        Symphony ('Resurrection')
        Khrushchev born; Kossuth dies
        Nicholas II becomes (last) Russian Tsar
        Dreyfus trial in Paris

1895   Hindemith born
        Dvořák, Cello Concerto in B minor
        Pasteur dies
        Marconi transmits messages by wireless; Röntgen discovers
        X-rays; first public demonstration of moving pictures by
        Lumière brothers
        Freud, *Studien über Hysterie*
        Wilde, *The Importance of Being Earnest*

1896   Bruckner dies
        R. Strauss, *Also sprach Zarathustra*; Puccini, *La Bohème*;
        Giordano, *Andrea Chénier*
        Verlaine dies
        First modern Olympic Games held in Athens
        Celebrations of the Hungarian millennium

1897   Brahms dies
        Dukas, *The Sorcerer's Apprentice*
        Second Colonial Conference, London
        War between Greece and Turkey
        Pissarro, *Boulevard des Italiens*

1898   Dohnányi, First Piano Concerto; R. Strauss, *Ein Heldenleben*
        Hemingway born; Mallarmé, Bismarck die
        Spanish–American War; First German Navy Bill hastens
        naval expansion
        Empress Elizabeth (Austria–Hungary) murdered in Geneva
        Discovery of radium by the Curies
        Zeppelin invents airship

1899   Poulenc born
        Schoenberg, *Verklärte Nacht*; Elgar, *Enigma Variations*;
        Sibelius, First Symphony
        The Hague Peace Conference; outbreak of Boer War
        Aspirin is invented
        Monet starts *Water Lilies* paintings (to 1926)

1900   Weill, Krenek, Copland born
        Sullivan dies
        Puccini, *Tosca*; Sibelius, *Finlandia*; Mahler, Fourth
        Symphony

Nietzsche, Wilde die
Boxer rebellion in China
Planck details quantum theory
Chekhov, *Uncle Vanya*

1901   Verdi dies
Ravel, *Jeux d'eau*, Rakhmaninov, Second Piano Concerto;
   Dohnányi, First Symphony
Disney born
Queen Victoria dies
Start of defence appropriation crisis in Hungarian parliament
Munch, *Girls on the Bridge*
Thomas Mann, *Buddenbrooks*

1902   Walton born
Debussy, *Pelléas et Mélisande*; Mahler, Fifth Symphony;
   Delius, *Appalachia*
Khomeini born
Zola, Rhodes die
End of Boer War; renewal of Triple Alliance between
   Germany, Austria-Hungary and Italy
Bayliss and Starling discover hormones
Conrad, *Youth*

1903   L. Berkeley born
Wolf dies
Sibelius, Violin Concerto; Schoenberg, *Pelleas und Melisande*
Pissarro, Gauguin die
Menshevist/Bolshevist split in Russian Communist Party
First premiership of I. Tisza in Hungary (to 1905)
First controlled aeroplane flight by Wright brothers
Hofmannsthal, *Elektra*
Shaw, *Man and Superman*

1904   Dvořák dies
Puccini, *Madama Butterfly*; Janáček, *Jenůfa*
Chekhov, Jókai die
Establishment of *Entente cordiale* between France and Britain
Start of Russo-Japanese War (to 1905)
Barrie, *Peter Pan*; Chekhov, *The Cherry Orchard*

1905   Tippett, C. Lambert born
Debussy, *La Mer*; R. Strauss, *Salome*; Lehár, *The Merry Widow*
Abortive revolution in Russia
Einstein enunciates his first theory of relativity
Freud, *Three Treatises on the Theory of Sex*

1906   Shostakovich born
        Schoenberg, First Chamber Symphony; Kodály, *Summer
            Evening*; Smyth, *The Wreckers*
        Cézanne, Ibsen die
        Stolypin introduces agrarian reforms in Russia

1907   Grieg, Joachim die
        Auden born
        Triple Entente formed between Britain, France and Russia
        Pope Pius X's encyclical *Pascendi gregis* against modernism
        Lumière invents colour photography
        Picasso and Braque pioneer Cubism
        Kokoschka, *Murderer, Hope of Women* (play)

1908   Messiaen, Karajan born
        MacDowell, Rimsky-Korsakov die
        Schoenberg, first atonal works; Ives, *The Unanswered
            Question*; R. Strauss, *Elektra*; Stravinsky, *Fireworks*;
            Ravel, *Rapsodie espagnole*
        Vasarely born
        Austria annexes Bosnia and Herzegovina
        Appearance of the Hungarian literary journal *Nyugat*
        Ady, *Blood and Gold* poems

1909   Rakhmaninov, Third Piano Concerto; Mahler, Ninth
            Symphony; Schoenberg, *Erwartung*; Kodály, First String
            Quartet
        First aeroplane crossing of the English Channel; Peary reaches
            the North Pole
        Kandinsky produces first abstract paintings
        Diaghilev's Russian Ballet starts Parisian seasons

1910   Balakirev dies
        Elgar, Violin Concerto; Stravinsky, *Firebird*; Berg,
            String Quartet
        Tolstoy, Twain, Edward VII (Britain) die
        Futurist manifestos in Italy
        Population of Hungary 18.2 million, of which 55 per cent are
            native Hungarian speakers (16 per cent Romanian, 11 per
            cent Slovak, 10 per cent German); 120,000 emigrate from
            Hungary to US in this year

1911   Menotti born; Mahler dies
        Stravinsky, *Petrushka*; Elgar, Second Symphony
        Schoenberg, *A Theory of Harmony*
        Reagan born

Chinese Revolution, leading to republic under Sun Yat-sen
Amundsen reaches South Pole

1912 Cage born
Massenet dies
Schoenberg, *Pierrot Lunaire*; Debussy, *Jeux*; Ravel, *Daphnis et Chloé*; Prokofiev, First Piano Concerto
Kádár born
R. Scott dies
Sinking of the *Titanic*
First Balkan War; Austro-Hungarian Army Bill; second premiership of I. Tisza in Hungary (to 1917)
Bernhardt stars in the silent film *Queen Elizabeth*

1913 Britten, Lutoslawski born
Stravinsky, *The Rite of Spring*; Debussy, *Préludes* Book II; Skryabin, *Prometheus*
Camus, Nixon born
Second Balkan War
Bohr discovers atomic structure; Hopkins isolates Vitamin A
T. Mann, *Death in Venice*
Proust, *Du côté de chez Swann*

1914 Stravinsky, *Pribaoutki*; Reger, *Variations and Fugue on a Theme of Mozart*; Dohnányi, *Variations on a Nursery Song*
Opening of the Panama Canal
Outbreak of First World War; German invasion of France; Russian attempted invasion of Hungary
Joyce, *Dubliners*

1915 Skryabin dies
R. Strauss, *Alpine Symphony*; Prokofiev, *Scythian Suite*; Debussy, *En blanc et noir*
A. Miller born
Increase in submarine and air warfare; Italy joins war on Allied side; Allies invade Gallipoli peninsula; Germans first use poison gas
Einstein's general theory of relativity enunciated
Picasso, *Harlequin*

1916 Menuhin born
Reger, Granados die
Stravinsky, *Renard*; Holst, *The Planets*; Bloch, *Schelomo*; Szymanowski, Third Symphony ('Song in the Night')
Mitterand born
Franz Joseph I (Austria-Hungary) dies

Allies reject peace offer from Central Powers; British first
use tanks
Easter Rebellion in Ireland
Dadaist anti-art movement in Zürich

1917   Prokofiev, First Symphony ('Classical'); Debussy, Violin
Sonata; Satie, *Parade*; Pfitzner, *Palestrina*
J. F. Kennedy born
Rodin dies
Russian Revolutions, leading to Communist state
United States joins war; increasingly bitter trench warfare on
Western Front; armistice declared on Eastern Front
Jung, *The Unconscious*

1918   Debussy dies
Stravinsky, *L'histoire du soldat*
Bernstein, Billy Graham born
Germans resume hostilities on the Russian front; general
Allied offensive on Western Front; Allies sign separate
armistices with Germany and Austria–Hungary; William
II (Germany) abdicates
Tisza assassinated in Hungary; liberal Károlyi regime
established
Influenza epidemics (into 1919)

1919   Falla, *The Three-Cornered Hat*; Prokofiev, *The Love for Three
Oranges*; Sibelius, Fifth Symphony
Renoir, Ady die
Communist revolts in Berlin, Bavaria, Hungary (leading to
short-lived Kun regime); Romanians occupy Budapest,
initiating period of 'White terror'
Nazi Party formed in Germany; Fascist Party formed in Italy;
Versailles Peace Conference
Weimar Bauhaus initiated by Gropius

1920   Stravinsky, *Pulcinella*; Hába's Second String Quartet, using
quarter-tones; formation of the 'Group of Six' composers in
France
Pope John Paul II born
Treaty of Trianon reduces Hungarian land area by two-thirds;
population of Hungary 8.0 million, of which 89 per cent
are native Hungarian speakers (German 7 per cent, Slovak
2 per cent)
Hungarian Regency of Horthy commences (to 1944);
Czechoslovakia, Yugoslavia and Romania form 'Little
Entente'

Inaugural meeting of League of Nations
First sustained radio broadcasting in Britain and US

1921   Caruso, Humperdinck, Saint-Saëns die
        Honegger, *King David*; Webern, Six Trakl Songs;
            Schoenberg develops serial techniques
        Two *coups d'état* of Charles IV in Hungary fail; Germany
            accepts reparations ultimatum
        D. H. Lawrence, *Women in Love*
        Munch, *The Kiss*

1922   Xenakis born
        Walton, *Façade*
        A. Bell, Proust die
        Mussolini's March on Rome
        Discovery of the tomb of Tutankhamūn in Egypt
        BBC founded
        Kosztolányi, *The Bloody Poet*

1923   Callas, Ligeti born
        Schoenberg's first systematically serial compositions written;
            Stravinsky, *Les noces*; Kodály, *Psalmus Hungaricus*; Sibelius,
            Sixth Symphony; Zemlinsky, *Lyric Symphony*; Honegger,
            Pacific 231
        USSR established
        Earthquakes in Japan
        Hitler's *coup d'état* in Bavaria fails; increasing inflation in
            central European countries (approx. 2,000 per cent p.a. in
            Hungary)

1924   Nono born
        Busoni, Fauré, Puccini die
        Gershwin, *Rhapsody in Blue*; Respighi, *The Pines of Rome*;
            Ravel, *Tzigane*; Dohnányi, *Ruralia Hungarica*
        George Bush born
        Lenin, W. Wilson die
        League of Nations reorganizes Hungarian and other central
            European finances
        Forster, *A Passage to India*

1925   Berio, Boulez born
        Satie dies
        Shostakovich, First Symphony; Nielsen, Sixth Symphony;
            première of Berg's opera *Wozzeck* (Berlin) and Busoni's
            opera *Doctor Faust* (Dresden)
        Thatcher born

Sun Yat-sen dies
Hindenburg elected German President
French evacuate Westphalia and Ruhr districts; treaties of
    Locarno
Hitler, *Mein Kampf*, Volume I

1926   Henze, Kurtág born
Berg, *Lyric Suite*; Krenek, *Jonny spielt auf*; Kodály, *Háry
    János*; Janáček, *Glagolitic Mass*; Hindemith, *Cardillac*
Elizabeth II (Britain) born
Monet dies
British General Strike
Hirohito becomes Emperor of Japan (to 1989)
Baird demonstrates television, in London
Milne, *Winnie the Pooh*

1927   Stravinsky, *Oedipus rex*; Schoenberg, Third String Quartet;
    Varèse, *Arcana*; Lambert, *The Rio Grande*
Allies relinquish military control of Hungary
Stalin consolidates his leadership of Soviet Union
Lindbergh flies solo across the Atlantic
Heisenberg states his 'uncertainty principle'
First talking films released

1928   Stockhausen born
Janáček dies
Weill, *Threepenny Opera*; Ravel, *Boléro*; Webern, Symphony
    for small orchestra
T. Hardy dies
Kingsford-Smith flies across the Pacific; German airship
    crosses the Atlantic
Móricz, *The Gentleman's Way of Having Fun*
D. H. Lawrence, *Lady Chatterley's Lover*

1929   Crum, Pousseur, Previn born
Walton, Viola Concerto; Schoenberg, *Von heute auf morgen*
Diaghilev, Hofmannsthal die
Byrd flies over South Pole
Stock Market crash in New York, eventually leading
    to Depression
Second Surrealist Manifesto
Hemingway, *A Farewell to Arms*

1930   Takemitsu born
Stravinsky, *A Symphony of Psalms*
D. H. Lawrence dies

Last Allied troops leave Germany
Discovery of the planet Pluto
Population of Hungary 8.7 million, of which 92 per cent are
    native Hungarian speakers (5 per cent German, 2 per cent
    Slovak). Population of Budapest reaches one million

1931   Melba, Nielsen die
        Walton, *Belshazzar's Feast*; Ravel, two piano concertos
        Gorbachev born
        Edison dies
        Revolution in Spain
        Major bank failures in Germany and Austria; Britain
            abandons gold standard
        Japan invades Manchuria
        Empire State Building, New York, completed

1932   Malipiero, First Violin Concerto; Shostakovich, *The Lady
            Macbeth of Mtsensk*; Schoenberg, *Moses und Aron*
        Neutrons and Vitamin D discovered
        Julius Gömbös leads radical right-wing government in
            Hungary (to 1936)

1933   Penderecki born
        Varèse, *Ionisation*; Kodály, *Dances of Galánta*; R. Strauss,
            Arabella; Prokofiev, *Lieutenant Kijé*
        S. George dies
        Roosevelt becomes US President; Hitler becomes German
            Chancellor; start of persecution of the Jews in Germany;
            numerous German artists and intellectuals emigrate, many
            to the US
        Orwell, *Down and Out in Paris and London*

1934   Birtwistle, Maxwell Davies born
        Delius, Elgar, Holst die
        Rakhmaninov, Rhapsody on a Theme of Paganini;
            Stravinsky, *Perséphone*
        Hindenburg dies
        Dollfuss, the Austrian Chancellor, is murdered during
            attempted Nazi *coup d'état*; Hitler becomes German Führer;
            start of purges in the Russian Communist Party

1935   E. Presley born
        Berg, Dukas die
        Hindemith, *Mathis der Maler*; Berg, Violin Concerto;
            Gershwin, *Porgy and Bess*
        T. E. Lawrence dies

Beginning of 'swing' period
Germany repudiates military clauses of Versailles Treaty;
    Italians invade Abyssinia

1936   S. Reich born
        Glazunov dies
        Varèse, *Density 21.5*; Prokofiev, *Peter and the Wolf*; Orff,
            Carmina Burana; La Jeune France group of composers
            formed
        Chesterton, Kipling die
        First commercial television broadcasts, in Britain
        Outbreak of Spanish Civil War
        Accession and abdication of Edward VIII (Britain)
        Three Power Pact formed between Italy, Austria and
            Hungary; German–Japanese agreement

1937   P. Glass born
        Gershwin, Ravel, Szymanowski die
        Shostakovich, Fifth Symphony; Bliss, *Checkmate*; Ginastera,
            Danzas Argentinas; première of Berg's incomplete opera
            Lulu (Zürich)
        Marconi dies
        Whittle builds first jet engine
        Japanese take major Chinese cities
        Exhibition of 'degenerate art' in Munich, arranged by Nazis
        Picasso, *Guernica* (mural)

1938   Chaliapin dies
        Copland, *Billy the Kid*; Benjamin, *Jamaican Rumba*;
            Stravinsky, 'Dumbarton Oaks' Concerto
        Atatürk, Čapek die
        Austria annexed by Germany; Munich Agreement between
            Britain, France, Germany and Italy
        First Vienna Award increases Hungary's land area by 13 per
            cent. First Jewish Law in Hungary
        Huizinga, *Homo Ludens*

1939   Kodály, 'Peacock' Variations; Shostakovich, Sixth Symphony
        Freud, Yeats die
        German annexation of Bohemia and Moravia; end of Spanish
            Civil War; outbreak of Second World War; Russo–
            German pacts; German and Russian invasions of Poland
        Hungary declares itself non-belligerent, although affiliated
            with Axis powers. Second Jewish Law in Hungary
        Gone with the Wind (film)

1940   J. Lennon born
        Stravinsky, Symphony in C; Webern, Orchestral Variations;
            Barber, Violin Concerto
        N. Chamberlain, Trotsky die
        German invasion of Denmark, Norway, Holland, Belgium,
            Luxembourg and France; Battle of Britain; warfare
            initiated in north Africa
        Second Vienna Award increases Hungary's land area by a
            further 52 per cent. Population of Hungary 13.6 million,
            of which 74.4 per cent are native Hungarian speakers
            (8 per cent Romanian, 7 per cent German, 4 per cent
            Ruthenian, 3 per cent Slovak)
        Disney, *Fantasia*

1941   Paderewski dies
        Martin, *Le vin herbé*, Messiaen, *Quatuor pour le fin du temps*;
            Tippett's *A Child of Our Time*; Shostakovich, Seventh
            Symphony ('Leningrad')
        Former William II (Germany), V. Wolff die
        German invasion of Yugoslavia, Greece and start of invasion
            of Russia; Japanese invasions in Far East, and attack on
            Pearl Harbor. United States enters war; Hungary actively
            joins the war on Axis side

1942   Zemlinsky dies
        R. Strauss, *Capriccio*; Schoenberg, *Ode to Napoleon
            Buonaparte*; Britten, *Hymn to Saint Cecilia*; Hindemith,
            Ludus tonalis
        Fokine dies
        Magnetic tape is invented
        Fall of Singapore; Japanese advances as far south as New
            Guinea; Allied forces move to the offensive in European
            and Pacific theatres
        Camus, *L'Étranger*

1943   Ferneyhough born
        Rakhmaninov dies
        Prokofiev, *War and Peace*; Vaughan Williams, Fifth
            Symphony; Rodgers and Hammerstein, *Oklahoma!*
        Penicillin first successfully used in treatment of disease
        Mussolini overthrown; Italy surrenders; Russian advances on
            Eastern Front

1944   Prokofiev, Fifth Symphony; Copland, *Appalachian Spring*;
            Messiaen, *Vingt regards sur l'enfant Jésus*; Stravinsky, *Babel*

Kandinsky, Munch, Rommel die

D-Day initiates Allied invasion of Europe; Philippines
    invaded by Allies; Germans occupy Hungary; abortive
    Hungarian attempts to withdraw from war; siege of
    Budapest by Russians commences

Mao Tse-tung starts campaign to take control of all China

1945   Mascagni, Webern die

Britten, *Peter Grimes*; R. Strauss, *Metamorphosen*; Stravinsky,
    Symphony in Three Movements

Hitler, Keynes, Mussolini, Roosevelt die

Russians reach Berlin; end of war in European theatre; use of
    atomic bombs against Japan leads to end of Pacific war;
    continuing occupation of Hungary by Russian Army

Founding of the United Nations

Orwell, *Animal Farm*

I
Hungary:
childhood, youth and Academy years
(1881–1903)

Bartók in 1886

Béla Viktor János Bartók was born on Friday 25 March 1881 in
Nagyszentmiklós, then one of the larger towns of the southern
Hungarian county of Torontál, now the Romanian town of
Sînnicolau Mare. His father, Béla, was aged twenty-five and had
been the director of the local agricultural school since 1877. His
mother, Paula, was one year younger than her husband, whom
she had met on being posted to the town as a schoolteacher in the
late 1870s. For the first twenty years of his life Bartók was subject
to an extraordinary number of illnesses, some so serious that fatal
outcomes were predicted. During his earliest years he frequently
had to be isolated from other children and even after starting
school still missed many days because of illness. Probably because
of this isolation and the trauma associated with the premature
death of his father, Bartók early assumed the traits of laconicism
and determination by which he was so frequently characterized in
later life. Between 1889 and 1894 the family moved from town to
town as Bartók's mother sought a suitable place for her children's
education and her own employment. The frequent changes of
school further hindered Bartók in developing normal friendships
with children of his own age. He only appears to have formed
such friendships during the subsequent, more settled years of his
secondary education in Pozsony (Bratislava), and while studying
at the Budapest Academy of Music from 1899 to 1903. Poor
health dogged him, however, even during his earlier years at the
Academy. Not surprisingly, Bartók's attachment to the one
constant element in his early life, his mother, was enormously
strong, and he remained utterly devoted to her until her death in
1939.

MRS BÉLA BARTÓK Sen. (née Paula Voit)
(1857–1939)

Bartók's mother was born and brought up in the northern counties of old Hungary. On the death of her parents, when she was sixteen, she moved to central Hungary to live with relatives, and trained as a teacher. After various posts in Hungarian provincial towns she was appointed, in 1894, to a position at a teacher-training institute in Pozsony, where she and her sister Irma continued to live, with only one interruption, until 1930. Bartók then persuaded his mother and aunt to leave Pozsony (by then part of Czechoslovakia) and to move to Budapest, where they saw out their final years. In August 1921 Bartók's mother started a series of letters to her ten-year-old grandson, Béla Jun., who had been curious to know what his father had been like at a similar age. This series of letters, from which extracts are presented below, provides the only detailed reminiscence of the composer's earliest years.

Pozsony, 14 Aug. 1921

My dear little boy,

This summer your mummy mentioned how good it would be if I were to write down a few things about your father's childhood, because that would interest you very much. I have also observed how you enjoy hearing me tell one story or another about the olden days. So now I'm setting about the task and each Sunday I'll write down a passage.

When he was born your father was a very strong, healthy child, but after a vaccination at 3 months (the doctor took the vaccine from another child) he got a rash on his face (in German it's called Vierziger) which later spread over his entire body. The poor boy suffered such a lot, and I suffered also with him, as I couldn't do anything about the pain he was in. He was actually under constant medical supervision and we gave him all different kinds of baths – alas, to no effect. The itching plagued him especially at night and only after 6 o'clock in the morning could he finally get some rest. This rash, which broke out sometimes in a mild form and sometimes more severely, lasted until he was five years old. (When he had a fever it almost completely disappeared, but as soon as the fever went away it broke out again more strongly.) The

Bartók and his mother, mid–1910s

doctor gave him arsenic drops, which could only be prescribed with parental agreement. This finally did the trick, and when he was 5 his face and his entire body cleared up, to our greatest joy. Since then he has never shown a single sign of that horrible and painful rash. In Pest, also, which we visited when he was 3, his condition improved a little; it didn't itch so much, but it didn't disappear. The poor child hid from people as it hurt him when they were always saying 'poor little Béla!'. You can imagine how I suffered seeing how innocently that good, gentle boy put up with such pain.

This condition was naturally detrimental to his physical development. He began to walk late, but otherwise became rather strong and fat. When he was 1½ years old an acute case of colitis greatly weakened him, and besides this, he suffered from pneumonia once in his earliest years. I was very worried, but each time, fortunately, he overcame the ailment. This trouble hadn't the slightest effect on his intellectual ability; although he only began to speak at 2¼ years, his understanding was very developed. Already at a very early age we realized that he liked singing and music a great deal. His nanny sang to him a lot, and he always listened to her with delight. Once, when he was 1½ years old, I played a dance piece, which he listened to carefully. On the next day he pointed to the piano and motioned (as he still couldn't speak) for me to play. I played several kinds of dance piece, but he shook his head at each one until I presented that particular piece. Then, with his smile, he indicated 'yes'. On the third day I put him to the test, to see if this had happened just by chance, but he behaved as on the day before until I finally came to the right piece. About this time, however, he became ill: he contracted colitis, and this lasted for a long time.

At the age of 3 he was given a drum, and was very pleased with it. When I played the piano he sat on his little chair, with his drum in front of him on the footstool, and gave out the exact beat. If I changed over from 3/4 to 4/4 time, he left off drumming for a moment, then resumed in the proper time. Even now I can visualize just how seriously and attentively he accompanied my playing. When from time to time gipsy music was played in our town (on some special occasion), he urged us to take him there and then listened to the music with amazing concentration. The guests never tired of observing how involved such a wee lad was with the music. When he was 4 he pounded out the folksongs which he then knew on the piano using one finger. He knew 40 tunes, and if we gave him the opening words to a song he could immediately play it. Even at that age he had a good ability to remember things. As he couldn't play with other children (only because of the rash) he was an exceedingly serious and quiet child – and little wonder. When he was sick and had to lie down, he always wanted me either to sing or to tell him a story, and liked it enormously if I stayed beside him. All in all, he loved his mother very, very much – and still does even now, which is my joy. He was always a good, loving son to me. He also greatly loved his father, but naturally spent less time with him, and unfortunately, when he was 7, his father passed away.

> In 1889 the family moved to Nagyszőllős (now Vinogradov, Ukraine), but Bartók's mother was not happy with the level of musical or general education there, and in 1891 he was sent to board with his aunt, Emma Voit, in Nagyvárad (now Oradea, Romania), where he attended the local grammar school.

Bartók's *The Course of the Danube* (1890–2) in his mother's hand

28 Aug. [1921]. In Nagyvárad a music teacher named Kersch taught him. He studied a vast number of works with him, but rather too superficially. Kersch gave him pieces which were too hard. He loved your father to play in a brilliant fashion, and was happy if he learnt a rather difficult piece in one week. A faultless performance was, naturally, impossible. His studies at the grammar school there didn't go well. The teachers were very strange. They liked only the children of wealthy parents, to whom they were also private tutors. They treated the others unfairly. They wanted to fail him in arithmetic and geography (later on, he continually gained 1 gradings in these two subjects). This greatly troubled him, and since he had meanwhile suffered an eye problem I took him away from the school lest, through failure, he have to repeat the grade. In April (of 1892), then, he returned home. On 1 May there was a charity song recital in Nagyszőllős, at which he also performed. This was his first public appearance. He played several pieces, including the Allegro of a Beethoven sonata (Op. 53) and, in conclusion, his own composition *The Course of the Danube*. The applause and enthusiasm were tremendous; he received 7 bouquets, among them one very cleverly made out of sweets. You can imagine our pleasure at this. Thanks to this appearance, the school inspector there showed his goodwill and helped me to gain leave for one year. I used this leave for us to move lock, stock and barrel to Pozsony, where I had hopes of gaining a position. There, at last, his musical education was in good hands. He learnt from László Erkel (the son of Ferenc Erkel), under whom he made great progress. He attended the 2nd grade of the grammar school here, and completed the year with outstanding success. He was, of course, exempt from school fees and received some books as well. Overall, his tuition – leaving aside his piano lessons – hardly cost anything.

Letters to Béla Bartók Jun., 14 and 28 August 1921, reproduced in Béla Bartók Jun., ed., *Bartók Béla családi levelei*, Budapest (Zeneműkiadó), 1981, pp. 315–16, 317

SÁNDOR ALBRECHT

(1885–1958)

After the year in Pozsony, Paula was forced to move once again, this time to Beszterce (now Bistriţa, Romania). There, Bartók attended the local grammar school, although he found the studies difficult as all instruction was conducted in German. Musically, he gained much experience with chamber music, but his mother could not arrange adequate piano instruction as he was already the best pianist in the town. In 1894 the family moved back to Pozsony, where Bartók continued to live until 1899. During those years he completed his secondary education, and resumed piano lessons with László Erkel, changing to Anton Hyrtl on Erkel's death.

Sándor Albrecht attended the same school as Bartók in Pozsony, although in a lower form. For some months, however, Bartók supervised his piano tuition. In 1907–8 this relationship was resumed at the Budapest Academy of Music, where Albrecht completed his piano studies under the newly appointed Professor Bartók. On returning to Pozsony Albrecht became the cathedral organist, and later, one of the city's leading conductors. The two corresponded frequently right up to 1940, when Bartók departed for America.

A couple of days later, when I was going into the school with my father, we happened to meet B. B. in the corridor. My father greeted him, but the two of us introduced each other: 'Albrecht' – 'Bartók' – and the acquaintance had been made. My father asked him one thing and another about his musical studies. B. B. was a gentle, courteous little boy who always doffed his hat when he spoke with his teachers. Looking ahead, I must say that later on he was decidedly hostile to such polite practices, without ever actually erring on the side of bad manners. Once, when he was already a professor at the Music Academy (he did not like this role) and I was a student, we were walking together on the street and I, out of courtesy, went across to his left side. He immediately reacted, saying: 'When you are with me, do not go in for such formalities!' (At that time we had still not adopted the informal forms of address, as there was a great distance between a professor and a student – even if not to the astronomical extent found between younger

Bartók in 1899

and older grammar school boys!)

I began my piano studies with dear old Mr Forstner, who was then well-known as the organist of Pozsony Cathedral. He was also Ernő Dohnányi's first teacher – to this day Ernő recalls him with affection. To my grief, old Mr Forstner suddenly died and I was placed in a dilemma: under whom should I continue my studies? With great discernment my father decided to summon the 'Grade 7' Béla Bartók and to entrust my further instruction to him. B. B. came round to see us. During conversation my parents asked him who his favourite composers were. He said: Beethoven, Bach and Brahms. He said them in that order, I remember. My father noted with a laugh: 'Well then, the 3 Bs will have to make room for Béla Bartók'. But afterwards, when asked to play something, he did not play music by these composers after all, but rather, something by Schumann: the first movement of the F sharp minor sonata. When my parents then implored him to play more, he said he would be happy to do so, but that it would be one of his own compositions. And he played the first movement of his very youthful sonata – which impressed us all. Once, when B. B. came to give me a lesson and I was still in the garden, my mother said to him: 'Play me something right now, while Sanyi is coming in'. 'What would you like?' – asked B. B. 'Your own sonata', replied my mother. 'I liked it so much!' He played it . . .

Studying with Béla Bartók was a thoroughly pleasant experience. I remember very many conversations we had at the piano. On one occasion, for instance, he spoke about the jolting or, alternatively, the mysterious effect created by leaving the third out of a triad. As an example of the former effect he cited the closing chord to the first (and also the final) section of Mozart's Requiem; for the latter, he played as a tremolo on the piano the dominant chord, likewise lacking a third, which is found at the beginning of [Beethoven's] 9th Symphony. At that time did I suspect how often I would conduct these works later on? (I think I did.)

On another occasion he mentioned the opinion which he had heard somewhere that a string quartet had to be performed as if only one person were playing, but a fugue as if different people were playing. – 'Well then, how must a fugue for quartet be played?' I asked in reply, and we had a good laugh.

Our grammar school even had a small chapel. One of the students always played the organ at the student mass on Sundays – some boy suitable for this task was always found. Béla Bartók was one such organist, succeeding Ernő Dohnányi, and being followed by me and then my successor Pista Németh. The participants were naturally the same at the school's festivities as well. Of course, we scored our greatest successes always with Liszt's rhapsodies . . .

One day [in February 1899] my father received a letter from Bartók's mother, in which she reported that Béla had to give up teaching me because he had vomited blood, was very sick, and had to lie completely still – in fact his career was surely at an end, and even his life could possibly be in danger. So the letter read. I remember it as if it were yesterday. After a few weeks they took Béla to the 'Friedliche Hütte' ['Peaceful cottage'] resort, which lay near the town, and there he soon started to get better. Later, in the summer, a holiday in Austria helped him to recuperate further. But I am convinced that when this serious illness attacked him, at such a vulnerable age, B. B. was helped in the struggle by his belief that he had so terribly much to express that he could not leave this life without seeing through his chosen calling. He certainly had every desire to keep on living and working. He was young, and therefore won out in the struggle with death.

"'B. B.' – ahogy én ismertem', *Muzsika*, vol. 1/10 (October 1958), pp. 5–6

GÁBOR PÁVAI VAJNA

Shortly before falling ill in February 1899, Bartók had visited Vienna and Budapest to assess the opportunities for music study in both cities. Following the lead of Dohnányi, he determined to study in Budapest under one of Liszt's leading piano pupils, István Thomán. Despite some confusion about course admission and a bout of illness during his first term Bartók completed the first year at the Budapest Academy of Music with fine results in all subjects. During a summer vacation in the Austrian province of Styria, however, he fell ill with a pneumonia so severe that his local family doctor feared he would not survive. The prognosis of the specialist Gábor Pávai Vajna, given below, proved more realistic, and by March 1901 Bartók was able to resume his music studies in Budapest.

Redevelopment in Pest to create Szabadság (Liberty) Square, about 1900

I, the undersigned, certify that Mr Béla Bartók, student of the Hungarian Royal Academy of Music, in August this year suffered from a right *pleuro-pneumonia* lasting for several weeks, and that this disease did not take its course propitiously, because *a part of the remaining pleural effusion has remained up to now, complicated by a right apicitis*, which complication is important in this case because Mr Bartók had some more or less serious *pulmonary haemorrhages*. I certify further that *this disease of Mr Bartók is curable*, because *there are numerous favourable circumstances*: he does not have a fever; his appetite is good; the pleural effusion is absorbed slowly; he is putting on weight; he does not cough etc. *These make recovery sure*, chiefly if Mr Bartók will spend at least 4–5 months in a climatic resort of the south. I certify, in addition, that *I could not recommend Mr Bartók to go to a sanatorium*, considering his delicate, tender and oversensitive character. Finally, I declare that Mr Bartók's recovery needs not only clear, dustless air and good food, but *tender nursing and careful attention are essential too*: this is why I hold it as irreplaceable that he should *be nursed by his mother*, that tender, loving, self-sacrificing mother, who because of the worries and anxieties and because of *sitting up so often at night* by the bed of her only, highly talented son, *is exhausted to such an extent*, that together with her son *she needs a holiday that lasts for several months*.

Pozsony, 23rd September, 1900
Dr Gábor Pávai Vajna, head physician of the state hospital; member of the National Council of Health etc.

In Béla Bartók Jun., 'Béla Bartók's Diseases', *Studia Musicologica*, vol. 23 (1981), pp. 430–1, with revisions

MRS BÉLA BARTÓK Sen. (née Paula Voit)

Bartók's mother continues her record of her son's education, including this account of several of the more important concerts he gave while a student at the Budapest Academy of Music.

On 21 Oct. 1901 the first public Academy concert at which your father appeared took place. He played Liszt's B minor Sonata. The papers all reviewed his playing in terms of high praise. It was at this time that I first read reviews of his playing from Budapest. I now quote from one of these for you: *Budapesti Napló*, on 22 Oct. 1901

First, Béla Bartók played Liszt's B minor Sonata on the piano, with a firm, well-developed technique. This young man has developed his strength incredibly over the last 2 years. One and a half years ago his constitution was so weak that the doctors sent him to Meran lest the hard winter do him harm. And now he thunders around on the piano like a little Jupiter. In fact, no piano student at the Academy today has a greater chance of following in Dohnányi's tracks than he.

A paper in Pozsony also published these reviews and we were all inexpressibly happy. I was particularly happy, because I had seen just how his state of health had improved. In this same year (on 14 Dec. 1901) he appeared at the casino in Lipótváros. He received this invitation through the mediation of Professor Gianicelli. On this occasion, too, some complimentary lines appeared in the Pest newspapers. This was the first appearance for which he was paid. He didn't say a word to me about this, however, as he wanted to give me a

surprise at Christmas time. So, when we lit up the Christmas tree and
Father and Aunty Elza were looking at their presents, I saw that a
package was lying there for me also. I kept on opening it, layer after
layer, until finally I found a teeny-weeny purse (I still have this little
purse today), In which there were 10 gold pieces (100 frt = 200
crowns in value). This was his first fee, and he had made it over to me.
I can't say what a joyful surprise this was. We were very happy on that
Christmas Eve of ours. From this deed you can see what a loving and
good lad your father was. He is still the same, even today. So, my little
boy, you be like that towards your parents, too. He always sought to
please me; you, too, should try to do this always.

Scholarships and subsidies	
In 1894	15 frt
In 1895	40 frt
In 1896	120 frt
In 1897	120 frt
In 1898	120 frt
In 1899	120 frt
In 1900	360 frt
In 1901	456 frt
In 1902	300 frt
In 1903	300 frt
In 1903 [sic]	800 frt
In 1904	800 frt
In 1905	500 frt
In 1906	800 frt
In 1907	800 frt

5,651 frt, that is, 11,302 Cr.

Well, this is a grand total, for money was worth much more then than
it is today . . .

His public examination concert was held on 25 May 1903, and your
father played Liszt's Spanish Rhapsody on that occasion. He himself
wrote to me at the time: 'I scored a brilliant success. There was great
applause. I was called back 7 or 8 times. Professors Herzfeld, Hubay
and Mihálovich were all very satisfied, and even Szendy congratulated
me, saying that I had played very nicely.' The papers brought out

wonderful reviews. Furthermore, on 8 Jun. 1903 works by students of the composition department were presented in performance. Your father's works were the most liked and he was again extremely well received. A violin–piano sonata and a piano sonata [sic; study] for the left hand were performed. This latter work practically caused a sensation. The papers again ranked him as the best. In this year he composed his symphonic poem for large orchestra called *Kossuth*, which he played in the presence of the famous conductor János [Hans] Richter. Richter immediately declared his willingness to perform this work in England during the winter, which did, in fact, happen. Your father completed his course at the Academy of Music in this brilliant fashion, and then stepped out into professional life. He has frequently had to confront real difficulties along the way, but he has finally now reached the position where he is mentioned time and again alongside the foremost of contemporary composers. I am proud not just that he has become a great artist, but that all the time he was a good, loving son to me, and still is today.

Letters to Béla Bartók Jun., 15 August 1922 and 5 November 1922, reproduced in Béla Bartók Jun., ed., *Bartók Béla családi levelei*, Budapest (Zeneműkiadó), 1981, pp. 321, 324

II
Earlier professional years
(1903–1920):
a sense of failure

Bartók in 1909

On graduating from the Budapest Academy of Music Bartók had every reason to look forward to a successful career as a pianist–composer, following closely in the footsteps of his colleague Ernő (Ernst von) Dohnányi. Between 1903 and 1905 he did secure performing engagements in such centres as Budapest, Berlin, Vienna, Paris and Manchester, and his Romantic-style compositions were occasionally performed, but as the decade progressed his dedication to this traditional type of career began to waver. His interest in folk music was kindled, and he embarked each year upon major collecting expeditions, often in collaboration with Zoltán Kodály. Partly under the influence of these new rustic experiences his compositional style became more radical. His new compositions found little favour at home or abroad, except among small bands of progressive, younger musicians and artists. By 1912 he was thoroughly disillusioned, and, apart from fulfilling his piano teaching obligations at the Academy of Music and folk music activities, withdrew from Hungarian musical life. In 1917, however, he scored a success in Budapest with his ballet, *The Wooden Prince*, which encouraged the authorities to mount his opera, *Duke Bluebeard's Castle*, in the following year. Also at this time Universal Edition in Vienna agreed to publish his compositions. During the turmoil which followed the end of the First World War in Hungary he was prompted to re-emerge into public life as a performer. He started to promote his music and ideas more vigorously and to plan for concert tours abroad.

With family

MRS BÉLA BARTÓK (née Márta Ziegler)

(1893–1967)

On 16 November 1909, at the municipal building of the sixth
district of Budapest, Bartók married Márta Ziegler, then aged
sixteen. He had known Márta since September of the previous
year, when he had accepted the Ziegler sisters as private pupils.
During their fourteen years together Bartók's first wife frequently
assisted him with his folk music transcriptions and the copying of
scores. *Duke Bluebeard's Castle* was one of several works which he
dedicated to her. The marriage, which produced one son, Béla, in
1910, was subject to many strains during and immediately after
the war, and ended abruptly in the summer of 1923. Soon
afterwards Bartók married another of his students, Ditta
Pásztory. This recollection dates from 1966, the year before
Márta Ziegler's death.

Our first flat in Rákoshegy (3 Jókai utca) was rather small, and Bartók
could not find the calm necessary for work there. So we moved very
soon to another, more suitable dwelling: a house with four rooms, a
garden and a small, separate summer-house. Next to us and behind us
there were empty allotments, and therefore our peace was undisturbed.
Still, he mostly composed at night. During the day he was busy for
most of the time with transcribing and ordering his folksong collections
recorded on wax cylinders, systematizing the Romanian, Slovak etc.
collections for publication, or reading and studying languages. For the
sake of his folksong collecting he learnt Romanian and Slovakian, and
even tried to learn Arabic before his trip to Africa. He knew of no
idleness, since even his idleness and rest were active in some way. It
was part of his daily programme to draw something or other for the
'child'. The child's ever-recurring wish was: 'Aputa, jazsoljak tocsit-
loat' (Daddy, daw horth and cart), which was what he got until one day
Bartók decided to draw something else. He acquired a painting-book,
with the usual drawing of 'horse and cart' parading about on its first
page, but the remaining drawings showed other things: a team of oxen,
a walk in the zoo etc. – Another game was to build card-houses. He
constructed these with an amazing dexterity, and not just the usual little

One of Bartók's drawings for his son Béla, around 1915: 'A family excursion'

houses, but also sophisticated fences and roads. He laid great stress on the unfettered development of the child, who did not participate in public education until the fourth grade of elementary school. (He took the examinations for the first three grades privately.)

Bartók would exercise each morning according to Müller's *Mein System*, and would take the sun as early as possible. He could stand the sun particularly well and while sunbathing he would go on working, studying languages, scoring his compositions etc. Each day he took a walk, mostly with the family but sometimes alone. If alone, he always brought something home: a strange pebble, a small wildflower etc. One of his hobbies was collecting beetles and butterflies. He always carried a small flask of alcohol with him for the beetles and one of chloroform for the butterflies. He never stuck pins into a living animal.

Besides the morning gymnastics and walks, for physical exercise we – and later our son as well – used to play a ball game which Béla had learnt in the 'Licht und Luft' Sanatorium in Waidberg [near Zürich], where he had spent a couple of weeks in the summer of 1911. The game was played with leather-covered drumlike rackets and ping-pong balls.

In the springtime, however, he had to keep to his room for shorter or longer periods, as he suffered particularly severely from the

Taking the sun, 1910s

so-called hay fever brought on by the flowering of acacias and hay.

The 'natural lifestyle' initiated in Waidberg also brought the vegetarian diet to our home, and he stuck to it for years. When he was abroad he did not stick to this diet so strictly, but tried out the specialities of the country or city in question, looking for what was new and interesting.

You never heard a loud word from him. When he was angry, he pursed his lips and kept silent. Besides, he was very taciturn and declared that he could not *speak* any language, not even Hungarian. He rarely laughed – mostly only when a letter arrived from abroad with an error in the address or he received first proofs of one of his works from one of his publishers abroad in which the Hungarian text was littered with misprints. I only know from hearsay that 'Tót legények tánca' ('Dance of the Slovak youths') was set as 'Tót lepények tánca' ('Dance of the Slovak pies'), but I do remember his amusement at the first proofs of one of the pieces in the Liszt Revision, published by Breitkopf und Härtel, which begins with Vörösmarty's ode *To Franz Liszt*, 'Zengj nekünk dalt, hangok nagy tanárja' ('Sing us a song, great master of sound') etc., where in place of 't' they had set 's' throughout. And when he heard or saw something amusing and related the incident to his family his smile was unforgettable.

He never drank alcohol and did not start to drink real coffee until after the First World War. During the war, as shortages of provisions became ever more pressing, he took up smoking as a substitute for food.

He endured illnesses with great patience and without complaint – even the extremely painful inflammation of the middle ear which he contracted during the big influenza epidemic of 1918. He was rather worried, however, when for a while after the opening of the eardrum (Kodály brought a specialist to Rákoshegy by car) he heard every note on the piano a fourth higher than normal. He complained, jokingly, that he constantly heard a composition by Hubay.

He harboured no professional jealousies. During the rehearsals for *Bluebeard*, for example, he carried the four-hand piano score of Stravinsky's *Sacre du printemps* around with him constantly, waiting for an opportunity to play it to the Intendant and so to persuade him to stage the ballet . . .

The picture of Béla Bartók's daily life would not be complete if I failed to tell about those who, in addition to his mother (his passionate love for her was often written about in the biographies), had a close relationship with him but scarcely gained a mention in the biographies known to me.

There was Aunt Irma, Bartók's mother's elder sister by 8 years, whom Bartók held as his second mother. She ran the household and, after Bartók's father had died, stayed with her sister for good. Bartók's mother had clung so much to Aunt Irma since her childhood that Irma gave her the nickname 'stickpin', reflecting how closely she always stayed around her, as if pinned to her skirt. This great, mutual attachment made Mama and Aunt Irma merge in the eyes of the family into one single person – as it were – for one could simply not imagine the one without the other. Mama was the breadwinner; Aunt Irma managed the household and shouldered the greater responsibility for the well-being of the family – as far as was possible – but above all for Béla whose constitution was rather weak. Aunt Irma cooked, mended things, did the darning – she was never idle for a moment – while Mama shared all her joys, sorrows and cares with her. Here is a typical example of Irma's all-pervasive care and concern: around midday she would keep a look out from the highest landing on the 4th floor (at that time they lived on the Teréz körút [Budapest]), watching for Béla's

Bartók and his first wife, Márta, 1912

coming – he never used the lift – so that she could serve up his soup immediately and he would not have to wait until the food cooled down, thereby losing a few minutes of his precious time. And how happily she would grumble if Béla sneaked behind her and undid her apron. *'Aba Béla!'* ['But, Béla!'], she would exclaim, and her eyes showed her joy at finding Béla in a good mood.

The other person who was very close to Bartók was his sister Elza. She was passionately fond of her brother, and extended her affection to all who belonged to his circle of acquaintances. She was married to the overseer of an estate in Békés county. At first they lived in Vésztő (actually, Szilad puszta, which was connected with it), then on the Rudolf farm, then in Kertmeg, and finally in Szőllős puszta (all these properties belonged to the Wenckheim Estate). Her house was always open to receive relatives and friends in search of relaxation and peace of mind. Bartók, too, often stayed at her home and – as is well known – collected many folksongs there. He had the farm-hands and day-labourers sing; indeed he made everyone who lived and worked there sing. Péter Garzó, Julcsa Varga, Róza Kocsis, Róza Ökrös and others sang the folksongs which he collected there. Once, when he played these songs on the piano, one of the above-mentioned girls left her work, positioned herself beside the piano, with feather-duster in hand, and sang all the songs one after another.

At Elza's everyone had to gain weight – Bartók, too, of course. He would be weighed once a week on the granary balance, and a note taken. Once Béla played a joke by putting weights unobserved into his coat pockets, but his amusement did not last for long as his face immediately gave the whole 'fraud' away.

The sounds of the night from his stay in Szőllős puszta unmistakably live on in 'Az éjszaka zenéje' ('The Night's Music' [from *Out of Doors*, 1926]).

That's as much as I want to say about the day-to-day life of Béla Bartók. Perhaps one day someone will manage to compile a fuller picture of him with the help of this account.

'Über Béla Bartók', *Documenta Bartókiana*, vol. 4 (1970), pp. 174–6, 178–9

BÉLA BARTÓK Jun.

(b. 1910)

Béla Bartók Jun. is the composer's elder son, by his first wife, Márta. After his parents' divorce in 1923 he maintained strong links with both, and only lost contact with his father after communications between the United States and Hungary were severed in 1941. An engineer by profession, Béla Bartók Jun. attained a senior rank in the Hungarian State Railways and taught at the Technical University in Budapest before retiring there. He is now a leading official of the Unitarian Church in Hungary and travels widely in that role. His writings about his father include two chronicles, a volume of family correspondence, and numerous articles.

Of all his qualities and virtues those which most impressed me were his love of nature, his sense of patriotism and ardour for national freedom, and his extraordinary diligence and capacity for work.

He loved nature greatly and everything to do with the natural sciences. He was most interested in astronomy – the 'great Universe' – and knew all about the stars and the great constellations, which he liked to explain to us on clear nights. His wonder and admiration for the

perfection of nature attracted him to many of its other manifestations as
well: he collected insects, plants and minerals, and would arrange them
with the help of textbooks. He did his best to make time for periodic
visits to the Zoo, for regular walks, and occasionally for long
excursions walking in the hills.

On his walks and outings he liked to take members of his family
along with him. We never tired of his explanations and comments; in
fact, they stimulated us to such an extent that geography and natural
history have remained among my chief interests, although I have
chosen a different profession for myself.

He loved the sort of human beings who lived close to nature –
peasants, whom he came to know mainly on his trips gathering folk
music. He would take advantage of these trips to add to his collection of
folk art; his home was furnished with carved and painted peasant
furniture which he had brought back with him from Körösfő, in the
Kolozs region. He had fine collections of peasant embroideries, pottery
and musical instruments. In folklore proper he was attracted above all
by folk poetry.

He had a great devotion to children; he regarded them as the raw
material from which a finer humanity could be shaped. His educational
activities formed an important part of his whole work – witness his
piano manuals, co-authored with Reschofsky; the cycle of works *For
Children*, which he revised several times; and the six volumes of
Mikrokosmos, composed with most careful attention to detail.

As for the kind of education he gave his own children, he believed
that they had independent personalities, and that education had mainly
to rely on good example and on constantly stimulating their interest.
He attached importance to regular physical exercise, plenty of sunlight
and fresh air, abstinence from alcohol, and a frugal and modern diet
based on vitamin-rich foods. I was still quite a little fellow when he
started to give me art reproductions; he encouraged me to trace on the
map the events described in the books I read. He would come back
from his trips abroad laden with pictures, and would give us a detailed
account of everything he had seen; it was from these accounts I began to
know about the world at an early date.

He looked upon both his sons as friends, and expected a similar
attitude from us. Believing it was for us to work for our own benefit, he
would never hear our lessons, nor would he ever call on teachers to

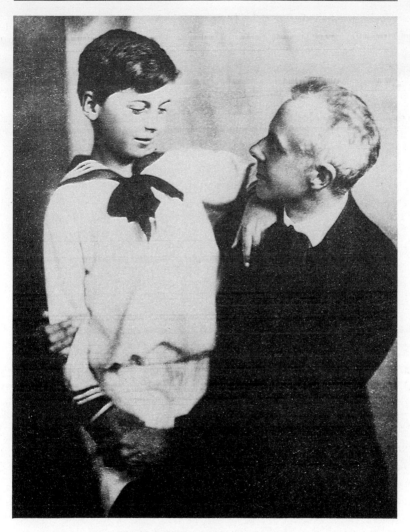

Bartók and his son Béla, about 1918

enquire about our progress at school; yet he was pleased whenever we brought home good school reports, and he would ask us questions about what had happened at school.

He thought our decision not to choose music as a profession was quite natural; but he liked to ask us to help him with the arrangement of folk music or other minor matters of that kind . . .

He always looked for a flat in quiet districts, for any noise coming through the walls upset him beyond endurance. He always chose the most isolated room for his study, and tried to make it sound-proof by fitting on a double-door by some means or other. For his part, he took great care not to disturb other people's peace; when practising, he would shut his windows, even on hot days, in order not to disturb other people.

The clothes he wore were plain and modest; he managed to keep them in good condition for many years at a time.

He ate sparely as a rule, and rarely drank alcohol. For many years a non-smoker, he only acquired the habit of smoking during the First World War. In later years, he made several unsuccessful attempts to break himself of the habit, and his failure to do so annoyed him considerably.

He had no recreations in the conventional sense of the word. He never visited the cinemas, cafés, or other places of amusement, and would seldom go to concerts. His principal pastime was – work. During the school year he would leave the house very rarely – with the exception of visits to the family or to give his lessons at the Academy of Music. He read the newspapers avidly and would buy one every day, sometimes more than one. He was interested in everything in it, editorials, economic news, politics and the arts.

His manner with strangers was reserved and to some extent cautious, owing to the tendency of some to intrude on his privacy. But those he conceived an affection for were fully appreciated; he was completely at ease with his relatives. He was very fond of explaining things, teaching people, showing them the results of recent research, recordings of folk music, etc.

He had a sure sense of vocation, but would never speak of it. He was modest and polite. On one occasion I went with him to Békéscsaba, where Mária Basilides, the famous contralto, and he were scheduled to give a recital. He noticed that his name was printed first on the poster, and Miss Basilides's second. He immediately complained to the concert manager, saying he deplored the practice of putting the names of the men before the names of women on concert programmes. Because of his diffident manner strangers thought my father a sombre, melancholy man; yet he had a good sense of humour, and enjoyed puzzles and riddles . . .

He made a point of remembering all family festivals, particularly each birthday of his mother. When he or I happened to be away from home, he would always remember my birthday in a long letter, no matter how great the pressure of work. His last letter to me was written for my birthday in 1941. War, which he hated so intensely, and death, which he had wished so fervently to delay, combined to prevent him from writing any more.

'Remembering my father, Béla Bartók', *New Hungarian Quarterly*, no. 22 (Summer 1966), pp. 201–3

He [Bartók] adapted himself to the school-years, not to the calendar years – when he was a student as well as when he was a professor – and we can note that after his holidays, when he had had a good time, he started the autumn season with good health; on other occasions he started it with an illness as early as September. – It can be considered regular, too, that during the winter he had a few slight colds in November and in December; and from the middle of January to the beginning of March he had a serious disease every year.

It is also interesting that in those parts of his life when he had political and economic problems, or he was occupied by his work, he could pay less attention to his state of health and he did not have any serious complaint. Periods like this were the times of the trips to collect folk songs, when he was never ill, the first year of World War I, the time of the difficulties in connection with the première of *The Wooden Prince*, problems during the Hungarian Soviet Republic (1919) and at the beginning of his last stay in America.

'Béla Bartók's Diseases', *Studia Musicologica*, vol. 23 (1981), p. 441

Q: Did the family know just what composition Bartók happened to be working on?

A: Yes. Although I was still a small child, even I knew about the stage works. This [Rákoshegy] was where he composed *The Miraculous Mandarin*. He only did the orchestration somewhere else. I also knew he was arranging folksongs. On the one hand, I listened to his talks about them, and on the other, sometimes performing artists visited us, to whom my father showed his recordings.

I knew quite certainly that the members of the Waldbauer String Quartet were here separately, and also together. I recall Waldbauer and Kerpely were here in uniform, being on war service. The Second String Quartet was completed on the occasion of a visit like this.

Q: What did the family see of the process of composition?

A: We had an opportunity to observe the writing of the scores, because owing to the poor lighting and other circumstances caused by the war I wrote my lessons at the same table where my father worked on his manuscripts. We had the illumination of two or three candles, which were themselves not easy to obtain, and were of poor quality. This left such a deep impression on my father that around 1935, when the Second World War was imminent, he bought a large quantity of candles so that if a war broke out again he could avoid difficulties of this nature . . .

Q: What did you think of Bartók's mathematical knowledge, and generally of his interest in the exact sciences?

A: He always had excellent grades in mathematics and physics, in contrast to languages, although his grades were never less than good in these, either. He loved to play chess . . . All the technical discoveries which began to accelerate with rushing speed in our century, already in his lifetime, interested him. For instance, the structure of the airplane, the technique of flight, and even radio . . . not only as art, but also as technical equipment.

Q: What kind of literature did Bartók give his son to read?

A: At quite an early age he gave me books which in some way developed my knowledge. This picture-book, for example, he gave me when I was four, on Christmas Day, 1914. I have preserved it for more than six decades. The book is written in German, and besides German, the names of the animals are also given in Latin. Where he could, my father also wrote the Hungarian names. On each Christmas, and on any occasion whatever, he always bought books. I hardly recall any other kind of gift . . . He had the series *Hungarian Master*

Writers, which he later gave me as a gift. He had a high regard for the modern poets – among them first of all his contemporary, Ady. For example, on my 20th birthday I received Ady's complete poems . . .

Q: How much time did Bartók have to follow the new Hungarian literature growing up around him? Ady was practically their banner, for both Kodály and him. Béla Balázs was close to him. But meanwhile the generation of Móricz and Babits grew up, all of whom would have sought the road to Bartók.

A: My father subscribed to *Nyugat* from the beginning; he was also in contact with its editors and a few of its contributing writers, among others, with Zsigmond Móricz, whom we also visited once at Leányfalu. My father bought every book by Móricz, and Babits's books, too. I received the *Stork Caliph* and other Babits works.

Q: Might we hear something about your father's connections with religion?

A: My father was born a Catholic. He attended the Catholic Secondary School in Pozsony, where after the graduation of Dohnányi – Dohnányi also attended the same school – he played the organ in the Cathedral, the Pozsony Coronation Church, at student masses. He felt the religious duties to be rather rigid. He displayed an interest in the most varied spiritual trends at the beginning of the century; among other reasons, this was why he strove to become a free thinker, and he also strove to convince those in his environment of this. Later he became an adherent of the unitarian faith, primarily because he held it to be the freest, the most humanistic faith. In the everyday sense of the term he was not at all religious. One could say rather that he was a nature lover: he always mentioned the miraculous order of nature with great reverence.

Q: What can you tell us about his patriotism?

A: He never gave up his patriotism. He served the brotherhood of all peoples – as an ideal of a higher order. He understood brotherhood to mean that the Hungarians should not be in the last place among peoples. Wherever he could help the Hungarians in any way, or heard that the Hungarians achieved anything at all in the world, he was more pleased than if it was news about other people. He regularly subscribed to the periodical *Magyarosan* [a language reform journal]. He fought against everything that was un-Hungarian. At his Academy [of Sciences] inauguration when he read his paper on Ferenc Liszt, among various themes he emphasized Liszt's Hungarian character as the most essential – the fact that Liszt was Hungarian, and everybody had to acknowledge it, despite the fact that Liszt did not speak Hungarian. In America he did not feel at home; in the Concerto [for Orchestra] and elsewhere many features indicate his nostalgia for Hungary. He wanted in every way to come home and finish his life here, because he did not emigrate – despite all such legends. He left all his belongings here, and went abroad only for a year; it turned out later that he had to stay longer, and finally he could never return.

In interview with László Somfai, published as 'Béla Bartók Jun. on his Father', *New Hungarian Quarterly*, no. 64 (Winter 1976), pp. 193–4, 195–6

With friends and associates
ANTAL MOLNÁR
(1890–1983)

During his long life Antal Molnár turned his hand to most forms of musical expression: composition, performing, teaching, criticism and musicology. On 19 March 1910 he played the viola in the Waldbauer–Kerpely Quartet's première performance of Bartók's First String Quartet. During the 1910s and 1920s he wrote frequently about Bartók's music, establishing many of the principles by which it has come to be assessed. In later years his writings ranged widely over the chief figures of Western music from the Baroque to the twentieth century. The florid style of his Hungarian has been imitated, where appropriate, in this translation.

The most striking characteristic of our gifted Master was his exceptional *laconicism*. The explanation I usually give for this is that Bartók limited his message to music and felt it superfluous to add anything in words. But I can also put it this way: he knew that his message was of a far deeper significance than could ever adequately be expressed in the medium of words. There is a very curious consequence to this. If someone did not know Bartók's music he would not gain the slightest idea from conversation with Bartók of the type of spirit that infused his personality. He would rather have imagined that the person he was talking to was hardly different from any other everyday, prosaic person.

Bartók's *intonation* in speaking contributed further to this impression, as it was exceedingly grey and monotonous. Very rarely did I ever hear the Master emphasize a particular word. Mostly, the whole text flowed out completely evenly, like a tranquil stream.

Although I dislike overstatements intended to startle the reader and want to avoid making them, I cannot help myself when it comes to reporting on Bartók's appearance. That is, I have to put on record that his external appearance was *exactly the opposite* of the revolutionary vigour of his art. It was all pure restraint, simplicity and natural ordinariness. Leaving aside the fire which shone now and again from his eyes, the appearance he presented to the world was no different from that of an ordinary person. I did not ever hear anything from his lips which went beyond the commonplace. Never did I gain from his manner the slightest indication of human greatness, exceptionality, or even just some interesting feature. As the Germans say: 'Grau in grau'.

As soon as the Master sat down at the piano all this turned at once into its diametrical opposite, as he bestowed on us the power of his artistry. There, a demon was at work – an equal to the greatest investigators of the human spirit - and it is scarcely an exaggeration to call his piano playing the outpourings of a prophet. I was fortunate to be present at the premières of his piano works, and so I can vouch for the fact that since that time Bartók's opuses have never been performed as perfectly as their composer interpreted them. The surviving recordings give only a very limited idea of these original conceptions.

Artist and *scholar* in the same person: this is by no means a rare phenomenon. Just think how many artists *teach* – that is, they have to deal also with questions of theory. I have to say that in Bartók's case, however, a totally unprecedented dimension was added to this dichotomy. There is hardly any case where, in one and the same person, a scholar's dedication to complete accuracy, precision and extreme scrupulosity is united with the most perfect intuition and inspiration of an artist. It is quite remarkable that to some degree Bartók carried across the precision of the scientist into his art, as, for instance, with the precision of his performing indications and calculation of exact timings, and, as a pianist, with his extremely precise adherence to the score and exemplary maintenance of tempos. In him, a genius merged

Bartók and Zoltán Kodály (both seated) with the Waldbauer–Kerpely String
Quartet, 1910. Antal Molnár is in the centre of the picture
looking straight into the camera

with a schoolmaster, if we take the best meaning of the latter. The
organic unity of such extreme opposites is rare, *indeed*. It is probably a
unique instance.

On one occasion I had to turn pages for the Master. So engrossed
was I in his inspired playing that just once – only once – I turned the
page a second too late. Of course, Bartók – according to the principles
of Schumann – went on playing smoothly, without a break, but at the
end of the performance he said sarcastically to me: 'You were late!'
Even such a bagatelle as this needed, in his opinion, to be denounced.

This *sarcasm*, which more than once in his compositions verged on the
grotesque, was introduced into our relationship on some other occasions
too, but always in a mild way, evidencing real tolerance. Once, for
example, he asked me to sing something from his latest collection of
Romanian folksongs. No doubt he wanted to check whether someone
who had not been present could gain an idea of the original folk mode of
performance. I tried, of course, to sing 'nicely', with due emphasis on
tone colour and other 'good qualities'. Bartók burst out laughing. 'Just
sing what's written. There is no *espressivo* marking!' In this way the trait

of the rough 'primitive man' which suffused the entirety of his art was revealed. But such deviation – such diversion – from his customary prosaic path occurred but rarely in my experience.

His all-embracing sense of intellectual honesty is shown in his response to my questioning of why he did not perform the late Beethoven [piano] sonatas. Those works were – he said – very difficult: they required a lot of practice, and, unfortunately, he did not have time for that. I objected that he did perform his own *Etudes*, which were among the most difficult works in the entire literature of music. 'That is true' – he replied – 'but their preparation took months, during which time I could not do anything else that was really worthwhile. It was wasted time!'

I record here my theory (also applied elsewhere) of how Bartók recovered from his almost superhuman cerebrations. When he was tired of composing, he played the piano; when he was exhausted by playing, he turned to his work with folklore; when the incessant transcribing led to cramp in his fingers, he would go to teach. This cycle allowed him to accomplish what would otherwise have been quite unimaginably taxing.

To sum up Bartók's personality: he was out-and-out a rarity; someone quite extraordinary; one of the world's deepest, most rousing composers, with so much to express yet having the simplest imaginable prosaic appearance. In speech he was even simpler and more modest than the average man; at the same time, his musical manifestations were stunningly rich, of high standard, and often almost touched the mystery of a magician. An utterly plain figure, with a thin build, cautious gait – and when this boyish character sat down to his instrument, his staggeringly powerful playing brought to mind the moral strength of the prophets. In his music he evidences a ravishingly rich imagination, and this same seer had the exemplary patience to spend hours, days, weeks with his phonograph cylinders, so that his transcriptions might be flawlessly erudite. He is the most bewildering composer of our age, and one of its most reassuring and sober scholars. Only life, only truth, can give rise to such an abnormality.

I would not like to dwell on the unfavourable reputation of musicians. It is perhaps sufficient to point out that those who look for moral purity should probably not look to musicians. Fortunately, however, there are some exceptions. But, even among these, Bartók's wide-ranging spiritual constitution was outstanding. Nowhere and never in the course of my life have I met a character comparable to Bartók in terms of moral rectitude, purity and unassailable puritanism. In conclusion I have this to say: the greatest musician and the superlative ethnomusicologist of our time was the real hero of duty, human solidarity and resistance in the name of humanity.

In Ferenc Bónis, ed., *Így láttuk Bartókot*, Budapest (Zeneműkiadó), 1981, pp. 53–7

BÉLA BALÁZS
(1884–1949)

Between 1905 and 1918 the poet, novelist and playwright, Béla Balázs was in close contact with both Bartók and Kodály. A one-act play of his, written in 1910, formed the basis of the libretto of the opera *Duke Bluebeard's Castle* which Bartók wrote in the following year. Balázs also supplied the plot to Bartók's ballet *The Wooden Prince*, which was completed in 1917. On account of his left-wing views Balázs was exiled from Hungary between 1919 and 1945. In his diaries Balázs provides several vivid impressions of Bartók in his twenties and thirties, during which time his opinion of the composer changed radically.

Sept. 5, 1906. Béla Bartók was here [Szeged]. We went collecting folksongs together for a week. He is naïve and awkward. A 25-year-old prodigy. A wonderful, quiet persistence dwells within him. He is a frail, thin, sickly little man. I was indeed already extremely exhausted, but he simply urged and drove me on, just to continue, and collect some more. – He plays lovely things in a beautiful fashion. – I have no knowledge of these things. But I did not sense his greatness from the man himself. He probes, he is impatient, restless, but he seems to be seeking a certain something that he has already sensed. He seeks with childlike *naïveté*, out of curiosity.

He studies the stars, hunts insects, engages in ethnography, etc. This avidity is obviously to be explained by the fact that so far he has not studied much of anything outside music.

Playing excites him. His face becomes entirely transformed: it lengthens, grows large, serious, at times it grows wonderfully beauti-

ful. He has a nervous tic of sniffing. I believe sometimes that perhaps
the only reason I do not sense anything great in him at other times is
because 'er ist ein Talent eingesperrt' ['his is an imprisoned talent'].
And this – by the way – is certain.

He is very modest, like a girl – but vain. And I can enjoy nothing
about him apart from his music. His *naïveté* is not fresh enough, and
his irony (because that is also present) lacks force. But sometimes his
head is very beautiful. Perhaps he is more than a grown-up prodigy – a
composer.

> In the summer of 1911 Balázs spent some weeks with the Kodálys
> and Bartók at a mountain camp near Zürich in Switzerland. At
> the time Bartók had nearly finished composing *Duke Bluebeard's
> Castle*.

Béla Bartók is a moving and most marvellous man. He, too, undressed
to the skin. His frail, weak, delicate little body, even when he ran after
the ball, seemed as if it moved in robes in front of an altar. It has
unbelievably magical dignity and nobility. You could peel his skin off
him, but not his unconscious dignity. The genius, in the most
schoolboyish romantic sense. And how much childlike charm exists
within it. He travels with a knapsack and ten cigar boxes, filled with
insects and flies, which he gathers with scrupulous care and constant
wonder. He will sit for hours on the edge of a dirty pond and fish for
water insects with Edith [Balázs's wife]. And the most awful thing is –
he says in a plaintive childlike voice – that when a person thinks he has
got one of every variety, he finds a new one. He gets up in the night
and brings in a 'glow-worm insect', as he says with careful precision,
because it is not yet a beetle. He studies it for an hour, then he carefully
takes it back out into the grass, because he doesn't collect worms. And it
is 'awful' that it has wings, and one can't know whether it is a pupa, a
worm, or what. He has taught me the names of the constellations and
the stars, for which I am extremely grateful to him. 'It must be more
difficult', I said to him, 'to learn them from a map. How did you learn
them?' 'Oh, that was awful. I had to sit outside all night with a lantern
and a candle and the wind kept on blowing it out,' he said complain-
ingly, as if complaining of being forced to do it. Meanwhile he worked
six to eight hours a day on the orchestration of *Bluebeard*. There is some
kind of miraculous paradox in his appearance. His figure, his features,

his movements were like some kind of rococo prince, yet he was marked by a kind of titanic dignity. A rococo titan! A 32-year-old [sic] dead-serious prodigy.

> Balázs also recollects how the privations and stresses of the First World War had driven Bartók to take up drinking and smoking.

March 24, 1917. Today dinner with Bartók, who wants to avoid sending his son to religious instruction. Bartók drinks and smokes!!! I would sooner have believed that I would become a woman-hating ascetic! The war is to blame for it. Everything is perishing, let us perish as well. Bartók, I believe, did not grudge himself, but rather the money for that sort of thing. But it is not worth while hanging on to money either. Who knows what will happen?

> Both Bartók and Balázs were intimately involved in the forty rehearsals which preceded the first performance of *The Wooden Prince* in May 1917. Some weeks after that première he recalled:

May 28, 1917. May 12 was the first night of the ballet. It was a success the like of which was never recalled at the Opera. They called me back at least thirty times. They raved for more than half an hour. The next day the papers gave Bartók full recognition, but me mostly abuse . . .

In the days before the opening night it was rumoured that the libretto would be successful, but not the music. This distressed me very much, and it would have been bitterly humiliating. That it happened the other way around might have pleased me if they had at least acknowledged one thing, or had just been aware of it: the fearful work I did for Bartók, and that I did it for him alone. That I broke his symphonic music down for the stage, since it is devoid of all stage timing and spacing (I, who am not a musician, and not a director!), that I drilled music which musicians do not understand into house-porters' daughters, that I got it across that every movement corresponded to a phase of the music (with ballerinas who were not even accustomed to doing this to the music of Delibes). That I held forty! hostile rehearsals, an author who was already a failure in advance, who worked them to such an unaccustomed extent, all in vain . . . The libretto – which naturally was in existence first – is a playful, light grotesque china knick–knack, the music to it is grave, tragic and demoniac. It was too late, nor would it have been right to be corrected by the direction. Of course they say I am the one to blame. At best, that I am not a suitable librettist for Bartók, as if this were my only style. They also write and say that the reason I 'jumped in' [and] terrorized Bartók to set my text to music was that in this way I hoped to share somewhat in his success, and secure myself a place 'at least in the history of music'. That is all. I am a little bit afraid that all these attacks and hatred will influence Bartók, whose literary judgement, after all, cannot be so impeccable, and for whom the most important thing nonetheless is that he should not tie a weight round the neck of his music, if I am one (although undeservingly). It would be painful for me, yet it is important that nothing disturbs his success (mine will come from some other source), and it is enough for me to know: this success was produced in part by my work.

> The highly favourable reception of Bartók's music to *The Wooden Prince* encouraged the Opera House to première the work on which Balázs and Bartók had originally collaborated, *Duke Bluebeard's Castle*. Relations between the two further deteriorated, and remained strained for many years.

May 25, 1918. Yesterday the first night of *Bluebeard* took place. Again a great assault on me by the critics. Again they are sorry for Bartók. I am a drag on his wheels. I wrote in the *Magyar Színpad* that it might be that these texts are not perfect librettos, but when I wrote them and offered them to Bartók, Hungarian writers were not yet thronging around him. He was a madman and a swindler then, and he was not a good investment. Now, of course, they send Sándor Bródy, and he is coming, too, to write a libretto for him. And they beat me the harder in order to hail the redeemer all the more loudly. – Very well. This does not hurt. I never would have believed that I could grow accustomed to attacks and remain so indifferent. But something else aches very much. I showed Béla Bartók what I wrote about the libretto. He squirmed about it at the time, that this was not the way to do it, that there was something like a reprimand in it, and it might make his dealings with Bródy morally somewhat difficult. And then he wrote his own statement 'About the Composer's Piece', in which he expressed his thanks to the Opera, to the conductor, the director, to the performers, etc . . . He did not even mention my name. It did not occur to him that he was the only man who could have repudiated these attacks, if he had only said that he did not set me to music *faute de mieux*, but because my librettos pleased him. Now he is associating with Bródy, and so, out of friendship, is Zoltán [Kodály]!!! (Yet they would be very astonished if I gave a libretto to Hubay or Zerkovitz, or even to Puccini himself.) They now throw me out of the rising balloon like a sandbag. They try to do it very tenderly, gently, so that no bitterness remains.

My heart aches over Bartók. He is a great musician, and as long as he does not compromise his music, it is all the same how he behaves as a person. But my heart aches. Because it turns out that he joined forces with me quite accidentally, without any inner necessity, and in doing so he sensed no kind of predestined meaning in it at all. He did not choose me out of admiration, as I did him.

And also the fact that Béla meant virtually more to me as a person than as a musician, I felt that here, too, I was cut off from something that was very important and very precious to me. 'You'll dig me out of the grave,' he used to say.

Bluebeard, by the way, is not a suitable opera libretto, because it does not have enough pantonic comprehensibility, and the text, naturally, cannot be properly understood in the singing.

In István Gál, 'Béla Balázs, Bartók's First Librettist', *New Hungarian Quarterly*, no. 55 (Autumn 1974), pp. 204–8

HUGO LEICHTENTRITT
(1874–1951)

For the first half of the century Hugo Leichtentritt's writings and lectures exerted a powerful influence over thousands of German and, later, American musicians. Although his few articles specifically about Bartók date from the 1920s and 1930s, he had met Bartók much earlier, probably in January 1909 (not 1906 or 1907, as Leichtentritt states). The piano piece described was perhaps from the 14 Bagatelles (1908).

My first acquaintance with Béla Bartók dates back to 1906 or 1907 in Berlin. One day my friend, the young Hungarian composer Erwin Lendvai (one of the few pupils of Puccini), paid me a visit, bringing with him a shy and modest-looking, slim youth, whom he introduced as his friend and fellow student, Béla Bartók of Budapest. They had both been pupils in composition of Hans Koessler at the Budapest Conservatory. Lendvai had often spoken to me with admiration of the scholarly and artistic teaching of Koessler. For that reason I was from the very start interested in young Bartók and expected great things of him even before I had seen or heard a note of his music. Bartók likewise must have had an exaggerated notion of my importance as a critic, even though at the time I was a beginner like my visitor. He showed marked signs of respect for me, but after a few polite introductory phrases we both settled down to business in earnest. He seated himself at the time-worn miniature piano (a grand piano was beyond my reach at the time), picked out from his bag a number of manuscripts, and began to play. I do not, after such a long lapse of time, recollect what works he played. Only one item impressed itself so vividly on my mind that I seem to hear it in my imagination even now: a set of little piano pieces with the oddest harmony that had ever come to my notice. It was not the extravagant Wagnerian chromaticism – the last word in advanced harmony in those years – nor was it akin to the refined *clair–obscur* impressionistic harmony of Debussy, at that time very little known in Germany. It gave the impression not of a polished refinement but, on the contrary, of a primitive, rustic, strong, instinctive feeling for colourful sound. In a word, the first brief acquaintance with Bartók's music revealed in a few minutes, even thirty-five years ago, Bartók's basic national trait, stemming from his native Hungarian soil. Everyone in those days had quite a definite notion of Hungarian music, derived from Liszt's Hungarian Rhapsodies and Brahms's Hungarian Dances. Yet this Bartók Hungarian music was different from these well-known models.

ANTAL DORÁTI

(1906–88)

Antal Doráti studied at the Budapest Academy of Music, learning from such professors as Bartók, Kodály and Leó Weiner, before embarking upon a distinguished conducting career, firstly in Europe and later in the United States and Britain. He knew Bartók well, both in Budapest and later in New York. Here he recalls their first meeting, in about 1916.

A few years later – I must have been ten by then – I went with my father to 'the Academy' – as the Franz Liszt Academy of Music was called for short. (Quite significantly, this distinctive abbreviation was accorded in Budapest only to the Academy of Music; the Academies of Science and Technology, etc., were always quoted by their full, cumbersome names.) Entering, my father stopped as we encountered a small, thin, grey-haired, clean-shaven gentleman, who said 'Good day' in a whisper, as my father addressed him.

'Good day, Professor Bartók'.

I looked, awe-struck; but strangely, not disappointed. There could not have been a greater difference between my fantasy-Bartók and the real man I saw then for the first time, but I immediately accepted the 'real man' as the 'right one'. Of course, that was the way he *had* to look: frail, rather small of stature, grey hair, certainly, that was in order, he always had to have grey hair (in fact he greyed very early), and very fine, sharply-cut features – small, thin-lipped mouth, an almost classic-Greek nose. And his eyes, my God, his eyes – large, knowing, penetrating, transfixing – the eyes of a prophet, just stepping out from the Bible.

'Good day' (whispered).

'Toni, greet Professor Bartók'. I greeted Professor Bartók.

'That is your son?'

'Yes'.

'Is he musical?'

'Yes. He plays the piano'. (My father was talking too much.) 'He also plays your pieces'. (My father was talking far too much.)

'Well, some time he shall play for me, maybe?'

'Certainly, he will be honoured to do so – won't you, Toni?'

By then I was already running up the stairs, very scared, my ears red like two small traffic signs.

From that day onwards I often saw Bartók, on the streets and at concerts. When we passed each other, I always greeted him, bowing politely according to the rules of good behaviour as I learned them at home. Bartók always acknowledged my courtesy, somewhat distracted, but amiably.

'Bartókiana (some recollections)', *Tempo*, no. 136 (March 1981), p. 7

ARTHUR HONEGGER
(1892–1955)

The Swiss composer, Arthur Honegger, studied in Zürich and Paris. In 1919–20 he joined such composers as Poulenc and Milhaud in forming 'Les Six', although he always remained on the group's more sober fringe. His major compositions, in a wide variety of genres, mostly date from the inter-war years.

I first met Béla Bartók in 1911 at Zürich when I was studying at the Conservatoire there. During a *Tonkünstlerfest* concert a slimly-built man, with delicate features and clear eyes, took a seat beside me while the orchestra was playing, and then, when the piece was finished, went up on the stage and played his *Rhapsody for Pianoforte and Orchestra* [Op. 1] under the baton of Volkmar Andreae. At once I was captivated: how fresh the colour and rhythmic the life of this work, so unlike the many similarly entitled pieces which then encumbered the repertoires.

Soon I had the opportunity of studying the piano *Bagatelles* (Op. 6), and I must confess that I was somewhat disconcerted by the surprising liberty of their idiom. Since then I have been able to familiarize myself with the work of this great Hungarian musician, and, from the *Second Quartet* to the *Music for Strings and Percussion*, my admiration has steadily grown. Soon after its publication, the quartet was performed by Yvonne Giraud, Delgrange, Darius Milhaud and myself, not without faults, for the work is quite difficult. Highly interesting, we found it, indeed we of the younger musical generation were captivated by Bartók, and to listen to a fresh work of his became an event, alas too rare, of capital importance.

Most writers have agreed to hold Schönberg and Stravinsky responsible for the reaction which set in after Debussy. Some have included Erik Satie; I personally would nominate Bartók instead. These three are the authentic representatives of the musical revolution of that generation. Less direct and sparkling than Stravinsky, less dogmatic than Schönberg, Bartók is perhaps the most profoundly musical of the three and best manifests a close-knit organic development . . .

Preface to Serge Moreux, *Béla Bartók*, tr. G. S. Fraser and Erik de Mauny, London (Harvill Press), 1953, pp. 9–10

With pupils
ERNŐ BALOGH
(b. 1897)

One of the most outstanding of Bartók's early piano students at the Budapest Academy of Music was Ernő Balogh, who studied with him between 1909 and 1915. In 1912, at the age of only fifteen, he gained the Liszt Prize. He later studied in Berlin. In 1924 he emigrated to the United States, where he worked as a pianist and composer, eventually settling in Washington DC. Balogh assisted Bartók personally during his concert tours of the United States and also during his final residence there.

Béla Bartók who lived and died as one of the most significant composers of the twentieth century – and who felt his greatest contribution to music was as preserver and annotator of the folk music of several nationalities – made a living practically all his life by teaching the piano. In this respect he shared the fate of Chopin, whom we know and remember only as a composer and delicate performer of his own works, but whose living depended on giving piano lessons.

Since Bartók spent a greater part of his lifetime, from his student days until he died, in teaching the piano there is considerable interest in what kind of teacher he was. Although I do not feel qualified to give a complete answer to this complex subject, since I studied with Bartók in the Academy of Music in Budapest only in the years 1909 to 1915, I can report my experiences of those six years. This belongs to the early phase of Bartók's teaching in that Institute, where he had started just two years previously (1907) and where he taught until 1934, when he retired and transferred his activities to the Hungarian Academy of Sciences, working on his collections of folk songs. He kept on teaching privately until he left Hungary for America in 1940 and he did some teaching until he died – working periodically with just a few pupils.

I played for him a few times in 1928, 1929, 1934, 1940 (mostly his own compositions) but my most vivid memory of him as a teacher is from those six years, when for ten months of the year I had two lessons a week – the most important moments of my life during those years.

Though I was only twelve when I began to study with him (the youngest of his class) his words, attitudes and approach are still clearly etched in my memory. He was under the age of thirty but already possessed a great reputation as the most respected and most controversial composer in Hungary, who challenged the critics and the public with his provocative music. All of his students admired and loved him for his genius, of which we were convinced, for his profound knowledge of every phase in music, for his gentle and kind manners, for his unfailing logic, for his convincing explanation of every detail. He was just and fair, but he could not conceal his annoyance with his less gifted students.

The essence of his approach as a teacher was that he taught music first and piano second. Immaculate musicianship was the most important part of his guidance and influence. He clarified the structure of the compositions we played, the intentions of the composer, the basic elements of music and the fundamental knowledge of phrasing.

He had unlimited patience to explain details of phrasing, rhythm, touch, pedaling. He was unforgiving for the tiniest deviation or sloppiness in rhythm. He was most meticulous about rhythmical proportion, accent and the variety of touch.

Bartók insisted on first solving the musical problems and then the pianistic ones. In fact, he was not deeply interested in pianistic problems. He had a natural technique and although he was recognized in time as a virtuoso, virtuoso problems did not interest him.

All Bartók students naturally copied his playing style, although it had a limited dynamic scale, was not effortless and did not exhibit 'Spielfreudigkeit', which is perhaps the most captivating element for the general audience. I refer to the type of playing in which neither the listener nor the player is conscious of details of execution, but the whole performance gives the impression of such spontaneity that the composition seems to be created right at that moment.

Bartók loved to explain, and endeared himself by doing so like one musician talking to another; never in an authoritative way. Our lesson started with our playing the whole composition without interruption (we had to play everything from memory the very first time we brought it) while he made his corrections on our music with light pencil marks. Then he played the entire composition for us. After this we played again, this time being stopped repeatedly and re-playing each phrase until we performed it to his satisfaction.

He demanded great exactness, particularly concerning rhythm. For instance, I remember clearly that he put great importance on the fact that in a 6/8 rhythm the last eighth should not be too short, and in a dotted 3/4 rhythm (   ) the third quarter note should be not too short. Let us say, generally, that the upbeat which is the chief indicator of the good beat should get its proper share of time, [and] never be rushed. He insisted that a sixteenth should be exactly a sixteenth, never less nor more, that every accent should be in the right place and in correct proportion. He did not permit any unnecessary accents and had a marvellous sense for the balance of voices and for the proportion of tempi and dynamics.

He was against excessive rubatos and ritardandos which prevent the continuous, undisturbed flow of the music. Within this continuous flow some freedom of tempi was permitted, but it had to be in the proper place and in the proper proportion.

He respected and encouraged the individuality of his students. He not only never demanded that they copy his playing (although all of his students did this to some extent either consciously or unconsciously) but he respected the individual's approach to a phrase as long as it was within good taste and the style of the composer.

Bartók had no use for sentimental playing, which does not mean that he forbade emotional expression. In fact my music has many of his pencil marks indicating either 'espressivo' or the same, in his shortened way, 'espr.'. There are also several 'dolce' marks, by which he meant gently, while by 'espressivo' he meant a singing tone with feeling.

Bartók was for clean use of the pedal, without overindulging in its use. On the other hand, he used the soft pedal frequently and

Bartók and Ernő Balogh during the composer's first visit to America, 1927–8

encouraged his students to do so. He also used and taught the half pedal for separating changing harmonies or for thinning out a sonority.

In his personal relations with his students he was friendly, but did not encourage the discussion of any subject which was not pertinent to the lesson. I was studying composition at the same time as piano and in the fifth year when the Budapest Philharmonic Orchestra played a composition of mine he learned of it by accident and was surprised that I was active in that field too. It never occurred to me to tell him anything unrelated to my piano lesson unless he asked me, and he asked very few personal questions, if any.

He taught us a very wide range of repertoire, from the oldest to such new music as Debussy and Ravel, which we learned in the same year that the works were published. But he didn't assign a single concerto during the time I studied with him. This did not leave one entirely unprepared for the concertos of Mozart and Beethoven, because after going over one single Mozart Sonata or Beethoven Sonata with him (and the first such work took a very long time) one had no doubt how to approach any other work of that composer.

He never assigned his own compositions and we had to ask for them if we wanted to learn them. At the same time he wanted all of his students to get acquainted with other contemporary music.

Did Bartók like teaching? Having known him for the last thirty-six years of his life, I believe I can answer this question. He surely would have preferred to earn his living by other means, such as ethnographic research or composing. But since teaching offered his only means of livelihood, he did it, as he did everything else, with utmost conscientiousness, doing his very best in a field for which he had so many qualities. His logical mind, clear presentation of any problems and his joy in explaining anything, made his teaching less taxing for him and enjoyable for his students.

'Bartók, the teacher – as I knew him', *Etude*, vol. 74/1 (January 1956), pp. 20, 51. © 1956, *The Etude Magazine*, used by permission of the publisher, Theodore Presser Company.

GISELLA SELDEN-GOTH
(1884–1975)

Gisella Selden-Goth studied piano in Budapest with Bartók's own teacher, István Thomán, and was one of the very few people ever to have received private lessons in composition from Bartók. That instruction occurred between 1906 and 1908. Selden-Goth then pursued a career as a composer and writer about music, in Berlin (1912–24), Florence (1924–38), New York (1938–50), and, during her later years, again in Florence.

His teaching was not orthodox, nor was it easy at first to follow his system, although in the long run it proved to be exciting and challenging. From the first, he insisted on my harmonizing the simplest four-part chorales in a 'progressive' way and not ending them on the usual cadences; he had me work out contrapuntally themes of Debussy, himself a vaguely frightening figure at that time; and he believed strongly that the music written for each instrument should be thematically independent – for example, in a duo-sonata the violin and piano should work out completely different thematic material, thus violating the constructive principles of traditional composition. Some lessons were devoted entirely to hearing him play by memory from Richard Strauss's *Salome* and *Zarathustra* – music forbidden at that time at the Academy as devilish and corrupting! – while I followed it closely with a pocket-score which he always carried around in his portfolio. Other lessons were spent in explanations of his own works, works that are today considered 'tame' but which at that time scared his colleagues as if they had been inspired by Satan himself. Sometimes, without warning, he would vanish for months, travelling through the Balkans to record an immense quantity of folk music, a task he felt to be one of the most important in his life. After months of absence, he would walk in again without a word of explanation and ask, 'What have you to show me today?' When after two years of strenuous study I had written an orchestral composition, he did not approve of it because he found it 'reactionary' and 'old style'. When I managed to arrange for a performance of the work at a Budapest Philharmonic concert, Bartók chose to regard my action as an unforgivable personal insult. He cut off our relationship immediately and we did not see each other for many years.

I met him again as a refugee in America – first in Washington, D.C., where he appeared at one of the Coolidge Concerts in the Library of Congress as a composer of already considerable but still very controversial fame; later in New York, where he had accepted a grant at Columbia University to do research in his beloved folk music, the only work that provided him with a measure of relief from the homesickness and general uneasiness that dogged him wherever he went. By then he had forgotten our quarrel, and we would sometimes meet in his modest apartment on West 57th Street, which I always left with the feeling that things were going from bad to worse. His health was failing, he suffered from frequent fits of depression, and material worries were increasing. But this is the story that has been told by many others . . .

I shall never forget the day when he told me that a most distinguished and lucrative position had been offered him by the Curtis Institute of Music in Philadelphia to teach composition, and that he had refused it. 'But why, for heaven's sake?' I asked anxiously. 'Why should *I* tell people how they should compose?' was his despondent answer. 'I just cannot.' 'But', I said, 'you could do it once, with me – why did you teach me at that time?' He shook his head sadly. 'Perhaps I did it because we were young, and because I thought that, maybe, you were a talent . . .'

"'I shall never forget . . .'": A vignette of Béla Bartók', *Musical Courier*, vol. 152/4 (October 1955), p. 14

With folk singers

LIDI DÓSA

(b. 1885)

Lidi Dósa was a Transylvanian-born nursemaid to a Budapest family. In the summer of 1904 she accompanied the family on a holiday to the resort of Gerlicepuszta in Gömör county (now Ratkó, Czechoslovakia). Bartók was staying at the resort at this time, devoting his energies to composition and concert preparation. Lidi Dósa's singing is credited with having first stimulated Bartók's interest in folk music. One of the songs sung by Lidi

Lidi Dósa, around 1904

Dósa, 'Piros alma' ('Red apple'), was published with an accompaniment by Bartók early in 1905.

Q: As far as we know, Lidi, during the time you were in service in Pest you sang some beautiful folk songs from Kibéd [now Chibed, Romania] to someone . . .

A: Yes, that's correct!

Q: To a music professor?

A: The man was not a music professor but an important artist: Béla Bartók! I had to keep on singing to him, but he only wanted to hear old village songs. He liked only those I had learned from my grandmother . . .

Q: How did you get to know Bartók, Lidi?

A: . . . I was staying there at a summer resort. Our rooms were next to each other. I heard Bartók practising all the time . . . and then, on one occasion, he heard me singing. I was singing to the child . . . The song pleased Bartók, and he asked me to sing it again because he wanted to note it down. When he had taken it down, he went to the piano and played it. He then called me and asked if he was playing it properly. Well, it was exactly as I had sung it.

In an interview reproduced in Péter Cseke, 'Aki Bartóknak énekelt', in Ferenc László, ed., *Bartók-könyv 1970–1971*, Bucharest (Kriterion), 1971, p. 91

SUSANA CÎRŢ

(b. 1898/9)

Susana Cîrţ (née Hord) lived in the predominantly Romanian-speaking village of Troaş (Torjás) in Arad county (now in Romania). She recalls Bartók's visit to the settlement in July 1917 to collect folk tunes. The second 'professor' mentioned was almost certainly the Italian conductor Egisto Tango, who was travelling with Bartók at this time. Two months previously Tango had conducted the première of *The Wooden Prince* in Budapest and would similarly introduce *Duke Bluebeard's Castle* in the following year.

I was a girl. It happened one Sunday. The old retired teacher from Săvîrşin, Givulescu, came over to me, together with his son and two professors from Pest. There were four of them. Givulescu had taught in Troaş, too, for a few years. The professors had relaxed expressions on their faces, and were tall. They were well-built men, young and handsome! They asked my mother to receive them and to agree to my singing into the gramophone for them. They called the machine a 'gramophone'. I sang one nice verse, and then another one. It came back sounding so beautiful. The whole village gathered around us. *The whole village*. Everyone was wanting to sing. The young men sang, the old women sang, and so did Ştefan Florcă, Hălmăgean Gligor, Cătană Maxim . . . I remember that the professors asked me not to sing songs we'd learnt from the soldiers, but only those from the mountain region here. So I only sang the ones from the mountains!

In Béla Csende, ed., *A népdalkutató Bartók Béla*, Békéscsaba (Kner Nyomda), 1981, pp. 96–7

Collecting songs in a Slovak village, 1907

RÓZA ÖKRÖS
(b. 1899/1900)

Róza Ökrös (Mrs Mihály Kira) was one of the more celebrated of Bartók's Hungarian folk singers. She sang for Bartók in 1917, while he was visiting his sister in Vésztő, Békés county. This interview dates from 1980.

I was seventeen when I met Béla Bartók, and doing work in the fields of the Wenckheim estate in Kertmegpuszta, next to Vésztő. Bartók's brother-in-law was the estate manager there. We were working in the fields when a man about thirty-five, with fair hair – not tall – came over to us and asked if anyone knew any old songs and would be prepared to sing them to him. There were many girls all together but they were all diffident and, in their shyness, said that they did not know any old songs. But I volunteered.

In the evening he came to our quarters and sat down on a worker's case, with a night-light beside him. I sat opposite him and sang. He noted it down. I sang two songs, the 'Fehér László' and the 'Angoli Borbála'.

Transcribing folk music, 1910s

I was undoubtedly awe-struck, for no more songs came to my mind at that time. He was such a modest man, and did not press me to sing any further.

There were many workers in the barn – the quarters – and in the evening everyone retired to rest. Only I sang. I well remember how careful he was that my singing and his work did not disturb the others. About myself I remember that I was then already a great lover of songs, and if I heard a new song I would set about learning it.

Mostly I learnt these songs while working. My father died when I was 10. I never heard my mother sing. I learnt very many songs, but now I'm getting old and I've forgotten so many of them. However, I haven't forgotten Béla Bartók – it's as if he were here before me today. He has always remained in my memory.

In Béla Csende, ed., *A népdalkutató Bartók Béla*, Békéscsaba (Kner Nyomda), 1981, pp. 67–8

III

Later professional years
(1920–1940):
a taste of success

From about 1920 Bartók was seen and heard more on both the national and international stage. His numerous concert tours, principally as a pianist playing his own works, led him to most countries of Europe and also, in 1927–8, to the United States. Receptions of these tours were usually mixed, but sufficiently encouraging – especially in the countries of Western Europe – to inspire a fairly regular flow of compositions. Many of these works, such as the violin sonatas, violin rhapsodies, piano concertos and piano sonata, were written with Bartók's own performing opportunities as a soloist or chamber player in mind.

As an ethnomusicologist he became more involved in the transcription and annotation, rather than further collection, of folk musics, although in 1936 he did engage in field work in Turkey. He prepared numerous volumes of Hungarian, Romanian and Slovak folk music, but could only gain significant international dissemination of a single-volume study of Hungarian folk music. In 1934 he was relieved of his piano teaching responsibilities at the Budapest Academy of Music and appointed to work as an ethnomusicologist in the Hungarian Academy of Sciences. Until his departure for the United States in 1940 this scientific work was from time to time interrupted by concert tours and the composition of some of his finest works: the final two string quartets, Music for Strings, Percussion and Celesta, the Sonata for Two Pianos and Percussion, and the Second Violin Concerto.

Before the Press

KELETI ÚJSÁG

(Transylvania)

In 1922 Lajos Kőmives was a writer for the *Keleti Újság (Eastern News)* of Kolozsvár (Cluj Napoca, Romania). As a result of the Treaty of Trianon the city, along with the rest of Transylvania, had recently been transferred from Hungarian to Romanian control. During Bartók's visit there on a concert tour late in October 1922 Kőmives arranged for an in-depth interview with him, from which the following portrait is extracted.

The door quietly swings open and the Master appears in its opening. At first sight he appears unpretentious and unassuming. The theatrical manner of internationally feted celebrities is completely absent from his demeanour. He is not robust, is rather shorter than average in stature, and his black clothes vividly set off the outline of his refined white countenance, from which his shrewd, stern eyes, radiating intelligence and ardent interest, attest to the presence of a superior spirit. His face is still thoroughly youthful, but above the smooth high forehead his short hair has already turned completely white. That is not a sign of old age but only of premature greying. It bestows on his whole head a quality of greater whiteness and interest . . .

'Látogatásom Bartók Bélánál', *Keleti Újság*, 31 October 1922

MUSICAL NEWS AND HERALD

(London)

During Bartók's second post-war visit to Britain, in May 1923, he was interviewed in London by Watson Lyle, a correspondent for the *Musical News and Herald*.

I think that the wish to meet M. Béla Bartók was formulated after listening to a performance of his 'Two Portraits', for orchestra, in Queen's Hall several months ago. The character of this work indicated a kind of Dr. Jekyll and Mr. Hyde, as the personality of the composer, united to vivid imaginative gifts and – as then appeared – a rather cynical outlook upon life . . . Admiring the work of the composer as I do, it is good to feel that cynicism is not a characteristic of his personality. There is in his nature the charitableness, the warm humanity, and the clarity of thought that are antagonistic to the harbouring of jaundiced views upon either Life, or its reflection, Art. My misconception may have been engendered by reading (to kill time while awaiting the performance of 'Two Portraits') one of those marvellous, high-browey programme annotations that acclaim cynicism, in music, as a virtue, and adjure us to listen to that which is about to be played as 'abstract' music.

Bartók would, I think, feel considerable amusement at such ideas. His humoursome smile, and simple directness in expressing an opinion, are alike free from pose.

Slight, physically; unassertive yet dignified in manner, his dark eyes often glow with a compelling intensity in his sharp-featured face. His hair is white. One feels, however, that he is of the eternally young in spirit, and of this his fiery exposition of some of his own music, at 9 Wigmore Street, on the evening after our talk, gave ample evidence. I have particularly in mind his interpretations of the remarkable 'Allegro barbaro', the Suite Op. 14, the Three Burlesques Op. 8c, and the Roumanian Peasant Dances.

Thus, indeed, did the far off, initial impression of a dual personality gain credence. It hardly seemed possible that the composer who strongly, sometimes almost defiantly, proclaimed the distinctive individuality of his art, and himself, when seated at the keyboard, could be the modest man I met the previous day who, when I referred at all to his music, was much more inclined to change the subject than to discuss it.

'Béla Bartók: A Personal Impression', *Musical News and Herald*, 19 May 1923, pp. 495–6

THE MUSICAL TIMES
(London)

Late in 1925 the London journalist Frank Whitaker visited
Bartók at his home in Budapest. The resultant article was
commended for its veracity by many, including Bartók himself.
In the following year Whitaker signed a contract with Oxford
University Press to write the first full-length book, in any
language, about Bartók and his music. Only the first chapter, now
lost, was ever completed.

Physically as well as mentally Bartók presents striking antitheses. His
loosely-brushed hair is white, though his tanned face is young for his
forty-four years. His rugged, strongly rhythmical music suggests that
he is big and powerful, but he is slight and lean, with hands and feet
almost as delicate as a woman's, and features as ascetic as those of Lord
Darling, whom he strongly resembles. On the platform, at the
pianoforte, he whirls tempestuously through his part; in private he is
gentleness itself – alert but not aggressive, precise without being
pedantic. In his grave, old-world courtesy there is not a trace of
affectation. One is conscious all the while of his virility, but it is of the
kind that burns inwardly – that glitters through the eyes rather than
spends itself in gesture. His eyes, indeed, stamp him at once as a
remarkable man. They are of a rich golden brown, and he has a habit
of opening them wide and slowly tilting back his head as he waits for a
question. A sculptor would seize at once on this backward poise of the
head; a painter on those fine eyes.

He received me with that warm-hearted hospitality which an
Englishman meets everywhere in Hungary, and for several hours, in
his cosy sitting-room, discussed with me his work and his plans. On the
wall behind us was a large portrait of Beethoven. That and a
photograph were the only pictures in the room. Instead, on the wall and
indeed in every corner, were the outward signs of Bartók's intense love
of country – strips of peasant embroidery, brightly-coloured bodices
which were once part of some national costume, pottery, and wooden
vessels of various kinds. Even the furniture was peasant's work, of
carved and stained wood . . .

Since the war Fate has made him amends, but even now I think

Budapest does not realise the high regard in which he is held abroad. His distinguished fellow-countryman Dohnányi, whom I also met while I was in Hungary, spoke of him with warm admiration, placing him at least on a level with Stravinsky. But he has still to become a national figure.

The cruel years of his early manhood have left their mark on Bartók. Several of his friends warned me that I should find him an embittered man. Embittered is, I think, too strong a word for one whose smile is so ready – his smile is beautiful: I can find no fitter word – and whose manner is so simple. I would describe him as a disappointed man, and a disillusioned man. No one of such acute sensibility could have withstood the buffetings of the world without being changed. But he shows it not so much in what he says as in an indefinable impression of aloofness from the world. Some of the things he knew about current musical life in London surprised me – *e.g.*, that a prominent newspaper was at that time wanting a critic: he discussed with interest who was likely to get the post. But of other matters of greater moment he spoke as from a great distance.

'A visit to Béla Bartók', *Musical Times*, vol. 67 (1926), pp. 220, 222

NOUVELLE REVUE DE HONGRIE
(Budapest)

In May 1932 the *Nouvelle Revue de Hongrie* released a special issue in celebration of the gathering in Budapest and Esztergom of the Commission for Intellectual Cooperation of the League of Nations, on whose Permanent Committee for Literature and the Arts Bartók served. That issue of the journal included an extensive interview with Bartók conducted by Magda Vámos, a career journalist with some experience in music criticism. Forty years later she recalled her impressions of the interview with Bartók.

The path up to the Rose Hill house where Bartók occupied a flat on the First Floor was pretty steep. The ground above and behind was still free of buildings at the time. Silence reigned, and horizons were distant; the Danube islands and the outline of the town built on the Pest plain were within reach of the eye.

Silence and eyes that reached distant horizons: that was the first impression I had of Bartók as we shook hands. He had only recently returned from Egypt, his complexion was tanned by the sun, but his handsome figure still looked fragile, and in need of protection. His manner reminded me of outstanding mathematicians whom I knew. There was nothing 'arty' about him. Simplicity, an effort to be precise, concealed wit – that is what I observed. The edge of his irony was playful rather than biting.

If I remember right we sat in two large leather armchairs, books, scores, magazines behind us. I had barely arrived and we had something to drink when Bartók's son Péter, who was eight at the time, burst in, showing no intention of leaving. His father told him not to disturb our conversation and he found a place under the piano opposite, between the pedals and the right-hand leg. He crouched there right to the end without batting an eyelid, observing us for a full hour. He came out from his hiding-place when we said goodbye. 'Why didn't you ask me anything?' he said with a certain sound of reproach in his voice. Then, like a little gentleman, he took me down to the gate, right down the steep slope of the garden . . .

The interview was first recorded in Hungarian, then I translated it into French myself. Bartók carefully checked both the Hungarian and French versions and signed them.

'A 1932 interview with Bartók', *New Hungarian Quarterly*, no. 50 (Summer 1973), pp. 143–4

In public and in private
MÁRIA LUKÁCS-POPPER
(1888–1981)

Through being a close relative of Bartók's piano teacher (István Thomán), Mária Lukács-Popper came to know Bartók while still a girl. Later, he taught her harmony and met frequently with her when she studied cello at the Academy. In May 1920, on the initiative of Ernő Dohnányi, the Bartóks moved to live in Buda at

the home of her father, the banker József Lukács, and stayed
there until March 1922. Mária Lukács-Popper was the younger
sister of the renowned Marxist philospher György Lukács.

Ernő [Dohnányi] was greatly concerned that Bartók, who lived at
Rákoskeresztúr with his family and commuted from there to the
Academy of Music, was not very well off. At Keresztúr there was no
gas or electricity, and no fuel – he even had transportation problems.
Ernő came to us and asked my father to do something for Bartók and
his family. It was easy to say this, but much more difficult to put into
practice. Béla was an extremely proud man: he liked to help others, but
refused from others what he could not repay. Finally my father hit
upon an excellent scheme. He asked Béla to do him a favour. Naturally
Béla replied: whatever I can do. My father represented the situation as
though he feared part of the house would be requisitioned, and if Béla
and his family moved in with us it would solve the housing problem for
all of us. And that was what happened. Béla and his family occupied my
father's apartment in the Gellért Hill house, which vanished completely during the siege of Budapest in the Second World War. Béla, of
course – thinking all this time that he was doing us a favour – wanted to
know what he owed for board and lodging for all three of them. We
assured him that everyday life would cost him no more hereafter than it
had done up to then. Much later, when he no longer lived with us, he
jokingly reproached me: you deceived me, life is much more costly
than you made it out to be then. But he was not angry about it. That was
when I got to know Márta, Béla's first wife, who devoted everything,
her whole life, to serving him. Life never rewarded her for her
exceptional self-sacrifice. Now that she is not with us any longer let
these few lines serve to honour her memory.

The Bartóks, as I mentioned, occupied my father's apartment. It
soon became apparent that this was not the best arrangement, because
Béla could only work in total seclusion, and thus he finally got the guest
room, which was completely isolated from the other rooms. Now he
was able to work to his heart's content . . .

In everyday life Béla was modest. He worked regularly, and lived a
normal middle-class existence. When he considered a cause to be good,
he immediately espoused it, not caring that he might thereby cause
himself harm. He was a reliable friend, with an over-scrupulously

pure and honest character. For this reason he undeservedly suffered much harm.

Few people have taken the trouble so far to point out why Béla was so difficult to reach. Let us admit, he did not possess that attribute which won Dohnányi so many friends: a bright affability in his dealings with people. Kodály's life was also easier side by side with his extraordinary life-companion, Emma . . .

Béla and Ernő's friendship was a good one, although both Béla and I criticized many things in Ernő's attitude. Especially the fact that for a time he yielded to his wife's wishes and played far too often at the request of right-wing institutions and organizations, without any particular protest. In this regard Ernő was not as unshakeable in his belief as Béla. This did not mean, of course, that Dohnányi sympathized with the extreme right-wing fringes – it was just that he did not attach any importance to the whole matter. We were sorry that things happened this way, but there was nothing we could do.

In the Gyopár utca house we were often together with Ernő and Béla. Once Béla mentioned that his Viennese publisher, Universal Edition, would like to publish a work from his youth, the *Piano Quintet*. He remarked that part of the manuscript was missing, and that he could no longer recall it. Ernő then asked him: 'Is this the quintet which you showed me at that time in Berlin?' (That must have been about sixteen to eighteen years previously.) 'Yes,' Béla replied. Ernő thought a bit, then said, 'Wait a moment, Béla.' He sat down at the piano and began to play, like a sleep-walker, groping for the notes. Suddenly Béla exploded: 'That's it, that's it! We've found it!' Ernő, who was not always strong in everything, had a remarkably keen memory.

When the Bartóks found a home at Szilágyi Dezső tér they moved from Gyopár utca, leaving a great void. We missed Márta in particular, who had practically lived amongst us, unlike Béla, the artist, who with an oblivious and selfless asceticism secluded himself exclusively in his art. A few days after they had moved away, my father happened to remark in passing that for the past few days he had been sleeping soundly. In reply to a question from me about this, he said: 'You know, dear, now I can tell you – Béla always played at night.' The piano had been located on the second storey just over my father's bed. I can hardly imagine a greater friendly sacrifice for a paternal friend and admirer to devote to Béla's genius. While Béla lived in our house my father did not mention this at all, not wanting to obstruct him in his work. For we not only admired Béla, we sincerely loved him.

'Bartók our House-guest', *New Hungarian Quarterly*, no. 84 (Winter 1981), pp. 104–5

DOROTHY MOULTON MAYER
(1886–1974)

The soprano Dorothy Moulton was an early British exponent of the vocal music of Schoenberg, Stravinsky and Bartók, and came to know Bartók well during the 1920s and 1930s. She collaborated with Bartók in at least two performances, and also, as the wife of the industrialist and philanthropist Robert Mayer, received him in her London home on several occasions. In later years the Mayers co-founded a series of children's concerts. This extract is drawn from the associated music magazine for children.

He never apologized for himself, he was incapable of writing a note he did not believe in, he was very reserved and very proud and all this did not help him to win the favour of the musical public in Budapest. This mattered less, because he was acknowledged abroad as one of the greatest of contemporary composers. He came to London in 1923, and I had the honour of having him in my house as guest; he played at a party to which all the pianists in London came – and though one of them afterwards said 'I wonder your piano could resist such treatment' – he had a tremendously hard and percussive touch – they all realised that he was a master.

'Bartók', *Crescendo*, no. 114 (October 1961), p. 10

PAUL ARMA
(1904–87)

The Hungarian-born French musician Paul Arma studied piano with Bartók between 1920 and 1924. He then performed and taught widely in Europe and the United States. Between 1931 and 1933 he worked in Germany with Brecht and Eisler, before fleeing to France, where he took part in the Resistance during the

Second World War. In later years he devoted his time to composition, performance and ethnomusicology.

He mapped out his own path with foresight and kept to it with singular firmness without ever departing from it.

He liked to argue with his friends. Bartók's curiosity and genius was not indifferent to art of any kind. He made me read Dostoevsky and Stravinsky, Victor Hugo and Darius Milhaud. We read and played new works together: with an infallible glance he took them to pieces, passed judgement on them and recomposed them.

Occasionally he made concessions, but not once to platitude, to tawdriness or to fashion. He was able to retain the reserve indispensable to any real force seeing its path and knowing its goal.

He was exceptionally modest, very kind, often fatherly, but not indulgent; a single injustice was enough to provoke his violent reaction, to bring out his toughness, to make evident his upright and intractable character. His nature, faithful to his ideas, to his conceptions, his convictions and his friends, did not allow him to tolerate disloyalty.

'Bartók: Man, Musician, Scholar', *New Hungarian Quarterly*, no. 81 (Spring 1981), p. 27

CECIL GRAY

(1895–1951)

Cecil Gray was one of the most provocative British music critics of the inter-war years. A close friend of the composer–critic Philip Heseltine (Peter Warlock), he helped to promote the works of such composers as Schoenberg, Bartók and van Dieren in the years immediately after the First World War. In 1920 Gray wrote a landmark article about Bartók for Heseltine's *Sackbut* journal. This led to an exchange of letters and Gray's visit to Budapest to meet Bartók and Kodály in the following year. As the 1920s progressed Gray became disillusioned with Bartók's compositional direction, in particular with his use of 'unrelieved dissonance', and their friendship faltered.

I seem to have lost, or temporarily mislaid, the touching letter which the composer wrote, thanking me for the article and inviting me to visit him in Budapest, which I duly did a few months later. But I still preserve the characteristic note he wrote to me (in English) shortly before my visit, of which the following is an extract:

Dear Mr Gray,
. . . Please let me know exactly by a telegram the time of your arrival. I shall expect you at the station and guide you to Mr Kodály. Here I send a more recent photograph of mine to you: you must try to address me on your arrival – I am very thin, have grey hairs, and am wearing spectacles. Besides, I shall have with me a copy of The Sackbut *in order to make for you easier to find me.*
> *Yours very sincerely,*
> *Béla Bartók*

All these secret code instructions proved unnecessary. He was charmingly unaware of the fact that, even in the vast surging crowd which confronted me on my arrival at the central station in Budapest, without the necessity of sending me a recent photograph or carrying ostentatiously a copy of *The Sackbut*, even with my more than myopic eyes, I would be able to identify at a glance the personality whom I had immediately recognized, from a mere glance at his works, to be one of the most outstanding masters of contemporary music.

And so, of course, it happened. As soon as I set eyes on him in the railway station there was no possibility of doubting his identity: he stood out in almost melodramatic relief against the dim, circumambient, neutral mass of negligible humanity, like a lighthouse in the midst of a stormy sea . . .

He was one of the saints and fanatics of music, and it is just that which makes him and his art intolerable to the *homme moyen sensuel* – that, and a strain of harsh asceticism which in some of his works amounts to almost physical cruelty: whether to himself or his audience, whether masochistic or sadistic – or both (for the two things, so far from being incompatible often, and perhaps generally, go together), it would be difficult to determine. But the flagellatory aspect of his art is very decidedly in evidence, particularly in his middle period, and was in the process of development at the time of my visit to him in Budapest. The art of Bartók which I had hitherto known, on which my enthusiastic transports of admiration had been based – the early volumes of piano pieces, the String Quartet No. 1, the orchestral

Images and *Portraits* – had given place to something very different; and
I found the change highly disconcerting.

I remember only too well the occasion when I was first introduced to
the recently completed music of the ballet, *The Marvellous Mandarin*.
It was a day of scorching heat in August (in Budapest), in a street in the
centre of the town where the din of the traffic was intolerable; and
Bartók played to me the piano score on an inferior instrument which
was also decidedly out of tune. Even in orchestral performance this
work is a severe strain on the nervous system, to say nothing of one's
aesthetic sensibilities; consequently my sufferings under the aggravated
circumstances of the performance can perhaps be estimated, without
much exercise of the imagination. I have seldom suffered so much
from music. It was even too much for the composer himself. About
three-quarters' way through the work he suddenly stopped playing,
saying that he did not feel in the right mood. I searched my brains
desperately for some complimentary and appreciative words which
would not sound too insincere, but failed. I could find nothing to say.
But later, when walking back with Kodály, with whom I was staying,
to his flat, I confessed my misgivings and disillusionment, and was
comforted to learn that my feelings were to some extent shared, and at
any rate completely understood. 'This harmonically exacerbated style',
said Kodály, 'is a phase through which Bartók has to pass. He will
emerge from it, you will see.' How prophetically right he was is shown
by the last works which, purged from all violence and perversity, reach
back to the early Bartók. But the intervening period lasted so long that
I gave up all hope of any such miraculous transformation. The quality
of sheer musicianship remains unimpaired and unquestionable
throughout all his works, and I never ceased wholeheartedly to admire
it; but much, if not most of his middle-period music, has always been
personally antipathetic to me, in marked contrast to my feelings with
regard to the early and late works . . .

I have said that there was a strong element of laceration in the music
of Bartók, a pleasure in the infliction of pain on himself or his audience
or on both, which became intensified during his middle period; but in
his personal relations he was the most courteous and kindly of men.
Indeed, his hospitality, and that of Kodály, during my stay in Budapest
was more than a little embarrassing in view of the conditions then
prevailing. Apart from the fact that neither of them was in prosperous

Bartók in the 1920s

circumstances at the best of times, Hungary was then (1921) under-going a severe bout of inflation and economic crisis; and I was keenly conscious of the heavy financial burden that I must have been to my friends, who would not permit me even to pay for a tram fare if they could possibly prevent me, such being the quixotically excessive nature of Hungarian hospitality, which one is compelled to accept at the risk of causing mortal offence. The irony of the situation consisted in the fact that with the advantages of the exchange I was in a very much better position to play the part of host than they were, and that I also yearned to make the acquaintance of the night life of Budapest, which even then was the most glamorous in Europe. But I had to forego these beckoning allurements, which I could have well afforded under the circumstances, in order to be a burden on my good friends. Since then I have frequently been inclined to regard excessive hospitality as a vice rather than a virtue. Apart from that, it lays the recipient under an obligation which he is not allowed to repay. It is unfair, but in saying so I hope it will be understood how deeply I appreciate the spontaneous kindliness and generosity which prompts such excesses.

Musical Chairs, London (Home and van Thal), 1948, pp. 180, 181–4

DARIUS MILHAUD
(1892–1974)

The prolific French composer Darius Milhaud was educated at the Paris Conservatoire in the years leading up to the First World War. During that war he worked in the French legation in Rio de Janeiro, where he became interested in Latin American dance and jazz. These influences were soon reflected in such works of his as *Le boeuf sur le toit* (1919) and *La création du monde* (1923). Along with other members of 'Les Six' during the 1910s and early 1920s, Milhaud looked on Bartók as a kindred spirit, although their musical styles remained quite distinct. Despite the apparent sharpness of Milhaud's recollection below it is factually inaccurate in several places. (In the fourth paragraph, in particular, he has separated by several years two events which took place in Paris during April 1922.)

I knew the music of Bartók *well* before I came to know him personally. As far back as 1909 I was going to the publishers Eschig, on Rue Lafitte in those days, to study their scores of Bartók, brought out in Hungary, and those of Schoenberg, published in Vienna, for which Eschig was the agent. It was there that I bought Bartók's first quartet. My Conservatoire friends and I were regularly performing quartets at my place and we had become passionately fond of this work, so full of life and such personal lyricism. But my fossicking at Eschig came to an end with the 1914 war: 'enemy music' no longer reached us in France.

I have turned up several letters which I exchanged with Bartók immediately after the war. At the time that I went to Vienna with Francis Poulenc and Marya Freund we were hoping to give a concert in Budapest, but we couldn't bring this about, and so I only came to know Bartók several years later.

In 1919, with the establishment of the Group of Six, we organized a concert of foreign music in Paris and Bartók's Second Quartet featured on the programme.

I made the acquaintance of the great composer in Paris, when he came for the Concerts de La Revue musicale at Vieux Colombier, and it was also in connection with *La Revue musicale* that I saw him again some years later when, after a dinner at Henry Prunières', he played his two *Dreams* [*sic*; *Sonatas*] *for Piano and Violin* with the violinist Jelly d'Arányi, an artist of exceptional, almost tumultuous, rapture. I admired him not just as a composer but also as a pianist of precision and lyricism who possessed a faultless technique.

In 1928 my wife and I went to spend a few days in Budapest at the home of our friend Audrey Parr, whose husband was then at the British legation. It was springtime: the Hungarian countryside was all a mass of flowers – in the meadows, on the fruit trees. I took advantage of this sojourn to visit the Maestro at his home. He received us even though his wife was seriously ill at the time. It was a unique experience when Bartók played for us a series of folk recordings which he had made in Transylvania, although not without difficulty! He told me stories of his travels, of the technical complications of recording folksongs up in the mountains and how he had to prise these songs out of the suspicious peasants . . . There were extraordinary songs and dances accompanied by rapid, brilliant and rhythmical violin playing.

We ran across Bartók at the festivals which took place between 1928 and 1936 (Baden-Baden, Florence, the Biennale of Venice) – he was generally with Kodály, and hardly ever parted from him on these trips – and we resumed our interrupted conversations . . . We met up once again [during 1939, in Paris] at a dinner at the Vicomtesse de Noailles' after the performance of his *Concerto* [*sic; Sonata*] *for Two Pianos and Percussion*, which he played with his second wife under Scherchen's direction. The political situation in Europe and the spreading of Fascism were intolerable to him and he was thinking of leaving for the United States. It was in California that I next came across him, in 1942 [1941]. He gave a recital of his works at Mills College and lectured at Stanford University. Although he made several tours at that time they were – alas – not sufficient to guarantee his livelihood. He was worn-out, and his health was already deteriorating. I saw him again, for the last time, in New York. I was giving a paper at Columbia University and he had the courtesy to come to it. I was rather unwell then and he said to me: 'Is it true, Monsieur, that you, like me, are afflicted with an incurable disease?'

It is always immensely sad when a great composer is denied the joy of witnessing his own glory. During his lifetime Arnold Schoenberg was afforded proof of the incredible influence his theories were exercising on young people the world over. Bartók died in hospital, and it was only then that glory came – one could say that it was waiting for the demise of dear Bartók in order brilliantly to assert itself. Knowledge of his output and the admiration which it had invoked among a limited circle of musicians only then became universal. Concert societies and record companies sought to outdo each other in activity. What a shame it is that the composer himself was never able to partake in this magnificent blossoming! His son, Péter Bartók, a specialist in sound recordings, is the sole witness of this rapid rise which hallows one of the truly great masters of our age.

'Hommage à Béla Bartók', *La Revue musicale*, no. 224 (1955), pp. 16–18

EUGENE GOOSSENS

(1893–1962)

After music studies in Liverpool and London Eugene Goossens pursued a career as a conductor, gaining positions in London (from 1916), Cincinnati (from 1931) and Sydney (from 1947). In his earlier years he also composed a considerable amount of music in a style resembling that of Debussy and Ravel. Through his support of the newly formed International Society for Contemporary Music (ISCM), Goossens came to meet Bartók in February 1924.

. . . the following day I departed for Zürich for the jury meeting of the first International Society for Contemporary Music Festival to be held later that year at Prague. My fellow jurors were the composers Bartók and Casella, with Ansermet, conductor of the Geneva Orchestra and one of the foremost interpreters of contemporary work, giving us invaluable help. We stayed with Dr Volkmar Andreae, head of the Zürich Orchestra, and waded through some two hundred and fifty orchestral scores during our three days' stay there. Casella, Ansermet, and I disposed of half that number in the first day, largely by eliminating at first glance the inferior or second-rate works. Bartók, however, having picked out a couple of MS. scores which seemed at first glance to appeal to him most, wandered away to another part of the house, and spent the entire morning digesting them there. In vain we pointed out to him that unless he speeded up his methods of score-inspection we would never get through our job in under a month. He refused to be hustled, and in the end we finished by ignoring him entirely, and selected the half-dozen best works at the end of the specified three days without his aid. Bartók admitted to having scrupulously read through only five manuscripts in that time, and we departed for home leaving him in Zürich browsing among the remainder to his heart's content! During our incarceration at Dr Andreae's house, it rained interminably. Ansermet and Casella smoked endless packages of cigarettes, and I contracted influenza.

Overture and Beginners: A Musical Autobiography, London (Methuen), 1951, pp. 222–3

THE BRITISH BROADCASTING CORPORATION

Telephone
TEMPLE BAR 8400

BBC

Telegrams
ETHANUZE, LONDON

SAVOY HILL, LONDON W.C.2

When replying please quote **BM/JL.**

14th November, 1930.

Béla Bartók, Esq.,
Budapest, III
KAVICS U.10.

Dear Sir,

NATIONAL - NOVEMBER 24th. 9.40 - 10.45 p.m.

Many thanks for your programme for the above date.
We herewith confirm the following items:-

1. Seven Pieces for Pianoforte   BARTÓK   (Charles Rozsnyai)
   (Nos.2,3,4,5,7,12, & 10
   from "Fourteen Bagatelles")
   Five Hungarian Peasant Tunes   "   (Universal Ed.)
   (Nos. 1-5 from "Fifteen Hungarian Peasant Tunes)

2. With Jelly D'Aranyi.
   Sonata in A major for Violin & Pianoforte (K.305) MOZART
   I   Allegro Molto
   II   Andante grazioso
   III Presto

3. Dances of Marosszék for Pianoforte   KODÁLY   (Universal Ed.)

Will you please let us have by return corrections, if any,
in the spelling of items etc.

Balance Test. Will you kindly arrange to attend at 9.15 p.m. in order
that a balance test may be taken.

We will try and arrange for you to have the use of either a
Bechstein or a Bösendorfer piano, but will let you know definitely at
a later date.

Yours faithfully,
THE BRITISH BROADCASTING CORPORATION.

Marosh-Sake

Joseph Lewis

MB.

for Director of Programmes.
(Music Department)

Letter from the BBC arranging a broadcast, 1930

FRANK WHITAKER

Despite abandoning his plans to write a book about Bartók, Frank Whitaker continued to promote his cause in Britain during the 1930s. This account of the composer in his early fifties was written as part of a British Broadcasting Corporation campaign in 1932 to present a more human image of Bartók to listeners.

Béla Bartók is a quiet little man with a springy walk and a complexion like faded parchment. His lean, alert face suggests the man of forty, his white hair and scholar's stoop the man of sixty. Actually he is fifty-one this month (March). His brown eyes shine like sunlight in a witchball, and seem to expand as his interest in a subject grows. He has a trick of tilting his head back as he talks. He speaks English and French fairly well and German fluently, in addition to his native Hungarian. The English words he uses oftenest to describe his music are 'provoking' and 'unaccustomed'. For instance, he will say: 'My *Bagatelles* were my first provoking work,' or 'My second string quartet was too unaccustomed for the public of the day.'

Nothing in his appearance suggests the musician. He would just as soon pass for a lawyer – indeed, he is not unlike the Lord Darling of thirty years ago. His temperament does not show itself either in the length of his hair or the breadth of his tie, and when I saw him last he had not fallen to the temptation to wear a sombrero. He does not pose and he has no fads. On the platform he is the picture of self-control, but he dislikes appearing in public. That is because he is incurably nervous. He is one of the finest pianists in Europe, but if someone were to leave him ten thousand pounds tomorrow, I doubt if he would play in public again. In his early twenties [*sic*; late twenties] he was invited by Busoni to conduct the Philharmonic Orchestra in Berlin. He was so flustered in the rehearsal that he did not know how to begin, and Busoni had to help him with the first down-beat. The concert went reasonably well, but Bartók has never conducted since.

His technical knowledge is profound. I believe he cannot play a single instrument in the orchestra, but he writes as though he played them all. I remember calling on him one hot afternoon at his flat in Budapest and finding him with a sidedrum on his knees and a rapt look on his face. In one hand he had a drum-stick; with the other he was fiddling with the snares, or catgut strings, that are stretched across a sidedrum to make it rattle. A pair of cymbals lay at his feet. I wish I remembered exactly what he was doing with them all, but I don't. However, the point is that he had discovered a new effect, and for the next five minutes or so, having motioned me to a chair, he alternately thwacked the drum with a startling vigour and listened to the echoes wide-eyed and still, like a thrush that hears a footstep on the lawn.

The same afternoon a question arose about the practicability of a passage in his Second Violin Sonata. In a flash the thrush became a hawk, and the hawk had run out of the room and fetched the queerest-looking fiddle I ever saw. Perhaps some peasant had made it, for the flat was full of rustic handiwork. It was a cross between a Norwegian wall-bracket and the sort of thing Mr Dolmetsch makes at Haslemere. But it served its purpose. Bartók proved his point and honour was satisfied.

'The Most Original Mind in Modern Music', *Radio Times*, 26 February 1932, p. 504

ANDOR FÖLDES

(b. 1913)

Andor Földes studied piano with Ernő Dohnányi and composition with Leó Weiner at the Academy of Music in Budapest. He first met Bartók in 1929, in the humble role of page-turner, and was immediately captivated by his distinctive musicianship. From the early 1930s on Földes frequently performed in Western Europe. He settled in New York in the same year as Bartók, 1940. In 1948 he returned to Europe, and has continued to perform all over the world as a pianist, and, more recently, as a conductor.

There was something strange, almost forbidding about this man. His slight, bird-like figure had, despite the obvious modesty inherent in his behavior, a great deal of dignity about it. He commanded respect in everybody who saw him or met him. No matter whether you liked the music he wrote, whether you professed to understand his compositions or not – you had to respect Bartók, the man.

There were all sorts of rumors going around in the musical circles of Budapest those days. Bartók was not popular among the many professors of the Royal Hungarian Franz Liszt Academy of Music

. . . He was much too severe, much too self-conscious, much too retiring. But his own pupils who knew him better and had daily contact with him, went all out for him. As a professor of piano he was very demanding, very severe. He was not content with anything less than perfection, especially rhythmically. He also insisted that his students should thoroughly analyze all works which they studied from every point of view. He never taught composition – he didn't believe in teaching it. But from the way he taught the interpretation of Bach's piano works or the Beethoven Sonatas one could learn more about musical forms than many a young and aspiring composer was able to pick up by studying harmony and counterpoint with other teachers of the Music Academy. The Academy was chock-full of 'masters' at the time, as most teachers insisted that they be called by that title. Bartók was an exception.

'Mr Professor,' or 'Professor Bartók,' was the only title the great composer ever kept. It seemed there was something in the word 'professor' – this rather cool and academic word – that rather appealed to Bartók.

Every once-in-awhile Professor Bartók gave himself to writing letters – letters of protest against this or that, against some injustice which he wasn't able to stomach. One of the old doormen at the Music Academy – well informed of all goings on – characterized the situation aptly: 'Professor Bartók,' he told me somewhat aghast one morning, 'keeps writing letters and all the gentlemen at the Academy keep scratching their heads . . .'

Apparently Bartók did not 'belong' to the 'gentlemen'. He came seldom to academic meetings and had few friends among his colleagues. Perhaps his only real friend and confidant was Zoltán Kodály, with whom he shared his great love and passion of folk-song collecting. Of the two, Bartók was definitely the more active, the more passionate, I'd almost say, the more dramatic personality. There is a characteristic story about Bartók and Kodály which sheds light on their respective temperaments. It tells of the yearly visit the two composers paid to the old and staid music publisher of Hungary, Rózsavölgyi and Company, in order to receive their accounting of the year. Bartók, it seems, was in the habit of putting up a big fight with the publisher, trying to prove that the company cheated both of them out of their meager royalties. While this went on and Bartók (who was much the smaller and more fragile of the two) kept pounding the table, the tall, lanky, bearded Kodály stood silently a step or two behind Bartók. After each particularly strong outburst Bartók would turn to Kodály: 'Am I right Zoltán?' 'Yes, Béla,' came the reticent answer. After having said all there was to say, Bartók, carrying his friend Kodály in tow, left the premises proudly.

One of those famous letters, which Bartók wrote [in 1935] and which the 'other gentlemen' were unable to answer, was the one he addressed to the committee in charge of distributing the famous Greguss Prize. This prize, perhaps best comparable to our own Pulitzer Prize, was given in succession every year to a composer, a writer, a painter, a sculptor, an actor or an architect. So every sixth year a composer was to be awarded it. After all other composers of Hungary had already been given this coveted prize, the arch-conservative committee had no choice left – Bartók had to receive the award. But they didn't want to let him off with it quite so easily. So they decided that instead of giving him the Prize for a work composed during the last six years (which was the original stipulation in the rules of the Award), they gave it to Bartók on the strength of his Orchestral Suite, Opus 3 – a work written more than 25 years earlier, which by no means represented the mature composer at his best. Bartók was infuriated. He took it as a calculated slap in the face and his answer, refusing to accept the prize for such an early and no more representative work, was printed prominently on the front pages of every newspaper in Budapest. 'It would be sad indeed,' wrote Bartók, 'if since my early youth I wouldn't have written anything worth while.' If such were the case, he argued, it would be best, perhaps, if they'd give the Award to somebody more deserving than himself. Bartók came out with a positive suggestion. He recommended Kodály instead of himself and finished his stinging letter with a sentence, which became the *motto* of many a Bartók-admirer for years to come: 'As for myself I have no desire to accept the Greguss Award – dead or alive.'

The Committee had no statement to make after receiving Bartók's letter. No composer was awarded with the Greguss Prize that year and a great silence prevailed concerning the matter. Many a name whose owner did get the award has been forgotten long since. The name of Béla Bartók shines more with each day and his letter is not forgotten.

On another occasion [in 1931] Bartók did an even more daring

Aylmer Buesst

thing. Admiral Nicholas Horthy, then Regent of Hungary, decided to establish a new award to be given to the 'best minds of Hungary.' It was to be called the Corvin Decoration, so named after one of the best-known kings of Hungary. There were 72 such decorations, 12 bigger ones for the 'really great' and 60 smaller, for the stars of second rank.

Eugen Hubay and Ernest von Dohnányi, both favorites of the Hungarian government of those days, were in line for one of the 12 big awards. But Horthy had no love for the daring and free work of Bartók. Hence, it seemed inevitable that he should be presented with one of the 60 smaller decorations; and so Bartók's name appeared at the bottom of the long Corvin Award list.

On a sunny morning, 71 of the best-known Hungarian artists, academicians and other members of the country's spiritual 'elite,' marched to the Regent's Castle on the left bank of the Danube to receive their decorations from the hands of Horthy himself. One by one, their names were called out in the pompous reception room of the Burg. They had to step forward and accept the decoration from the hands of Nicholas Horthy. The name of Béla Bartók was read out aloud, too, in due time and the Regent stood there with the decoration in his hand, waiting for the composer to step out like all the others to accept the plaque. But nobody moved. No person stepped out of the line to get his share in the glory. Bartók simply didn't show up for the occasion. The Regent placed the plaque back into its case and nobody ever spoke of the affair anymore. There was no mention of it in any of the Hungarian newspapers. It was unthinkable to report on the case – but those in the know spread the news and laughed about it for weeks to come, chalking the matter off as another of the silent triumphs of Professor Bartók.

'My First Meeting with Bartók', *Etude*, vol. 73/3 (March 1955), pp. 12, 49–50. © 1955, *The Etude Magazine*, used by permission of the publisher, Theodore Presser Company.

AYLMER BUESST

(1883–1970)

Educated in Melbourne and Brussels, Aylmer Buesst gained his first conducting position with the Beecham Opera Company during the First World War and then worked extensively with the British National Opera Company in the 1920s. In 1933 he was appointed Assistant Director of Music at the BBC, working under Adrian Boult, and in May of the following year conducted the world première of Bartók's *Cantata Profana* at a BBC concert in London. In this capacity he did not impress Bartók, who accused him of being merely a 'time beater'.

It would seem as though he did not make a strong impression on me – as a man. My recollections are of a quiet, rather negative sort of personality which would seem to be quite at variance with his music.

He had lunch with me twice, at Pagani's (the restaurant of wonderful memories, destroyed, alas!, by enemy action). The first time was on the day before the concert, and Hermann Grunebaum was with us; we spoke German, of course. And, in entering this fact in my Diary I have written 'Funny little man – Bartók! He complains of suffering from indigestion. So, I invoked the interest of the Manager of Pagani's – Arturo Meschini, who had some beef boiled in a particular manner especially for Bartók. And, when I saw it I could not help thinking that had I eaten it I would have had indigestion for a week.'

Another thing I remember is that B. appeared a little surprised (if not shocked) when I removed my dinner jacket before conducting. It was a warm night, and to conduct in shirt-sleeves did not seem to me a very heinous crime. (I have since often thought, though, that perhaps it was not quite correct as the concert was a public one, in the Concert Hall of Broadcasting House.)

Unpublished letter to David Clegg, 1962

DIANA CHISHOLM

In 1932–3, when Bartók made two visits to Scotland, Diana
Chisholm was Secretary to Glasgow's Active Society for the
Propagation of Contemporary Music, of which her husband,
Erik, was President. On both visits Bartók performed for Society
members and stayed with the Chisholms. He also became an
Honorary Vice-President of the Society.

When we knew Béla Bartók was coming to Glasgow to stay with us, the
first thing which worried us was – language difficulty. None of us, of
course, could speak one word of Hungarian: would our famous guest
be any better with English? I immediately bought an 'English-cum-
Hungarian' dictionary (by the time I left Scotland I had entertained so
many continental composers, musicians, and singers that I had a very
comprehensive collection of 'English-Cums'). I pictured myself standing on the station platform anxiously scanning the face of every male,
who, in my opinion, looked 'foreign', and gesticulating wildly with the
dictionary.

However, I was rescued (or thought I was) from this predicament
by the Hungarian Consul in Glasgow, Sir W. (William, I think)
Burrell, who telephoned me the day before Mr Bartók's arrival to say
that he also would like to come to the station to receive this
distinguished visitor from Hungary. 'Luck', I thought, 'this let's me
out'; so you can imagine my disappointment when, on meeting Sir
William Burrell a few minutes before the train was due to arrive (8.35
p.m. on 28th Feb. 1932), he said he hoped that either my husband or I
could speak Hungarian because he couldn't! 'Well', I said laughingly,
'you're the official representative so you can get on with it.' But we need
not have worried! When the 'Flying Scotsman' arrived and the
passengers alighted from the train it was quite simple to recognise him.
There was only one Béla Bartók! A small, white-haired man, wearing a
black Homburg hat, thick black coat with a heavy astrakhan collar, and
armed with a music case in one hand and an umbrella in the other.
Who, I wondered, had forewarned him about Glasgow's weather?

Sir William went forward at once to greet him, and I swear I saw a
look of relief flit across the Consul's face when Bartók said in a softly
spoken, broken English accent, 'Bartók is my name'. After that all
went smoothly. Later in the day, my husband and I admitted to each

Season 1931-32

FIFTH
ACTIVE SOCIETY
CONCERT

STEVENSON HALL. GLASGOW

ST. GEORGE'S PLACE

CHAMBER CONCERT

THE MUSIC OF

BÉLA BARTÓK

MONDAY, 29TH FEBRUARY, 1932

AT EIGHT O'CLOCK

BÉLA BARTÓK, PIANIST

ANGELA PALLAS, SINGER

BESSIE SPENCE, VIOLINIST

BOSENDORFER Piano kindly supplied by
Messrs. PATERSON SONS & CO., Ltd., 152 Buchanan Street, C.1.

Announcement for a concert in Glasgow, 1932

other that we had both felt ashamed that not one of the party who came to receive him could reply to him in his language, least of all the Consul.

Bartók was of a very shy nature. Where music was concerned he would and could talk at length, but apart from the fact that he told us he had a wife and son, he spoke very little about himself.

He made a great fuss of our baby daughter Morag and seemed to be extremely fond of children, yet I felt he had built an invisible barrier of defence for himself against the outside world. We do know that he was really badly off financially, and that apart from his heavy overcoat, which was beautifully warm and looked new, his suits though well tailored and well pressed were equally well worn, his shirts too were frayed at the cuffs and collars – although he gave one the impression of 'putting a face' on things generally, and being harassed by some secret worry. The face of a pathetic little man – but an intensely proud one who was also a musical genius.

His stay was a very pleasant one for us. He was almost fanatical in his passionate love for folk music – not just Hungarian or Slav, but the folk music of all countries. He told us something of his experience in searching for and collecting the folk songs of his own country. Normally his face looked rather stern and taut, but his whole face lit up and his eyes became pools of liquid fire when recounting what was obviously the most vital interest of his life. At first he did make one feel he was unapproachable and distant, but when he found that he could relax, and was in no danger of being 'lionised' (the soul-searing penalty the celebrity pays for being a celebrity) and that he was among simple, friendly, sympathetic people, his whole personality seemed to change, to become electrified. Then it was one became aware of the terrifically forceful personality of this seemingly quiet, shy, self-effacing musician. Here was someone with dynamic strength of will to achieve what he had set out to do with his life.

My husband asked him if he had ever come across the folk music of Scotland, and in particular, if he had heard any of our ancient Piobaireachd (Pibroch) music. Bartók confessed that this was one branch of folk music he had had no opportunity to study. In fact, I think he had not quite realised just what scope there was in it. To many continentals Scotland just seems to be the top part of England with no particular characteristics of its own. How wrong they are! If they travel to the north of Scotland and make contact with the Gaelic-speaking population, see our tartans, Celtic Crosses, and hear our Piobaireachd music, they may realise that we have certain Asiatic qualities which are not shared by the Sassenach.

Now Scottish folk music and especially Piobaireachd happened to be my husband's pet subject and particular study at this time. For years he had been doing considerable research in this line, so of course, he brought out various collections of folk music and gramophone records, and Bartók listened and studied these for hours. The result of this conversation was that the very next day Bartók went to a well-known shop in town which supplied all Highland requisites and came home with a tartan rug, a chanter, all the Piobaireachd music he could lay his hands on, and told us that the manager of the firm had arranged with one of our most noted Pipe-Majors to come next day to the Grand Hotel to play the bagpipes to him (this was one thing my husband hadn't been able to do!). Bartók was enchanted.

In Erik Chisholm, 'Béla Bartók', unpublished paper delivered in Cape Town, 1964, pp. 9A–11

YOLAN HATVANY

(b. 1903)

Yolan Hatvany was the wife of the writer Lajos Hatvany (1880–1961), who early in the century had been a backer of the innovative literary review *Nyugat* and a supporter of the poet Endre Ady. When the German author Thomas Mann was on a brief visit to Hungary in June 1936 he stayed with the Hatvanys at their home in Budapest's prestigious Castle district. Mann had come to know Bartók through their common work for the League of Nations and asked the Hatvanys to invite the composer to dinner. (Mann's account of the evening can be found in his published diary for this year.) Yolan Hatvany still lives in Budapest.

. . . there were only Bartók, the Manns, ourselves and Béla Reinitz, the composer of the musical settings of Ady's poems and an ardent admirer of Bartók's, who were present, and my duties as a housewife did not preoccupy me too much. I was thus able to watch these two

Bartók's proposal about artistic and scientific freedom to the Permanent Committee for Literature and the Arts of the League of Nations' Commission for Intellectual Cooperation, early 1930s extraordinary men throughout the evening, and I was so intensely aware that this was a unique and wonderful experience that the very recollection still thrills me today, almost thirty years later.

After dinner, when the time came for Bartók to sit down to the piano, I felt rather embarrassed at having to make apologies, but since my husband did not allow music near him, they would have to come down to the nursery on the ground floor, where there was only an upright piano available. Bartók asked what make, and I told him it was a Förstner. He reassured me that that would be quite all right, for, he said, 'a good upright is very much better than a bad grand'. It really did seem to be all right, since, allowing for some short intervals for conversation, he played for almost three hours. Wonderfully modest and thoughtful, he asked Mann after each piece what he would like to hear next. Mann, who expressed his admiration by murmuring 'beautiful! very beautiful!' at intervals, named one Bartók work after another. Each time Bartók wanted to stop, saying that so much music had no doubt exhausted his listeners, Mann made his accustomed gesture of protest to say that he was not tired. 'Please go on!' And so this little concert continued till the small hours of the night.

As I look back on that evening I see before me the thin, fragile figure of Bartók, his marvellous head that was translucently clear and brilliant, as though carved from a cube of ice. Thomas Mann's bony, angular face, like a German etching, was tranquil as he reclined at ease on my child's couch. And beside him sat Katia, the most suggestive and most significant of wives.

We held our breaths enraptured, watching and listening to them.

'An Evening with Thomas Mann and Béla Bartók in Budapest', *New Hungarian Quarterly*, no. 19 (Autumn 1965), pp. 74-5

BENCE SZABOLCSI

(1899–1973)

Bence Szabolcsi received a broad education in the liberal arts and music in Budapest before specializing in musicology at the university in Leipzig from 1921 to 1923. In the succeeding half century he held many important posts in Hungarian musical life, eventually becoming Director of the Institute of Musicology in the Academy of Sciences. In an article written in 1942 Bartók recognized him as 'one of Hungary's foremost musicologists'.

Bartók's figure imprinted itself with unforgettable sharpness on the minds of all who ever met him, although he never sought to draw attention to himself or acted conspicuously. He could permit himself the greatest luxury of his age: to be true and sincere. And though there is hardly any evidence of it in his art, his family, his acquaintances, his peasant singers and young pupils all bear witness to the warm and simple human feelings concealed in the depths of his infinitely complicated creative personality.

He was of middle height and had a nervously delicate build, but his frail body bore a head radiant with inner light; his hazel eyes had a penetrating look. They dilated and blazed up in the heat of discussion or when he was playing the piano; his forehead domed, and the once wavy, later short-cropped hair turned prematurely grey, especially at the temples; his nose was finely shaped and his lips thin and energetic – all this gave the impression of a medieval, ascetic monk. His hands were narrow and artistically moulded, but they expressed extraordinary power. In public his movements often seemed to be hesitating and somewhat stiff, but there was a rhythmical, purposeful sway in his gait. The way he threw back his head expressed forcefulness. Those who saw him playing the piano will remember that in his movements, his stretchings and sudden starts there was something of the panther, predacious and fearful. He wore spectacles only for work; in his youth he used a pince-nez for some time (around 1912). Several times he grew a moustache and a beard, but each time for a short while only. His almost excessively deep, disciplined and serene voice formed a peculiar contrast to his vivacious, nervous constitution; his speech was unusually clear, plain and, at the same time, restrained, matter-of-fact and concentrated. At one time he was a heavy smoker, and his well-known photographs, with a cigarette in his hand, immortalize one of his most characteristic poses.

This is the picture of Bartók in the prime of life between the ages of forty and sixty, as we knew him in the 'twenties and 'thirties . . . He presented the picture of a personality filled with great tension, of an artist and fighter powerfully moved by all the contradictions and revolt of his age. He was a source of current, an antenna reacting with unprecedented sensitivity and awareness to every vibration in the world, and forming in himself the new voice of a changing epoch, of humanity in travail.

Bence Szabolcsi, 'Introduction' to Ferenc Bonis, ed., *Béla Bartók: His Life in Pictures*, London (Boosey & Hawkes), 1964, pp. 5–6. This extract is included by permission of Boosey & Hawkes Music Publishers Ltd.

The performer
LAJOS HERNÁDI
(1906–81)

A pupil of Bartók, Dohnányi and Schnabel, Lajos Hernádi (Heimlich) maintained a reputation as a leading performer and teacher of the piano from the 1930s into the 1970s. He was Professor of Piano at the Budapest Academy of Music from 1945 to 1975, during which time he helped hone the talents of such leading pianists as Gábor Gabos, Tamás Vásáry and Péter Frankl. He performed with Bartók in a Budapest radio broadcast of 1929.

To sum up Bartók as a pianist: Putting it quite simply, the age-old saying held true of his playing: it was beautiful because it was true. It was true from two aspects. Bartók as a person always remained true to himself, he was one of the most immaculate, austere characters I have met – and the man is always inseparable from the artist. But his playing was true in a strictly musical sense too. Whatever he chose to play, every single work sounded genuine under his fingers, from the ideal tempos and phrasings to the most lucid larger outlines of each piece. The inner truth of his interpretation shone through the work as a whole as well as in the tiniest phrases, stresses and shades. His playing was devoid of all superficial, irrelevant flourish – Bartók was not a colourist when he played the piano. Probably this was the only deficiency in his playing, and it appeared only when – very rarely – he played works by composers like Chopin, whose colours and specific, instrumental sounds are inseparable from the fullness of the aesthetic effect. These pieces sounded somewhat strange, as if they had been carved in granite – but they were granite-masterpieces all the same. He prepared for his recitals with incredible devotion and deadly seriousness, even if those five to six hours of practice a day meant less time for composing. For Bartók it was *morally* inconceivable to mount the concert stage or face the microphone if ever so slightly unprepared. The musical experiences of the audience would probably have been just as magnificent if he had not prepared as thoroughly as he did, yet – as in other things – he never compromised.

'Bartók – Pianist and Teacher', *New Hungarian Quarterly*, no. 30 (Summer 1968), pp. 197–8

ANDOR FÖLDES

(b. 1913)

While turning the pages for the Bartók–Hernádi broadcast in 1929, Földes came to realize what a master of interpretation Bartók really was. Although one of Dohnányi's leading students at the Academy, he started to take occasional private lessons with Bartók.

. . . The love and reverence which Bartók doted on every single note of the Schubert [F minor] Fantasy first stunned, then enchanted me, and as the playing went on, my preconceived thoughts and ideas, as far as Bartók the man and Bartók the composer was concerned, vanished into thin air. I could not help but believe my own ears. Anybody who could play the piano with so much heart, who could interpret the work of another so basically different a composer with such humility, could not possibly be a rabid revolutionary, a dangerous radical. I knew that everything I had been told about Bartók was wrong. The message coming to me from Bartók's piano playing was clear, forceful and unequivocal. It spurred me to immediate action. Next morning, I

At the piano, late 1920s

hurried to a music store and asked for some music by Béla Bartók.

. . . I can name the two characteristics in Bartók's piano playing which fascinated me most. First was his almost uncanny sense of rhythm – combined with a wonderful flexibility that characterised perhaps more than anything his playing. His rhythm had always iron logic to it – but it never became rigid. His sense of rhythm always allowed for flexibility and elbow-space, so to speak.

The second characteristic was his unbelievable sense of tone-colour and tone quality. In the course of one of our many afternoon sessions in his house, he brought home to me a point which I had never thought about before. He pointed out that dynamics and colouring in music come about only by relating one sound to another. He gave me a vivid illustration of his point. 'Ask the greatest piano virtuoso in the world to hit a note on the piano', he said, 'just one single note – then ask the nearest taxi-driver to do the same – and you will find that each note was hit by the two men exactly alike – one didn't sound a bit finer or more beautiful than the other. In order to discover the difference between the taxi-driver and the great artist – they have to hit *two* notes . . . there each will reveal himself, for it is the *relationship* between the sounds upon which the colouring hinges.'

There was one other pianistic suggestion of Bartók's which I accepted immediately and without hesitation, although when he first mentioned it to me the thought was very strange and completely new. His suggestion came at the end of a long session, when I happened to play Mozart's G major concerto, K.453. 'Why don't you play the grace notes as short as possible,' he advised, 'I play them almost simultaneously with the main note . . .'

I tried, and the result amazed me. This technique brought special flavours out of the melodic line. It gave it a vivid, contemporary twang, and added charm and spice to the music. Not for a moment did I doubt the rightness of this suggestion, but I am not yet certain whether I personally could follow another one of his suggestions – one that concerns the playing of a passage in Beethoven. In order to illustrate a particular point, which he suggested in the third movement of his own Sonata, Bartók played for me the last movement of Beethoven's F sharp major sonata [Op. 78]. What he advocated here was that when two even notes are tied with a *legato* sign the other note should be played very short. While this approach is entirely convincing in Bartók's music, I think it might be questioned when it comes to Beethoven. But Bartók's music, of course, often demands it.

'Béla Bartók', *Tempo*, no. 43 (Spring 1957), pp. 23–4

IVAN MARTINOV

(b. 1908)

In January 1929, while still a student, Ivan Martinov attended a piano recital given by Bartók in Moscow. After his graduation in 1936 from the Moscow Conservatory, Martinov taught music history in Tashkent, Khar'kov and Moscow, before joining the folklore section of the journal *Sovetskaya muzika* in 1948. Since then he has held leading positions in the Russian and Moscow Composers' Unions, in 1969 becoming president of the latter's musicology committee. His extensive writings include a book about Bartók, which appeared in 1968, and one about Kodály (1970).

Bartók's music was heard for the first time in the Soviet Union at the beginning of the 1920s, as soon as cultural relations broken off during the First World War had been re-established. His two string quartets and Dance Suite were performed in Moscow, the violin sonata in Leningrad, and the *Two Portraits* in Khar'kov. His piano pieces featured frequently in concert programmes; the transcription for violin of his Romanian dances gained widespread popularity. We could continue this listing further, as a keen interest in Bartók had been aroused both among performers and audiences. The Press wrote much about him, and as early as 1925 the journal *The Music of Today* dedicated a special issue to his output.

It was natural, then, that when he came to the Soviet Union as a guest artist in 1929 he was very warmly received and was duly praised for his accomplishments as composer and performer. The present writer had the good fortune of being present at Bartók's concert in Moscow. To this day Bartók's disciplined, exact and wonderfully expressive playing has stuck in my memory. The 'Allegro barbaro', which he performed at a moderate tempo, deeply impressed me, but I was especially struck by 'The Night's Music' from the cycle *Out of Doors*, which surprised me with its colours and its revelation of the psychological content of the music. The unique poetry of it all and the depth of the composer's creative personality could be felt.

I took note of his appearance, too: the face of a visionary, with radiant eyes, a penetrating gaze, an unaffected bearing and an

BRITISH MUSIC SOCIETY.
(LIVERPOOL CENTRE)

RUSHWORTH HALL   THURSDAY EVENING
ISLINGTON.   MARCH 30TH, 1922 AT 8.

M. BELA BARTOK
(The Eminent Hungarian Pianist-Composer)

IN

A PIANOFORTE RECITAL OF HIS OWN WORKS.

PROGRAMME:

I.

(a) HUNGARIAN PEASANT DANCES (Composed in 1914) .. .. *Bartok*
These are very old Hungarian Tunes, known now only to aged peasants. They were used
only for dancing, and played generally on bagpipes, but sometimes sung to the dance.

(b) EVENING IN THE COUNTRY (Composed in 1908) .. .. *Bartok*
This piece has two tunes. Both are in a certain pentatonic scale, being imitations of old
Transylvanian-Hungarian folk tunes, which are based on this scale.

(c) BEAR DANCE (Composed in 1908) .. .. *Bartok*
Impression of a bear dancing to the song of his leader
and growling to the accompaniment of a drum.

(d) ALLEGRO BARBARO (Composed in 1910) .. .. *Bartok*

II.

(a) SONATINA (Composed in 1915) .. .. *Bartok*
Roumanian dance tunes are used here in their original form without alteration. They
are not sung, but are played only on instruments (violin, bagpipes, peasant flute).

(b) TWO DIRGES (Composed in 1916) .. .. *Bartok*

(c) SUITE (Opus 14) (Composed in 1916) .. .. *Bartok*

(d) FIRST ROUMANIAN DANCE (from Opus 8a). (Composed in 1909) .. .. *Bartok*
The themes, while original, are not themselves folk tunes but are inspired by
Roumanian Folk music.

An Interval of 15 minutes, enabling members to adjourn to the
Clubroom and Library, where refreshments may be obtained.

III.

(a) VARIATIONS ON A HUNGARIAN FOLK TUNE (Composed in 1918) .. *Bartok*

(b) ROUMANIAN PEASANT DANCES (Composed in 1915) .. .. .. *Bartok*
Roumanian dance tunes are used here in their original form without alteration. They
are not sung, but are played only on instruments (violin, bagpipes, peasant flute).

(c) FIRST ELEGY (from Opus 8b.) (Composed in 1908) .. .. *Bartok*

(d) FIRST BURLESQUE (A Quarrel) .. ⎱
    SECOND BURLESQUE (un peu gris) ⎰ (Opus 8c) (Composed 1909-1910) .. *Bartok*
    THIRD BURLESQUE .. .. .. ⎰

With the indulgence of the Ladies smoking is permitted.

Programme for a concert in Liverpool, 1922

Programme for a concert in Sepsiszentgyörgy (Sfîntu-Gheorghe, Romania), 1927

unpretentiousness on stage. In the atmosphere of the concert room he accordingly drew attention to himself. We young Moscow musicians were completely bowled over by Bartók's artistry, and felt a deep respect for his personality. I think his concerts had this effect on all who heard them – they remain indelibly in the memory.

While he was staying here Bartók met with many colleagues, and chatted with them about the most burning questions facing modern art. He also listened to recordings of folksongs and dances. In summary, his visit was an important milestone in the strengthening of musical relations between the Soviet Union and Hungary.

'In memoriam 1945. szeptember 26.', *Muzsika*, vol. 13/9 (September 1970), p. 5

ALEXANDER JEMNITZ
(1890–1963)

The Hungarian composer and music critic Alexander (Sándor) Jemnitz studied composition in Budapest with Bartók's teacher, Hans Koessler, before undertaking advanced studies with Reger in Leipzig and Schoenberg in Berlin. He returned to Budapest in 1916, where he became a popular music critic, writing for one publication, *Népszava*, for over a quarter of a century. His compositions, which were appreciated more abroad than at home, showed the influence of his teachers in their frequently complex polyphonic textures. In 1937 his study *From Bach to Bartók* appeared in Hungarian.

Our second meeting outside Hungary took place in August 1933 in Strasbourg, at the International Music Festival organized by Hermann Scherchen, where again our works were performed together. It was quite emphatically a 'counter music festival' against Hitler, and his rallying cry against 'musical Bolshevists'. The German participants from the Reich were aware that with this gesture of opposition they had sung their swan-song at home; the non-Germans were elated by the feeling of having paid tribute to the freedom of the creative spirit. Béla Bartók participated with wrathful joy and played his 2nd Piano Concerto. His presence was a symbol of the attack on the anti-intellectuals, and the struggle: just the element in which he felt most at home. Ede von Zathureczky, the eminent violinist who died so young, told me that once when he was on a concert tour of Italy with Bartók a noisy disturbance developed during a performance of Bartók's 1st Sonata for Violin and Piano. There was shrill whistling; but against this, applause could be heard; it did not end before several punches had been thrown. Zathureczky was shocked and wanted to stop, but he heard Bartók playing on unperturbed. When the violinist turned around with a questioning glance, Bartók cheerfully called out to him: 'I like this! My partisans are standing up for their views!' That aggressive approach of his towards any kind of 'backwood' attitude, which breaks out so often in his own music, had found its mark in Strasbourg, too, where his presence represented a definite stance of resolution and action. Not long afterwards, after all, although he was not a Jew he was so hugely incensed that he filled out the infamous questionnaire of the German Reich with 'Jew'! Just like the magnificent Hungarian singer, Mária von Basilides, who, when that decree had been passed was so outraged that she wore the yellow star . . . Struggle against the anti-intellectuals, struggle against the suppression of human rights, against organized oppression of any kind: this was his battle cry throughout life. How often it comes through in his works!

And it was no heroic deed – was it? – no overt, ostentatious attitude of gallantry, when that Hungarian, whose strong affinity with his people was so fervently acknowledged and proven, relinquished his pleasant home in the Buda hills and left behind his beloved country, which had been poisoned with the intolerable ideas of an undignified ideology!? . . . 'I really work best at home, in my study', he told me as we were talking about the way many composers need distant, beautiful scenery to inspire them to accomplish their works. For the creation of larger compositions he merely required absolute quiet. At such times, those in his household had to tiptoe around and conversations had to be whispered, since every harsh word about bland everyday affairs would have wrenched him from that sound-world of his, that hitherto unexplored virgin territory. The creation of such incredibly bold sound structures required an undistracted concentration, helped by an unwavering, absolutely logical sense of order!

'Persönliches über Béla Bartók', in Erich Marckhl, ed., *Festschrift aus Anlass der Erhebung des Steiermärkischen Landeskonservatoriums zur Akademie für Musik und darstellende Kunst in Graz*, Graz (Leykam), 1963, pp. 87–9

OTTO KLEMPERER

(1885–1973)

For an incredible sixty-five years, from 1907 to 1972, Otto Klemperer conducted the leading orchestras of Europe and America. With the accession to power of the Nazis in 1933 he left his native Germany, undertaking some work in Vienna before moving to a position in Los Angeles. After the Second World War he conducted the Budapest Opera, and later, the Philharmonia Orchestra in London. (Klemperer is, incidentally, incorrect in thinking Bartók came to the rehearsal in Vienna with both wives. He was probably accompanied by his second wife, Ditta, and their friend Mária Lukács-Popper.)

That summer [1933] I conducted Bartók's Second Piano Concerto in Vienna with him as soloist. That was a great experience for me. He was a wonderful pianist and musician. The beauty of his tone, the energy and lightness of his playing were unforgettable. It was almost painfully beautiful. He played with great freedom, that was what was so wonderful. He was a strange man – very reserved, very shy, but very sympathetic. He had a new wife at that time. But the old also came to the rehearsal, so he appeared with two wives.

In Lotte Klemperer and Peter Heyworth, *Conversations with Klemperer*, London (Faber and Faber), 1985, p. 71

FRANCIS POULENC

(1899–1963)

Poulenc was another founding member of 'Les Six', and is today probably the most recognized representative of the group. His youthful works show, variously, strong influences of Satie and Stravinsky upon his style; much of his later writing is character-ized by a suavity of melody interrupted on occasion by jocular or enigmatic outbursts. Although he was not inclined to imitate Bartók's techniques in his own compositions, he maintained a keen interest in his output. Here he recalls two of Bartók's concerts of the 1930s. (The first was probably in February 1932, when the First Piano Concerto received its Parisian première; the second dates from November 1938.)

When Bartók came to Paris to play his Second Concerto [*sic*], in about 1930, there weren't many of us there in the vast Salle Pleyel to applaud him, despite the fact that he was as noteworthy a virtuoso as a composer.

The last time that I saw him was a short time before the war, in Holland. His countenance reflected a wonderful asceticism, as Falla's also used to. We knew we were in the presence of a true Master, one who was dejectedly heading towards an exile which he knew had to come – alas, without return.

Bartók and his wife played his Sonata for Two Pianos in a small hall in Amsterdam; some days before, they had performed Mozart's Double Concerto with orchestra. I have rarely been as upset as I was in

26

1936 jan. 7-én   II. zongoraverseny és
Rondó és Meditatio; vezényelt
Sir Henry J. Wood.   London

1936 jan. 8-á   II. zongoraverseny vezényelt
Willem van Otterloo   Utrecht

1936 jan. 9-én   Rádióhangverseny   Hilversum

1936 jan. 11-én   A fából faragott királyfi
VII. előadás   Budapest

1936 jan. 16-án   Szonataest Székely Zoltánnal
Mozart A dúr és C major, Bartók Szon.
Nr. 2. Román népi táncok   Liverpool xxx

1936 jan. 17-én   II. zongoraverseny vezényelt
Leslie Heward /. zongorasuit./   Birmingham

1936 jan. 18   Rádióhangverseny, ugyanaz Birmingham
a műsor, mint a 17. iki hangversenyen.

1936 febr. 3   A Magyar Tudományos Akadémián szék-
foglalóját tartotta Béla, benne Liszt Faustból Budapest

1936 febr. 3-án   Az Ujságirók Szanatórium Egyesületének
Liszt-díszhangversenye. Béla előadta
Liszt Haláltáncát a filharmóniai zenekar
kíséretével; Dohnányi vezényelt   Budapest

1936 febr. 18   A Székesfővárosi Zenekarig
/. nyilvánosbi./ előadásán játszotta Béla Liszt
Haláltáncát, vezényelt Vaszy Viktor /. Ujjai./ Budapest

1936 febr. 27-én   Bach c-moll kettős zongoraversenyt
előadta Béla Fischer Edőinnel /. sársi Lukics./ Budapest

xxx *Ehi rhapsódia Bélától, Szonata Raveltől*

A page from the listing of Bartók's concerts compiled by his mother that rather empty hall on seeing these two pale emigrants before their pianos. It has always seemed to me a peculiar lesson of fate that Bartók should be the only famous musician of our age to die in want and, what's more, in America. Such genius, purified by the fire of a wonderful creativity, must, in the end, fall prey to martyrdom. I don't know what Bartók's religious convictions were, but when I think of him it is the image of a saint which comes to my mind.

'Hommage à Béla Bartók', *La Revue musicale*, no. 224 (1955), pp. 18–19

PAUL SACHER

(b. 1906)

Born in Basle, Paul Sacher has maintained an association with the city ever since. He received his musical education there, specializing in conducting and musicology, and then quickly established a reputation as a conductor of works outside the standard orchestral repertory, particularly pre-Classical and contemporary works. He has commissioned numerous compositions from such varied composers as Strauss, Hindemith, Tippett, Stravinsky and Henze. Several landmark Bartók compositions – Music for Strings, Percussion and Celesta (1936), Sonata for Two Pianos and Percussion (1937) and Divertimento (1939) – were the result of direct or indirect commissions from Sacher, and he participated in the world premières of these works in Basle. The extract below refers to the first performance of the Sonata for Two Pianos and Percussion on 16 January 1938.

Whoever met Bartók, thinking of the rhythmic strength of his work, was surprised by his slight, delicate figure. He had the outward appearance of a fine-nerved scholar. Possessed of fanatical will and pitiless severity, and propelled by an ardent spirit, he affected inaccessibility and was reservedly polite. His being breathed light and brightness; his eyes burned with a noble fire. In the flash of his searching glance no falseness nor obscurity could endure. If in performance an especially hazardous and refractory passage came off well, he laughed in boyish glee; and when he was pleased with the successful solution of a problem, he actually beamed. That meant more than forced compliments, which I never heard from his mouth . . .

His impassioned objectivity penetrated everything. He was himself clear to the smallest detail and demanded from everyone the utmost in differentiated precision. Therefore in rehearsals he showed great patience and was never annoyed when the realization of his intentions did not take place without trouble . . . Bartók had summoned me to conduct during rehearsals and eventually at the concert as well. This proved superfluous, however, when the time came, since Bartók and his wife had mastered the two piano parts irreproachably, while the percussionists solved their problems skilfully and to the complete satisfaction of the composer. In these rehearsals Bartók gave proof of his genuine modesty. He undertook with the greatest matter-of-factness all the irksome requirements of the work, and treated both the assisting musicians like colleagues despite his characteristic proud reserve.

'Béla Bartók zum Gedächtnis', *Mitteilungen des BKO* (Basle), 17 November 1945, as translated in Halsey Stevens, *The Life and Music of Béla Bartók*, New York (Oxford University Press), 1953, pp. 73, 83–4

JOSEPH SZIGETI

(1892–1973)

A pupil of the famous Hungarian violinist Jenő Hubay, Joseph Szigeti had already established an international reputation as a soloist by his early teenage years. Over the following six decades he helped to popularize, in particular, the works for violin of Prokofiev, Ravel and Stravinsky, as well as those of Bartók, whose First Violin Rhapsody (1928) was dedicated to him. Szigeti performed frequently with Bartók in Europe and America, including a number of trio performances with Benny Goodman of Bartók's *Contrasts*. A recording of the three playing this work was issued by the Columbia Gramophone Company in 1940.

Generally speaking . . . it was Bartók's reluctance to 'promote' that must be one of the reasons for the dearth of authentic historical documents of his playing of his own works. How else [can one] explain the failure to record him in London in some of his piano works when at my instigation around 1928 [1930] we made discs at Abbey Road of the Rumanian Dances and transcription of his Hungarian Folk Tunes?

This was an opportunity if ever there was one: we had been playing joint programmes in London, Oxford and elsewhere, and his pianistic repertoire was at his finger tips – in both senses. Yet the only recordings of his from the late 1920s and the 1930s were either made by the Budapest affiliates of the 'big' companies or else from broadcast performances on labels such as Continental, Patria, Pacific and Qualiton . . .

Still one cannot understand that someone who was as 'conscious' of the importance of the gramophone as Bartók was (his whole life work as a folklore researcher was bound up with the instrument, from its cylinder days on) could be so patient and long-suffering about the neglect that persisted even in the exciting and enterprising mid-thirties of the gramophone industry . . .

To play Mozart's K.526 or K.454 Sonatas with him, or the Beethoven *Kreutzer* or G major, Op. 30, No. 3, was that kind of unique experience when one starts anew with a clean slate – that is the only way I can attempt to describe it. I find among my sparse diary notes, under April 12, 1940, after rehearsing for the Coolidge Festival in Washington: 'What a contrast, this rehearsal after the usual hair-splitting affairs! Somehow, a feeling of rightness, of security.' I still remember how those biting syncopated basses in the coda of the last movement of Beethoven's Op. 30, No. 3 became the folksy, outdoor music that so many emasculated interpretations fail to convey to the listener. (At a rehearsal of this same movement of Op. 30, No. 3, Bartók spoke to me of Beethoven's bagpipe effects in the *Pastorale*.)

'Working with Bartók', *Music and Musicians*, vol. 11/8 (April 1963), pp. 8–9

STUART HIBBERD
(1893–1983)

Hibberd was 'the voice of the BBC' during its formative years. He was appointed an announcer with the fledgling organization in 1924 and gained the position of Chief Announcer in 1942. Although he resigned from the BBC in 1951, he continued casual work as an announcer for many years. His volume of 1950, *'This – is London'*, contains vivid recollections of the inter-war years, including this portrait of Bartók in the BBC's studios on 6 November 1933.

The eminent Hungarian composer and pianist, Béla Bartók, gave a recital of works by Bach and himself in the studio in the first week of November. He was a tall, thin, clean-shaven man in the middle fifties, with a rather lined face and a pleasant smile. He began by playing some Bach from memory, then he played a piano sonata of his own, in three movements, and for this he asked me to turn over. This was not too simple a matter, because the music was in manuscript and not very clear, and he proceeded to use the piano as a percussion instrument, and in some of the louder passages lifted his hands so high that it was difficult to get near enough to the music to follow it. It was all very exciting, almost thrilling at times, because the music was full of excitement, but I was thankful when it was all over and I was able to relax once more.

'This – is London', London (Macdonald and Evans), 1950, pp. 91–2

TIBOR POLGÁR

(b. 1907)

After studies in composition and piano, Tibor Polgár became one of the first musicians to be employed by Hungarian Radio. From 1925 to 1950 he worked with the organization as a composer and a conductor, in 1945 becoming head of its music department. In the 1920s and 1930s he was frequently present in the studio when Bartók gave broadcasts. He settled in Canada in 1964, where he has devoted much time to composition, especially in the field of opera.

Once radio had passed its first infancy and started to gain a reputation, the time came to invite great artists to avail their services. I still consider one of my greatest experiences as being the privilege of being able to sit in on Bartók's concerts given in the studio, as a volunteer page-turner. He practically never played without a score – even his own compositions. He was a short, thin, frail man, with the wonderful eyes of a real genius. He had a light, floating walk, as if he were always walking an inch or two above the ground. Bartok's playing was strong and defined, in complete contrast with his speech. He was quiet and gentle, his speech was colourful but never loud. He was always

Tibor Polgár rehearsing the Hungarian Radio Orchestra in Budapest. His wife,
Ilona Nagykovácsi, sings Bartók songs

thorough and accurate; for example, he took such care over tempi, that
before starting to play, he would take a pendulum-type metronome out
of his pocket and check the speed – even of his own works.

I remember one occasion towards the end of the twenties, when
Bartók was giving a performance of his own works. Behind the glass
walls of the recording studio sat the musical producer with a frown on
his face. He was an elderly gentleman: old-fashioned, conservative,
and he hated modern music. He even avoided personal contact with
Bartók, considering his straight-forward open manner as rude. Thus I
became the mediator between Bartók and the official 'functionary'. At
the time the performer didn't necessarily meet any of the collaborators
working at the radio at all. The microphones were arranged in a set
position, the instrument was moved by attendants, and a signal was
given by the announcer. When the bell sounded and the red light came
on, the performer could begin to play, without actually having met a soul
in the whole mysterious building. Then at the exit, in the so-called
information room, his fee would be there waiting, sealed in an envelope.
Like this, one could go on the air without any sense of excitement. Bartók
was at ease in the padded studio and never unfriendly. Not even on the
occasion when he sent me to the announcer – the legendary Uncle Scherz
– with a message 'please tell the town-crier . . .' This was not meant to

Broadcasting over Hungarian Radio, 1930s

offend, it was just his way. The programmes for Bartók's broadcasts were chosen by himself, and nobody interfered with them. He corresponded with the radio by letter.

I can't remember any of the sort of stories people always like to hear. In fact there could hardly have been any, as Bartók only ever dealt with the essentials; in the studio he concentrated on the broadcast and was very withdrawn. He always took off his coat and hung it over the back of the piano chair. Once I took him and his wife to their home. Not a word was passed in connection with the broadcast. His radio concerts always provided a very special experience for his admirers, and I'm delighted that some of them have survived in the form of X-ray foils. And now an anecdote to finish with, told by Tibor Kazacsay. He was one of my colleagues at the radio and was present at the recording when Uncle Scherz, who enjoyed a sip of wine, even on duty – fell asleep. Bartók completed his performance, thoughtfully gazed at the peacefully sleeping Uncle Scherz, then stepped towards the microphone and in his quiet voice announced: 'I'm afraid our town-crier has fallen asleep' . . .

In a telephone interview, reproduced in László Somfai, János Sebestyén and Zoltán Kocsis, eds., *Bartók Record Archives*, Budapest (Hungaroton), 1981, accompanying booklet to LPX 12334–38, pp. 22–3

The composer
ERNEST LERT
(1883–1955)

The Austrian Ernest (Ernst) Lert produced Bartók's opera *Duke Bluebeard's Castle* at the Opera House in Frankfurt am Main during May 1922. He also assisted with the production of the ballet *The Wooden Prince*, which featured on the same programme. These performances, conducted by Jenő Szenkár, were the first outside Hungary for either work. Although Lert here depicts Bartók as being ecstatic at the success of the productions, the composer's private views at the time were less positive, as were many of the published reviews. Having held numerous positions in the opera houses of central Europe in the 1910s and 1920s, Lert spent more time in America in his later years. He died in Baltimore in 1955.

When I first read the scores of both works I was so absorbed in the music that I completely forgot about the production as a technical problem. Here was a play which challenged traditional playwriting. Bluebeard's 'Castle', not Bluebeard himself, was the hero of the story. A weird castle, tucked away in a paradise-like oasis, deep within a primeval forest. Its owner is a lonely tyrant and victim of a tragic obsession. For no clearly defined reasons he makes the woman he marries the ruler of his castle and household. Yet one room she was forbidden to enter – the huge subterranean hall. Particularly, the seven huge doors in the hall were taboo to her. Of course no woman is steadfast enough to suppress her curiosity. One bride after the other disappeared, and Bluebeard remarried again and again. We witness the tragedy of his last wife. The librettist, Béla Balázs, tells her story in a dialogue of thrilling symbolisms which hold the audience in constant suspense.

Words and music made me visualize the Castle as an immense mystical abode with enigmatic doors. When the curious woman opened one door after the other, the music carried me through enchanted huge rooms of gold and glittering jewels, through endless fairy gardens and through the last door, to a host of incredibly beautiful women floating in mid-air through endless blue spaces. Still drunk of the dream I reached for the telephone and contracted for the premiere of both, the opera and the danced play.

For weeks fantastic ideas fermented in my skull. What my mind heard was of a surrealistic reality – what my mind saw looked like a moving kaleidoscope of exuberant shapes in challenging colors. All these visions sprang up with such an intensity and clarity that I had to start working at once. I put my model of the opera house stage on my desk, collected my lumps of plasticine, assorted pieces of colored cardboard and, armed with knives and scissors, I was ready to let my dreams come true. The score of *Bluebeard's Castle* at my left, I switched on the lights which illuminated the stage model. At once my dreams burst into a nightmare.

Did you ever imagine a dreamhouse of your own and, when you saw it built and ready, your heart sank? This is exactly what happened to my heart. There was my stage, as dull and naked as an empty barn. Wherever my fancy flew it hit against walls, posts, and lighting paraphernalia. Any door on a stage is a makeshift and looks always fictitious. Now I had to build seven doors, each one huge, solid and mysterious – each of them different and all of them somehow alike, just as their music describes them. When a door opened the music must float inside of it and expand our view to the infinite. Yet that barn of a stage could not expand one single inch. Shall I change the whole scenery at each opening of a door and let the door itself disappear? The music not only left me no time for such a change, but whatever I make the stage look like, it will be as crafty and cheap as a county fair fireworks.

Suddenly an idea flashed through my mind. If Bartók's music could kindle and blaze up my own imagination, it could do so to any other listener. Why not show, then, a stage which looks like an infinite void and have each vision grow out of the dark emptiness as a gigantic symbol – like a cascade of gold coming from nowhere and going nowhere; or like a few huge white lilies pointed up to a deep blue sky; or like a group of women in white silk against a green sail? It worked!

The same system worked for *The Woodcarved Prince.* Dancing birch trees look clumsy and ridiculous. But have the *spirits* of the trees jump out of the tree-trunks and these human-like spirits will master the most graceful bendings, bowings, pirouettings and jumpings the music demands. *Eureka!*

The last few rehearsals were under Bartók's own supervision. The orchestra evoked heaven and hell rolled into one. Weird unisons announced leading themes working up to symphonic polytonal polyphonies, sometimes carried along by heavily groaning obstinate basses. In gigantic transformations folk themes in ancient modes weathered storms of violin and woodwind runs, while elsewhere brasses climaxed in wild bursts or in chorale-like transfigurations. Yes, Otto Gombosi was right, Bartók's use of folklore was less an artistic device but rather the expression of his 'peasant-like closeness to the elemental forces of nature'.

My best two artists lived the lives of the only two characters of the play with incredible veracity. Their superhuman personalities expanded the stage to the infinite – the infinite I had visualized.

Bartók stayed silent. His short fragile figure won significance only through his narrow firmly-locked lips and his blue-grey-green watchful eyes. His right ear was always bent forward. No criticism, no suggestion unlocked his lips. Just as Gombosi characterizes him: 'His character was hard and clear . . . radiating his inner heat without getting warm and soft on the surface.'

The premiere was a hard-hitting success. With a slightly ironic smile Bartók performed his many bows before an enthusiastic audience. When the last curtain closed he ran to his dressing room. On the way he fiercely grasped my arm and pinched it till it hurt. His eyes blazed in intense joy and enigmatic determination.

Yet, this premiere was a turning point in his career as a composer. He never wrote another opera. Like Beethoven, after *Fidelio*, he understood that the 'make believe' of the stage was too fictitious for his genuine ideas. *Bluebeard's Castle* is a drama of abstract ideas, not a battle of human beings. It is a powerful cantata or, if you prefer it differently, a symphony with voices. The stage is too narrow for such a work. *The Woodcarved Prince* is different. Its fairy tale character calls for a pantomimic performance.

Today I, for one, am eagerly looking forward to hearing *Bluebeard's Castle* with closed eyes and have Bartók's music stir up again all the beauty and all the terror I felt when I first read that great score.

'Bartók's Stage Works: Some Problems in Presentation', *The Long Player*, vol. 2/10 (October 1953), p. 25

BASIL MAINE

(1894–1972)

After his undergraduate years at Cambridge, Basil Maine devoted most of the 1920s and 1930s to a career as music critic for several London papers and occasional side-line activity as an actor and narrator. During May 1925 he visited Prague to attend the first large-scale festival of the International Society for Contemporary Music, about which he writes below. In another account of Bartók's contribution to this festival, published in the London *Music Bulletin*, he asked: 'Where will you find among contemporary musicians a mind so swift, so fiercely bright?'

Indeed, this performance [of Vaughan Williams's *A Pastoral Symphony*] and that of Bartók's *Suite des Dances* (composed in 1923 to celebrate the reunion of Buda and Pest) proved to be the peaks of that Festival. Talich, the Czech conductor, directed the latter. At that time, except for two violin sonatas, which Jelly d'Arányi had played in London, I had heard few professional performances of Bartók's music. The *Suite des Dances* at Prague was immediately compelling, the more so since I had met Bartók several times during the Festival and had felt something of the elemental power which was contained in that small, spare frame and was always flashing from those piercing eyes. In some degree that power is let loose at the end of the *Suite des Dances*, a scintillating score unified by means of a *ritournelle*. Purposeful – that was the feeling conveyed by each of the movements. Already, through the precise rhythms, the bold orchestral colours, the drive, we knew that this was the music of an exceptionally strong, not to say tough, mind.

Twang with Our Music, London (Epworth), 1957, pp. 108–9

ADOLF WEISSMANN
(1873–1929)

Adolf Weissmann was one of Germany's most prolific music
critics in the early decades of the century. Although based in
Berlin, he wrote for numerous newspapers and journals on both
sides of the Atlantic and thereby became an important link in the
world-wide dissemination of information about the latest trends in
central European music, particularly during the 1920s. This
sketch of Bartók's compositional personality dates from the
mid-1920s.

[Bartók] has abandoned traditional methods, but his interest in the
fruitful study of folk-lore has kept him in touch with primitive
emotion. He may claim that he has never bowed the knee to the gods of
sensationalism and he is undoubtedly one of the most genuine and most
powerful of the moderns. He takes his art very seriously and demands a
like attitude in his audience. Bartók's music diverges widely from the
beaten track and is bound to be received as a hard saying by many.
There is nothing flattering about it, nothing Southern or Latin, and it
does not rely on the persuasions of tune; nevertheless even an
unsympathetic hearer must feel that it is the work of a master musician
and a man of character. He early abandoned clearly defined tonality,
but the sonata-form with thematic work is still perceptible in his
chamber-music, while his treatment of part-writing and harmony
shows that he has no doubts as to the end in view, original as are his
means to that end. His work has great intellectual force, born of
solitude and intense concentration. He is most himself in a somewhat
gruff humour which his staccato rhythm and perverse harmony render
arresting and convincing. His lyrical work is more difficult, his
idiosyncrasy preventing the normal linking of emotion with sweet
sound; but, even apart from this, it is doubtful if he has any strong
lyrical impulse. He is drawn more strongly to those aspects of music
where intellect checks the free flow of imagination. Nevertheless he
believes that music is straying too far from its origin, that it is
becoming over-civilised, and on that account he has been a persistent
collector of folk-song on many journeys in the Balkans and the East.
He collects and arranges, but cannot originate, folk-music. It is a thing

of sunshine and brightness and it withers under Bartók's intellectualism; something perverse in his nature mingles with the dance, giving a misplaced suggestion of bitterness, and his work serves to emphasise the contrast between folk-music and intellectual modernism.

The Problems of Modern Music, London (J. M. Dent), 1925, pp. 203–4

JENŐ SZENKÁR
(1891–1977)

Although born and educated in Hungary, Jenő (Eugen) Szenkár's professional career was mainly spent outside that country. He popularized the orchestral and stage works of many of his contemporaries, in particular Prokofiev, Wellesz, Honegger, Kodály and Bartók, whose controversial pantomime *The Miraculous Mandarin* he premièred in 1926 during his term as chief conductor of the Cologne Opera. He left Germany in 1933 and only returned there in 1950, having meanwhile fulfilled conducting contracts in Moscow and Rio de Janeiro.

. . . one grand world première must receive special mention: 'The Miraculous Mandarin' by Béla Bartók – a magnificent work, which later found world-wide acclaim, and was first performed under me. We needed to have countless rehearsals with the orchestra, since the piece was very difficult and unusually complicated for an orchestra of that time! But how can I describe the uproar which this work caused with the audience and the Press! At the end of the performance we were confronted with a chorus of whistling and booing! Bartók was present – even during all the rehearsals he generally sat in the auditorium. The uproar was so deafening and threatening that the safety curtain had to be lowered! We did not give up, however, and were not afraid even to go out in front of the curtain – at which the whistling redoubled! There were, in fact, a few voices calling out 'bravo', but these were quite drowned out by the uproar. Then, on the following day came – the reviews! What was published, especially in the Catholic 'Volkszeitung', the paper of the Centre Party, can barely be repeated! But my good friend was not to be deterred. He insisted on making a small correction in the clarinet part, and his only concern was to go to the Opera as soon

Ára 5 korona.

Szombaton, 1921. április 23-án este 6 órakor
a Zeneakadémia nagytermében

DEBUSSY-SZTRAVINSZKY-EST

Közreműködnek: BARTÓK BÉLA, H. GERVAI ERZSI
és SZÉKELY ZOLTÁN

MŰSOR.

1. DEBUSSY CLAUDE . Préludes (1909—1912)
  1. Danseuses de Delphes. 1.
  2. Le vent dans la plaine. 2. Voiles
  3. Feuilles mortes.
  4. La puerta del Vino (Habanera).
  5. »Les fées sont d'exquises danseuses«.
  6. »General Lavine« — eccentric — (Cake-Walk).
  7. Ce qu'a vu le vent d'Ouest.
  8. La terrasse des audiences du clair de lune.
  9. Ondine.
  10. Les collines d'Anacapri.   (Zongora.)
2. SZTRAVINSZKY IGOR 1. Quatre chants russes (1918).
  a) Canard (Ronde).
  b) Chanson pour compter.
  c) Le moineau est assis . . .
  d) Chant dissident.
  2. Histoires pour enfants (1917) No. 2.
  (Les canards, les cygnes, les oies . . .).
                    Ének és zongora.)

S Z Ü N E T.

3. SCHÖNBERG ARN.   op. 11-ből (!909) 1. és 2. szám.
  SZTRAVINSZKY IGOR Piano-Rag-music (1919).   (Zongora.)
4. DEBUSSY CLAUDE . Szonáta zongorára és hegedüre (1916—1917.)
  Allegro vivo.   Intermède (fantasque et léger)
  Finale (très animé).

FODOR rendezése.

A „Bösendorfer"-féle hangverseny-zongorát CHMEL J. és FIA cég szállította.

Zeneakadémia.   Vasárnap, 1921. április 24-én.

M. HAVAS GYÖNGYIKE

DALESTÉLYE.   (FODOR rendezése.)

VIGADÓ.   Szerdán, 1921. április 27-én

FEUERMANN ZSIGMOND hegedű-estje.

Műsor: CSAJKOVSZKY: Hegedűverseny, BACH. PAGANINI, SARASATE stb.
                    (FODOR rendezése)

Programme from a Bartók piano recital of recent music, Budapest, 1921 as possible to find the part in the orchestral material! That's what Bartók was like! Meanwhile, however, a call came through from the Lord Mayor's Office that I was to report there right away. I feared the worst! Dr [Konrad] Adenauer received me in a cool and reserved fashion, but then promptly blurted out the most bitter accusations: how could it ever have crossed my mind to perform such a dirty piece? And he demanded that the work be dropped immediately! I tried to convince him that he was wrong, that Bartók was our greatest contemporary composer, and that one should not make oneself the laughing stock of the musical world! But he stuck to his view that the work had to disappear from the season's programme! I felt very despondent and considered offering my resignation! When Bartók heard about this, he implored me to do nothing of the kind: I was to continue! He was convinced that his time would certainly come! He was so moving, so great, so simple! To me he appeared to be a martyr who believed in himself! He expressed the hope that I would not tire of continuing the struggle on his behalf! I should not throw in the towel! So I felt in a way 'bowled over', and I stayed in Cologne! But I could never overcome my wrath against Adenauer, and when as the years went by I observed an ever-increasing awareness in musical circles of Bartók's importance I was happy and proud in the knowledge of my own lifelong commitment to such a great man! Meanwhile he has conquered the world, and New Music would be unthinkable without Bartók!

Memoirs, as recorded in Annette von Wangenheim, *Béla Bartók 'Der wunderbare Mandarin'*, Overath bei Köln (Ulrich Steiner), 1985, item 59

IGOR STRAVINSKY

(1882–1971)

The ever-evolving ideas of Russian composer Igor Stravinsky were some of the most influential upon Western musicians from the 1910s to the 1960s. Bartók, too, was fascinated by Stravinsky's music, particularly the early ballets, and on several occasions freely stated that Stravinsky was, in his opinion, 'the greatest of the moderns'. This respect was not reciprocated by Stravinsky, who always avoided any direct praise of Bartók's work or personal collaboration with him.

It's a pity that I have not had the opportunity to get to know the compositions of Bartók and Kodály in their entirety. But I did hear *one* Bartók work in Philadelphia last year. It was a great success. It was a joy to me that the national character of the Hungarians was not considered alien in America.

In Jenő Feiks, 'Igor Stravinsky', *Pesti Napló* (Budapest), 14 March 1926

R.C. [Robert Craft] Did you know Bartók personally?

I.S. [Igor Stravinsky] I met him at least twice in my life, once in London, in the nineteen-twenties and later in New York in the early forties, but I had no opportunity to approach him closer either time. I knew the most important musician he was, I had heard wonders about the sensitivity of his ear, and I bowed deeply to his religiosity. However, I never could share his lifelong gusto for his native folklore. This devotion was certainly real and touching, but I couldn't help regretting it in the great musician. His death in circumstances of actual need has always impressed me as one of the tragedies of our society.

Igor Stravinsky and Robert Craft, *Conversations with Igor Stravinsky*, London (Faber and Faber), 1958, p. 74

JENŐ ANTAL

(b. 1900)

Antal graduated from the Budapest Academy of Music in 1925, and in the following year joined the Róth String Quartet as second violinist. In July-August 1931 he was an artist-in-residence at the Mondsee Austro-American Conservatory of Music and Art of Stage. Bartók was also 'in residence' at the school, unenthusiastically teaching a small number of students piano, composition and harmony.

We taught chamber music, and the members of the quartet collaborated, as needs be. Our principal activity, however, was to present a concert once a week in the castle, not so much for the students of the course as for members of the public taking their summer holidays there.

And so it happened that in one of our concerts Feri Róth and I presented 5 or 6 pieces chosen by Bartók from his 'Violin Duos'. (At that time only 25 or 26 of the pieces were ready.) When Bartók handed over the manuscript of the duos he said that he would be arranging the pieces in a progressive order of difficulty, intending them as some kind of instructive course. He asked me to look through the bowings and, if I found something amiss, to correct it. I don't need to say that I didn't find a single mistake!

While there we also began to practise the Fourth String Quartet (his most recent then) under Bartók's guidance. Afterwards, at the end of the summer, we performed this in Venice at the Biennale. He came to several of our rehearsals and helped us in analysing the movements. We asked him to listen also to the First String Quartet, which we had already played a number of times in our concerts. He directed our attention to the fact that the metronome markings in the printed score were wrong. The 'Pro Arte' String Quartet has followed the wrong metronome indications in its gramophone recording, resulting in far too slow a tempo.

In Lili Veszprémi, 'Bartók és a Róth-kvartett', *Muzsika*, vol. 14/3 (March 1971), p. 19

ERIK CHISHOLM
(1904–65)

The Scottish pianist and composer Erik Chisholm came to know Bartók personally in the early 1930s through his position as President of Glasgow's Active Society for the Propagation of Contemporary Music. By that time, however, he had already performed numerous works by Bartók at concerts in Canada and Scotland. As already described in Diana Chisholm's recollection, Bartók stayed with the family during his visits to Glasgow. Shortly after the end of the Second World War Chisholm was appointed Professor of Music at the University of Cape Town. There he became particularly involved with the University Opera Company, which performed Bartók's opera in South Africa and Britain during the 1950s. Chisholm himself composed extensively throughout his professional life.

On both of his visits to Glasgow, he stayed at my house. On the second

HUNGARIAN COMPOSER IN GLASGOW.—Mr Erik Chisholm and Mr Ernest Boden (left), president of the Active Society, greeting Bela Bartok, the Hungarian composer and pianist, on his arrival in Glasgow to play in the St Andrew's (Berkeley) Hall to-night.

Bartók arriving in Glasgow, as recorded in the *Bulletin and Scots Pictorial* of 2 November 1933

occasion, November 1933, he had with him in his music case the full score of his 2nd piano concerto. I asked Bartók if I might look at it. It was written in the composer's own precise, clearly pointed and highly characteristic pen work on transparent draughtsman's paper ('Sympax' is the trade name we now give it). I asked him why he didn't write on ordinary manuscript paper; he replied that these transfers served as photographic negatives and allowed his larger works, which would be very costly affairs to engrave, to be printed at a very moderate cost . . .

Bartók knew I had played the solo part of his first piano concerto and asked me how I thought the piano writing compared in the two concerti. Turning over the pages – Bartók was sitting on the edge of his bed, I on the armchair – I saw that No. 2 did not seem so rhythmically complex as No. 1, and that there were some uncomfortably big stretches – chords consisting of two piled-up perfect fifths in each hand; a whole string of rapid semiquavers in block chords. Bartók said that he himself had not particularly large hands, and yet managed to play these passages without undue difficulty. I knew from the previous

A page from Bartók's travelling copy of the Second Piano Concerto year's concert that he had wrists of steel, and was a virtuoso pianist of a high order.

The opening of the second movement struck me as a typical Bartók slow movement: a quasi-chorale theme clothed in dissonant, acid, arid harmonies: less relentless, perhaps, than the adagios in the piano sonata and the first concerto, where the augmented octave interval seemed to have replaced the common octave. I passed over some pages until I reached the *Presto* section of this two-sided movement which combines slow movement and scherzo, and raised my eyebrows enquiringly at my first sight of tone-clusters. He smiled, then replied in that soft, almost inaudible voice of his: 'Not my invention, I'm afraid. I got the idea from a young American composer, Henry Cowell.' . . .

Many years later, when I was in Boston in 1954, I met with Henry Cowell quite by chance . . . He told me that when he was in London in 1923 Bartók accidentally overheard him playing some of his own music which employed tone clusters. He [Bartók] was extremely interested in this new technique, and later wrote asking if he might be permitted to use similar tone clusters in his own compositions. Cowell said that his chance encounter with Bartók was one of the most exciting episodes of his life, as Bartók invited him to come to Paris and demonstrate his revolutionary technical devices to some of Bartók's friends, including Ravel, Roussel and Manuel de Falla . . .

But, to return to our conversation in the bedroom. Bartók spoke also about another educational project he had in hand: the collection he called 'Mikrokosmos'. 'Beg pardon' I said, the word being new to me. 'Mikrokosmos' he repeated and spelled it out for me . . . In the quiet earnest manner in which Bartók spoke about this novel piano 'tutor' it was clear to me he was extremely interested in the project, and that it was one very much after his own heart. As a matter of fact he had a very personal interest in this collection, as he intended it primarily for the musical education of his nine-year-old son Péter and, indeed, dedicated the first two volumes to Péter. Péter later said that while he could cope with the earlier volumes, and struggle through the middle volumes, the last two books were quite beyond him.

'Béla Bartók', unpublished paper delivered in Cape Town, 1964, pp. 1–5

PÉTER BARTÓK

(b. 1924)

The composer's younger son, by his second wife, received his primary and secondary education in Hungary, then late in 1941 attempted to follow his parents to the United States. Because of the United States's entry into the war at this time he experienced great difficulty in reaching them, but did finally arrive in New York in April 1942. After military service he trained as a sound engineer and initiated the Bartók Records label, under which several recordings of his father's performances were issued in the late 1940s and early 1950s. Péter Bartók now lives in Florida, where he manages the American Bartók Estate. Bartók dedicated the first two volumes of his *Mikrokosmos* piano pieces (1926–39) to his son, who gave the 'first performances' of many of these pieces.

During the period when I knew him my father generally accepted only advanced piano students. Nevertheless, when I was about nine years old (1933), he agreed to start teaching me from the very beginning.

His teaching programme did not follow an accepted 'piano school' technique. At first I was to sing only. Later, exercises were improvised, directed partly at the independent control of the fingers. In the course of our lessons he sometimes asked me to wait while he sat down at his desk, and I would hear only the scratching of his pen. In a few minutes he would bring to the piano an exercise, or a short piece, that I was to decipher right away and then learn for the next lesson.

So were born some of the easier pieces in these volumes. However, he kept on producing others at a much faster rate than I could learn them. He wrote the little compositions as the ideas occurred to him. Soon there was a large collection to choose from, so I could learn those assigned to me from a fair copy of the manuscript.

Eventually my father arranged the pieces in a progressive order for publication . . .

Foreword to *The Definitive Edition of 'Mikrokosmos'*, London (Boosey & Hawkes), 1987, p. 4. This extract is included by permission of Boosey & Hawkes Music Publishers Ltd.

Bartók and his son Péter, mid-1930s

ERNEST ANSERMET

(1883–1969)

Trained initially in mathematics, Ernest Ansermet was in his mid-twenties before he conducted his first concert. During the years of the First World War, however, he became the principal conductor of Diaghilev's Russian Ballet, and in 1918 founded the Orchestre de la Suisse Romande, which he continued to direct until his retirement in 1966. During his long career he was associated with premières or early performances of numerous leading works, including several by Stravinsky, Britten and Bartók.

Bartók's character, on the one hand, inclined towards that clarity, precision, and most subtle distinction of thought, which would lead him to technical and documentary research, and to constructions of pin-point accuracy and refined, aural proportions.

Bartók is a musician in the old and even Germanic sense of the word; he is a 'Tonsetzer'. The 'Tonsetzer' sets up rather than composes: a melody is not a combination of notes; in a flash it is set up – and this is one of the meanings of 'setzen'. Here the other side of Bartók's personality becomes apparent: his blazing heart, which aims for the high and the distant, and which Music emboldens to lofty enterprises. In this way he forges a connection with the Classics and their synthesizing formal endeavours. But he cannot confine himself to traditional thematic material, which had been so debased by the musicians around him. He was looking to a radical renewal of it.

'Quelques souvenirs sur Béla Bartók', *Labyrinthe* (Geneva), 15 October 1945, reproduced in Werner Fuchss, *Béla Bartók und die Schweiz*, Berne (Nationale Schweizerische UNESCO-Kommission), 1973, pp. 109, 111

JOSEPH SZIGETI

(1892–1973)

Szigeti recalls the circumstances of the creation of Bartók's *Contrasts* in 1938. Bartók's original idea was for a piece of only two movements, but he later added a third movement between these two.

I have never commissioned any work for my own exclusive use; I somehow always managed to have my hands full without that. The nearest I came to commissioning a work was when I had a brainwave about suggesting to Benny Goodman that he authorize me to ask Bartók to write a work for the three of us – Goodman, Bartók, and myself – to be underwritten financially by Benny. The result was *Contrasts*, which we repeatedly played and also recorded; about the rehearsing of this Benny has some interesting things to say in his autobiography, *The Kingdom of Swing*. There were all sorts of complications, chief among them Benny's hope – though not his proviso – that the work should be just the right length for a double-sided twelve-inch disc. This was not the case, and Bartók was somewhat apologetic about the 'overweight' when giving me the timings of the work.

In his scores, by the way, Bartók sets down the timings to the split second, like this: '6 min., 22 seconds'; whereas Alban Berg in his Violin Concerto allows, apparently, a latitude of fully five minutes by noting on the flyleaf of the work: 'Duration 25–30 minutes.' This difference in outlook on the part of two contemporary masters, both trail-blazers, always puzzled me. I asked Bartók for the reason. 'It isn't as if I said: "This *must* take six minutes, twenty-two seconds,"' he answered; 'but I simply go on record that when *I* play it the duration is six minutes, twenty-two seconds.' An essential distinction, this.

Bartók wrote, when sending the score to Benny and me: 'Generally the salesman delivers less than he is supposed to. There are exceptions, however, as for example if you order a suit for a two-year-old baby and an adult's suit is sent instead – when the generosity is not particularly welcome!'

A good deal has been written about this work, but one angle has been neglected: that it was completed, according to the manuscript which is before me as I write, 'in Budapest on September 24, 1938' – the very

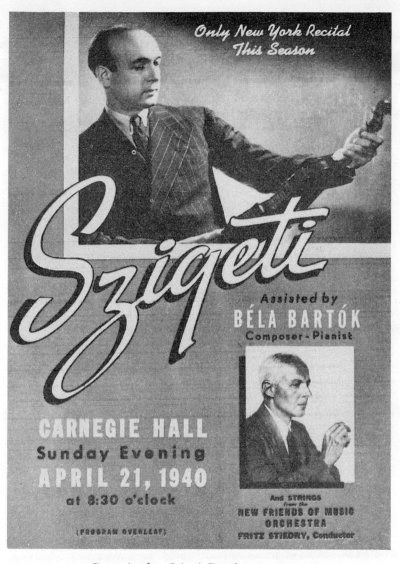

Promotion for a Szigeti–Bartók concert, 1940

day when Hitler's Sudeten demands had *almost* succeeded in setting flame to the Europe that was to give him another eleven months in which to arm . . . The picture of the creative artist meticulously putting the finishing touches to a work – during days when the whole world was holding its breath – is consoling and inspiring. But this same Bartók, anti-Fascist that he has always been, did not hesitate to answer the summons from the new parliament in liberated Hungary, in the spring of 1945, with an unequivocal yes. He had been elected to parliament by the people along with three other Hungarian exiles: former President Count Michael Károlyi; Professor Rustem Vámbéry (president of the New Democratic Hungary movement) and George Boeloeny, writer, who had been active in the French underground.

With Strings Attached: Reminiscences and Reflections, New York (Alfred A. Knopf), 1947, pp. 129–30. Copyright 1947, (c) 1966 by Alfred A. Knopf, Inc. Reprinted by permission of the publisher.

PERCY GRAINGER

(1882–1961)

Percy Grainger pursued a flamboyant career as pianist, composer, teacher and ethnologist through his various residencies in Australia, Germany, Britain and America. His folk music activities interested Bartók in the period before the First World War; later, in 1933–4, the two exchanged opinions on the topic of 'Melody versus Rhythm' in the pages of the *Music News* of Chicago. Both also taught the American pianist Storm Bull, and it was Bull's continued championing of Bartók's music, above all his Second Piano Concerto, that led to the following outbursts from Grainger in 1940–1.

As a gifted Norwegian–American playing Rachmaninoff & Bartók (playing the Grieg Concerto I do not count. It is not a novelty. And not a good example of Nordic music, it seems to me) you merely are an enemy of my hopes & intentions. I do not ask you to share my hopes & intentions. But I do ask you not to be so 'independent' as to ignore all my clearly-expressed ideals & still expect me to be interested in yr career. What are these careers for? To show how *abject* we Nordics have to be before every Hungarian & ½-Jew that appears on the horizon? . . .

Sketch of letter, Grainger to Agnes, Eyvind and Storm Bull, 26 October 1940

I suppose all this will seem fanatical to you – as it did to my English friends when I said: 'make a darkeyed man Britain's premier? He will lead you to disaster!' Now the Italian campaign has started badly, they must (of course) set a fair-colored man at the head of the army. Do these things have to happen a 1000 times before people understand them? If you, Storm, understand these things, you would not throw yr energy into playing a dark man's music? (Why do you want to interest *me* in Bartók's music? He belongs to the enemy group. That is all I know, or need to know. Furthermore, everything I know of his is energetic, harsh, ambitious. You know what I worship in music: the smoothness of Bach, the smoothness of Fauré. I rate all music by its closeness to *peace*.) . . .

Letter, Grainger to Eyvind and Storm Bull, 16 November 1940

One cannot make a paying career on Grieg & Rachmaninoff concertos – nor on Bartók, who, whatever else he may, or may not be, is hardly a melodist, &, therefore, hardly a man to thrill the big public.

Letter, Grainger to Eyvind Bull, 23 February 1941. All the above held in the collections of the Grainger Museum, Melbourne

(In a letter of 20 March 1941, Eyvind Bull, Storm's father, replied to Grainger's accusations against Bartók:

There are, of course, the most legitimate grounds for a difference of opinion as to Bartók's music. Personally I find it most enjoyable, of much musical worth and in many places even very melodious. And I cannot agree with you that place of birth necessarily means that the person in question MUST have any sympathy for the political or any other philosophy of the country of his birth or residence. If ever there was an *ANTI-NAZI*, or even anyone who was opposed to the accepted way of life in Hungary – it is Bartók! And if you think that Storm's enthusiasm for Hungary was based upon any sympathy for the so-called upper classes you are mistaken . . .)

Ernst Roth

ERNST ROTH

(1896–1971)

Educated in law, music and philosophy in Prague, Ernst Roth moved to Vienna in 1921 to further his musical studies under Guido Adler. In the following year he joined the staff of the music publisher Universal Edition. By 1928 he had become Head of Publications. On the annexation of Austria by Germany in 1938 Roth moved to London, where he worked for Boosey & Hawkes, of which he became Chairman in 1963. Bartók, too, changed his publisher from Universal Edition to Boosey & Hawkes in 1938–9 and so Roth was involved with the production of his scores for over twenty years – a not altogether enviable task, as he reveals below.

. . . unaffected by theories new or old was Béla Bartók. This small, thin, taciturn man was not an easy person to deal with, and his silences could drive a visitor to despair without his so much as noticing it. He never looked you straight in the eye and his finely chiselled face was like a mask, seldom changing beyond the occasional fleeting shadow of a distant smile or momentary anger. He spoke with visible effort, he seemed embarrassed to talk of himself or of his own or any other music.

Behind the unapproachable façade lay an extreme intolerance in both artistic and human matters. I cannot agree with the romantic descriptions of him which insist that he was the kindliest of men but was ashamed of himself and took refuge behind a wall of reserve. His reticence and intolerance were no deliberate protection from a world which would not understand him. They were his very nature and only in his music could he escape from it. Did this trouble him? Bartók was not an unhappy man in the usual sense, but neither was he a happy one who enjoyed himself and his music. In artistic and political matters alike he was an idealist, without practical objectives. It was said that he might have been chosen for the highest office, perhaps for the presidency of the Hungarian Republic after the Second World War, if he had not been doomed by then. His integrity was certainly unequalled, but I cannot think of anybody less suitable, and if his death prevented it, then at least he was spared another disappointment, of which his life had more than its fair share.

He never mentioned the music of other composers. He lived close to the aggressive Schoenberg circle but utterly ignored it. He admired Liszt, which was then an unfashionable thing to do, and played his works passionately, although he was not himself a showy virtuoso. Occasionally one was reminded that he had an astonishingly wide knowledge of music which one might otherwise have thought did not really interest him. In a letter he once quoted to me a few bars of cellos and basses which neither I nor anybody to whom I showed them could identify. They were harmonically so strange that I thought he had quoted from a new work of his own. But later he confessed with some irony that they came from the first act of *Lohengrin*.

Engravers and proof-readers dreaded him. He was the most scrupulous writer himself and would not tolerate the slightest carelessness in others. If now and then he abandoned the usual musical orthography he always had a definite purpose in mind and his wishes had to be followed unconditionally and unreservedly. Only rarely did he condescend to explain his intentions.

Once he partly let the mask slip. It was at the beginning of the 1930s. The general economic crisis all over the world had hit new music hard: public subsidies were cut, orchestras had to economize and give up all experiments. With Bartók himself things had gone badly. His works were hardly ever played, he had no satisfactory position in Hungary, he had few friends and none of those were influential. A journey through Turkey, collecting folk-songs in the vastnesses of Asia Minor, was a short escape from all his disappointments. The music which he wrote in those years testifies to the artistic, social and financial crisis in his own life. It became a mirror of himself, withdrawing into a hard shell of harsh, intolerant, unbending contrapuntal despair which accepted the inevitable with utter contempt.

He then did what he had never done before: he complained. He complained that even his piano works, apart from the 'Allegro barbaro', found no favour with the public. He rightly called himself the only legitimate contemporary composer of piano music, being a pianist himself and knowing how to write not only good but real, effective piano music. I could speak only from my own pianistic experience: from J. S. Bach to the Romantics every stylistic period had its educational literature which taught the beginner about both musical style and its technical problems; after Schumann this up-to-date literature of exercises and easy pieces began to disappear and the young player still had to start and finish with Czerny, which gave him all the equipment for Mozart and Beethoven but was no help with Chopin and Brahms, let alone what followed. 'But I am always writing short, easy pieces for beginners,' replied Bartók, 'I have drawers full of them.' This was not enough, I said. What was required was a system, a method . . . Bartók listened attentively and said he would think it over. The result was his *Mikrokosmos*, which I published in London in 1940.

The Business of Music: Reflections of a Music Publisher, London (Cassell), 1969, pp. 164–6

HANS W. HEINSHEIMER

(b. 1900)

Hans Heinsheimer headed the Opera Department of Universal Edition, Vienna, from 1924 to 1938. Like Ernst Roth, he left Austria at the time of the *Anschluss* and migrated to the United States, where he joined the New York office of Boosey & Hawkes. After the war he moved to the publisher G. Schirmer, eventually becoming its vice-president in 1972. Heinsheimer is now retired, but continues to live in New York.

I had met Béla Bartók many years ago in Europe when I was a young man with Universal Edition in Vienna, his publishers. Frequently he came through Vienna on his way to or from his native Budapest, and every time his short, businesslike calls were very special occurrences in the routine of our establishment. He was already an important composer, famous in an esoteric, not easily defined way, but not at all successful if success is measured by the usual yardstick of earth-bound public acclaim. Yet his visits – never improvised, always announced in a formal letter which stated not only the day but the exact hour of his appearance, arrangements which he would keep unfailingly – caused nervous fear and uneasiness. The deep respect extended to him by everybody from the doorman to the president of Universal was of a special brand, an intensity and seriousness that was rarely extended to any other of the many famous composers who walked through our doors from morning to night. Even the great Arnold Schönberg, so terrible in his wrath and so easily hurt by a wrong word or a seeming lack of submission, could sometimes quite easily be pacified by a well-placed joke or induced to tell a couple of them himself, and if he could get in a pun he came right down from his pedestal, grinning and relaxed, enjoying himself tremendously and becoming almost human. Bartók lived in an unsmiling, hushed world where there was little room for our human frailties and no pardon for our sins.

Fanfare for 2 Pigeons, New York (Doubleday), 1952, pp. 105–6

RALPH HAWKES

(1898–1950)

Thrust into a leading position in the family's London business by the death of his father in 1919, Ralph Hawkes went on to oversee the amalgamation with Boosey & Company in 1930 and the expansion of the joint publishing operation into the United States and Canada later in the decade. During these years he added such names as Britten, Stravinsky, Richard Strauss, Kodály and Bartók to the Boosey & Hawkes catalogue, and established a personal as well as a professional relationship with most of these composers. Bartók was sometimes critical of Hawkes in the middle years of the war, perhaps not realizing the extent to which the company's operations were restricted by the war, but he did retain the firm as his music publisher until the end.

As soon as the *Anschluss* with Austria was proclaimed, I realized that both Bartók and Kodály were, so to speak, marooned in Budapest. Their works were published largely by Universal Edition, and as this house was obviously going to be 'put in order' by Hitler's propaganda minister, these great composers, Aryan though they were, in view of their liberal and free attitude, would be in difficulty. A few days after the sensational news of the occupation of Vienna, I phoned Kodály in Budapest and said that I would immediately fly there to talk with him and with Bartók. I arrived the next evening and met them both. There was certainly no reticence on Bartók's part in agreeing to publish all his future works with us. He had several manuscripts in preparation, such as the *Sonata for Two Pianos and Percussion* and *Mikrokosmos*, which

Boosey & Hawkes
LIMITED
EVERYTHING IN MUSIC.
295·Regent Street·London·W·1

April
29th.,
1938.

IN YOUR REPLY PLEASE QUOTE
REF No RH/EJ.

Mr. Bela Bartok,
Csalan-Utca 29,
BUDAPEST II

My Dear Mr. Bartok,

You will no doubt recall my mentioning when I saw you
the intimate little Concerts we give in our Organ Studio here in
London.   We had the 2nd. Concert of the series last Monday
evening and I enclose herewith a Programme,showing the items
played.   Approximately 85 people were present and it was a
highly successful little show.

As you and Madame Bartok will be in London during the
International Festival of Contemporary Music in June,I would like
to extend to you an invitation to appear at one of these Concerts,
which we shall be having during that week and I should be most
greatful if you would give us 20 minutes of some of your newest
Piano pieces.   I am sure it would be a great attraction to the
Concert and we should be more than delighted to have you with us.
Actually,during that week we shall have two Concerts and amongst
the works performed will be probably:- one modern American work,
some Russian works and two modern English String Quartettes,
together with a new Trio by John Ireland.   The actual dates
for the Concerts are not yet fixed and I shall be grateful if
you will let me know whether you have arranged any engagements
that week,so that we may not clash with these.

Hoping you are well and awaiting the favor of your reply.

Yours very sincerely,

Representing

BOOSEY & CO.LTD   HAWKES & SON(LONDON)LTD   WINTHROP ROGERS LTD   EDITION RUSSE DE MUSIQUE   PHILHARMONIA MINIATURE SCORES
M P BELAIEFF   EDITION GUTHEIL   W BESSEL & CO.   CARL FISCHER INC   JOHN CHURCH CO
BOSTON MUSIC CO   OLIVER DITSON CO   C C BIRCHARD & CO   G SCHIRMER INC   UNIVERSAL EDITION

One of the earliest letters of Ralph Hawkes to Bartók, 1938

were partly done, and the *Divertimento* for String Orchestra which he was sketching for Paul Sacher and the Basle Chamber Orchestra. We talked about future plans and other forthcoming works far into the night. Thus, the foundation of Bartók's association with Boosey & Hawkes was laid. Kodály was less ready to do anything; his output as a composer was far less prolific than Bartók's, but he was in complete sympathy with my ideas.

Later that year, Bartók and his wife came to London for the ISCM Festival of 1938 and they played the *Sonata for Two Pianos and Percussion* at one of the concerts. It was then, I think, that I realized what was the tremendous force of the man. The intensity in his music was only a reflection of the man himself and as one knew him better, this became more and more apparent. He had no illusions as to the monetary value of his publications. He never expected the public to like them and play them and he told me so. He was the epitome of reticence and shyness about his work and remained so until his death . . .

My last meeting with Bartók was [in New York] in December, 1944, just before I left for England. At this time, I had commissioned and arranged to pay him for a Seventh String Quartet which he had expressed a desire to write. I vividly recall this meeting over dinner at the Gotham Hotel during which we discussed an article he had written for 'TEMPO' on the pronunciation and spelling of names in music. He was a great authority on languages and had profound knowledge of the subject as applied to music.

'Béla Bartók: A Recollection by his Publisher', in *Béla Bartók: A Memorial Review*, New York (Boosey & Hawkes), 1950, pp. 14, 16. This extract is included by permission of Boosey & Hawkes Music Publishers Ltd.

The teacher

JÚLIA SZÉKELY

(1906–86)

Júlia Székely studied piano with Bartók at the Budapest Academy of Music between 1923 and 1926. Upon graduating she worked as a music teacher and critic, and in later years wrote factually based novels about Liszt, Beethoven and Chopin. She has provided some of the most detailed recollections of Bartók's pedagogic interests and methods, including those found in her classic study of 1957, *Bartók tanár úr* (Professor Bartók). These passages are taken from the revised edition of that book issued in 1978.

Bartók did not like teaching. He said this a number of times, and to various people, and a few of his letters published after his death bear witness to the fact, as well. He never told this to his students, however, nor did he make them feel that teaching was a burden to him . . . According to the Music Academy's official timetable piano teaching was to take place between three and six, although it was sometimes possible to find Professor Bartók in the No. 14 teaching room even at half past eight. He sat before the writing desk or at the second Bösendorfer piano, listened to the student's playing, or himself played parts or the whole of the sonata, study, performance piece or Bach brought to the lesson. (He was never concerned with scales and technical exercises, considering these to be the student's own concern.) . . .

His teaching system was one not of explanation, but of rendition. When the student brought a newly-learnt piece to the lesson for the first time, he sat at the writing desk and heard it through without interruption. (Except, of course, if the student made an error of interpretation, reading or rhythm, in which case he intervened immediately and pointed out the error.) After he had heard the new piece right through he got up from the writing desk and sat down at the second piano. (This was also a Bösendorfer, like the first, at which the student played.) He did not say a word, and left the student without any idea of whether he had performed well or poorly. (In my case it was usually poorly, as later became evident.)

Júlia Székely, mid-1920s

At the second Bösendorfer, then, he played through the same piece himself, mostly without music if Bach or Beethoven were involved. He left it to the student to work out what conclusions could be drawn from the alternative renditions. He did not give any explanation to the student. Only in the next lesson did the nature and extent of the student's learning from the professor's performance come to light. Mostly, of course, it was not enough. At such a time he no longer heard the piece right through without stopping, nor sat at the writing desk, but stayed by the second piano. At each point of difference in conception he stopped the student, made a correction, made the student play the passage again and again, and also demonstrated single bars repeatedly until he could hear back his own conception absolutely exactly. While doing all this he kept a serious, cheerless countenance, without a smile; he said very little and did not lose his patience for a moment. We did not have tape recorders then, but if we had I suspect that even their faithful reproductions would not have been deemed sufficient. No: he certainly did not put up with the slightest divergences, even ones much less substantial than the differences between recorded and real sound.

Bartók never allowed so-called 'personalities' to develop freely; sooner or later it was impossible to stop turning into a slavish imitator. Now and then I tried to disagree with him. Once, when he had already played a section of a piano piece with me more than ten times (because it was still not precisely as he conceived it), I ventured the question:

— Well, am I playing this badly?

— I should like it otherwise.

This, of course, sounded like an order.

He was especially fastidious about rhythm. And accentuation. Rhythm and accentuation – in these two the true character of Bartók's piano-playing is found. On account of a single accent he was not averse to making the student get up from the piano fifteen or twenty times. First of all, he demonstrated at the second piano the accentuation he had in mind – which alone was deemed correct. Then, if the student did not succeed in adopting this exact sound from him, he stood up, took his place at the first piano, and demonstrated the same thing there. In this way the difference in timbre between the two pianos had also to disappear. And if the timbre heard back from the pianos still did not fulfil requirements at this stage he made the student stand up again and again, because again and again he wanted to demonstrate the same accentuation or rhythmic figure – a dotted or doubly dotted rhythm. This latter distinction conceals in itself an enormous difference, which most pianists, even today, still fail to heed . . .

Bach

In teaching Bach's works Bartók repeatedly directed our attention to the need to think of these piano pieces as being principally for organ, and only occasionally for cembalo. He stressed the conception for organ more since Bach himself had been primarily a performer of the organ. Therefore we had to think of his piano works – even the preludes and fugues from *Das Wohltemperierte Klavier* – not in terms of pianistic waves of crescendos and diminuendos, weakenings and strengthenings of tone, but in terms of exact, fixed angles, in a fabric of registers. Every voice had to be presented with a different tone colour, and lived its own special and autonomous 'register life', without fluctuations of tone, since on the organ it is not possible to change the tone colour within a register. But as the work has several voices, it is possible to show just as much tone colour on the piano as on the organ, for it is within the pianist's powers to elicit from the piano as many colours as are possible from the organ . . .

Mozart

In teaching Mozart's piano works Bartók checked whether the student was clear on the rules of scoring in Mozart's orchestral works. We had to know which voice Mozart would have given to the strings, which to the clarinet etc., should he have written the work in question as a movement of a symphony rather than of a piano sonata. By clearing up these issues of scoring it became easier to tackle the performance of the work . . .

Through Bartók we could come to know a new Mozart – the real one: hard, almost rapping *forte*s; *piano*s which were not delicate but spoke with a uniform voice; hard-set, closed formal articulations. Nowhere was there any emotional turn or sentimentality. Never was there any affectation or theatrical mannerism, still less any display of virtuosity . . .

Beethoven

According to nearly all Bartók scholars Beethoven's works were of decisive importance to Bartók's own creative make-up. The deep spiritual and intellectual affinity between the two was most in evidence when Bartók interpreted Beethoven's works. This affinity can only be comprehended by someone who has managed to hear Bartók perform a Beethoven sonata. Alas, such people are becoming ever fewer among the ranks of the living.

He included a Beethoven sonata in nearly all of his solo piano recital programmes, and, for the most part, this work was the greatest success of the evening. A number of foreign and Hungarian music critics hailed Bartók as the world's most correct and authentic interpreter of Beethoven's works . . .

By my recollection, he liked the Opus 110 sonata in Ab major best of all the Beethoven sonatas. I never heard him play this sonata in the concert hall, but he played it numerous times in lessons. The first time I heard this sonata from our professor was when he played it to Lajos Hernádi in a lesson. Never has Beethoven been played like this! The testimony which Beethoven and Bartók jointly produced in this exquisite sonata was just staggeringly personal. I decided that I would learn it, even if it killed me. It was not an easy task. But even today I know the work, as I have not allowed my first great Beethoven experience to sink into oblivion – neither in its details, nor in its totality. For me, that experience was Bartók's performance of the Ab major sonata.

Chopin

Chopin had an important place in the prescribed syllabus: the Preludes in the first year; the Etudes in the second. I studied all the Preludes, but some of the Etudes went beyond the capacities of my technique and physical strength . . .

It was seldom, indeed, that Bartók placed Chopin's works on his concert programmes. Only once did I hear the G minor Ballade from him in a public concert. The audience did not like it: the applause was sparse; people pulled faces. His interpretation of the piano music of Romantic composers did not accord with the prevailing opinions. It is a pity that I was so immature that I could not free myself from those opinions.

— No! — he objected, more with the movement of his hand than the word itself, when I took the C minor 'Revolutionary' étude to a lesson. — Not like that! — And he made me get up from the piano so that he could perform the C minor étude himself. He played more slowly than I had, and with precision, almost coldly, and without passion. I did not like the way he played it at all, but did not dare utter a word. He gestured for me to start again.

By the third bar he had stopped me. What kind of rhythm was that? Did I not notice that the rhythm was dotted? The composer had written the dot there so that the note would be lengthened, and the following note, correspondingly, be shortened. Why then did I play the Ab and the G as if they had equal value?

I did not dare to reply with what I was thinking, namely, that this was the work of a Romantic composer. Again I began the piece . . .

Liszt

This was not a part of the set curriculum. Liszt's works only appeared in the teaching list as suggestions for performing pieces. Bartók liked Liszt greatly, but not his virtuoso piano pieces . . .

[In 1901, while a student, Bartók had played Liszt's B minor Sonata in an Academy concert, to considerable acclaim] . . . in 1925, in the No. 14 teaching room of the Music Academy – from this time named after Ferenc Liszt – the B minor Sonata again appeared on the programme. Several students were studying it and taking it to their classes. I did not dare even to attempt it. I knew I did not have the strength for it. But this was not important. What mattered was that our professor performed the work. This performance now became a personal experience for us, and not just a fact of history, as with the student concert back in 1901. I do not dare to put down the experience of hearing it, as I am afraid that it might be similar to the case of the 'Kreutzer' Sonata [recorded in 1940, with Szigeti], where the recording has made me ashamed of my own lack of memory. Unfortunately, there is no question of that here. No one took a tape of this B minor sonata, which he performed with the tension of a Shakespearean drama. It cannot now be regained . . .

Debussy

I could bring as many of Debussy's works to my lessons as I wanted. He did not tire of them. He was especially fond of the Preludes. Sometimes I took three or four of the 24 Preludes to the one lesson. He did not finish the lesson until he had heard all of them right through and also played them himself on the second piano. Apart from the Preludes, I studied the following: *Poissons d'or*, *Children's Corner*, *Soirée dans Grenade*, *Jardins sous la pluie*. As he played these works on the second Bösendorfer right then and there in the lesson, it would have been possible to record them without making any changes, since these works emerged from beneath his fingers in such a finished form.

Now we had to forget everything which we had learnt for playing Bach because precisely the opposite considerations were involved. This is verified by the pencil annotations on the Durand edition of Debussy's works which I have before me. Here, for example, is the score of *Poissons d'or*. It was forbidden to pedal in Bach. ('We pedal in Bach's works only when it is absolutely necessary', he said.) Looking at my score of *Poissons d'or*, there are many pedal signs. The score is crammed with pedal signs, muted accents, huge *sforzato* and *marcato-piano* signs. This last is a typical marking of Debussy, with his impressionistic blending of colours, and Bartók also underlined twice with his red pencil the composer's marked *marcato-piano* sign. The following pencil annotations bear witness to Bartók's goals of dynamic playing, comprehension of the whole and appropriateness of interpretation:

'non fermata'

'non ritenuto'

'egybe!' ['together!'].

And there is every imaginable grade of accent from *marcato* to *sforzatissimo* marked in black and red pencil . . .

Kodály

He always recommended Kodály's works when someone came up with a request to study a work by a modern Hungarian composer which was not on the set curriculum . . .

Among Zoltán Kodály's piano works 'Epitaphe' [Op. 11 No. 4] and 'Rubato' [Op. 11 No. 7] were Bartók's favourites. He performed these two works with a dramatic tension the like of which we had not heard, either in the concert hall or the teaching studio. At one piano recital he played these two masterworks – long, slow, serious, still little known and not popular at that time – so effectively that the members of the audience listened motionless, in silence, and holding back their breath until the end. Then there was a storm of applause, as if they had been witness to some exhibition of bravura virtuosity, and the pieces had to be repeated. Bartók was the most authoritative interpreter, guide and popularizer of Kodály's piano works. Kodály's name was never absent from the programmes of his solo piano recitals.

Whenever I brought a work by Kodály to my lesson he would remain behind in the teaching room until late in the evening, and tirelessly help me in solving every problem in it. Only for Kodály's works did he give advice, as well, on how to surmount technical difficulties.

I learnt the *Dances from Marosszék* while it was still in manuscript. Professor Kodály even came in from the No. 18 teaching room to hear his work. He was not satisfied with me. Bartók drew his attention to the extremely difficult technical problems posed by the piece. He recommended that Kodály rewrite the final page of the manuscript, as the octave leaps of both hands in opposite directions were virtually unplayable. Professor Kodály gave me such a look that I would most happily have disappeared completely, and said:

It's not unplayable. You just need to know how to play the piano.

However much I would even have liked it, the earth did not open beneath me. On the contrary, Professor Bartók hastened to my defence.

— *I* can't play it, either — he modestly declared.

— *You* don't know how to play the piano, either — was the reply.

At this, Bartók laughed more heartily than was ever heard, before or after. Kodály was the only person who could inspire him to laugh in such an uninhibited way. Of course, Kodály was not serious about what he had said. He knew exactly how Bartók could be amused and how he himself could have some fun at the same time as well. Now and then they teased each other in this way.

However it happened, someone did nonetheless revise that troublesome section of the manuscript for the published copy. Whether it was Bartók or the composer himself, I don't know – I didn't dare to ask . . .

Bartók

How did Bartók teach his own works?

Many studied the works of Bach, Beethoven, Mozart, Liszt and Chopin with Bartók. They recall their experiences, and can speak and write about them. But among my peers I was the only one who took works by our own teacher to a lesson. None of my colleagues was sufficiently impertinent to do so . . . Then, without asking before-hand, I took Bartók's Sonatina to my lesson. This was the first Bartók work which I had dared to take to him. At a concert I had already heard him play this work for piano, with its Romanian folk inspiration, and I could feel from the way he played it how much he loved the work . . . With an indifferent expression on my face – as if this were the most natural thing in the world – I placed the score in his hands. He assumed an even greater expression of indifference. He sat down with the score at the writing desk, and became engrossed in it – as if he did not know the piece without the score – while I, tongue-tied with excitement, played the three movements without a break.

Not once did he interrupt me, not even in the short breaks between the movements. I recall that although I had prepared for this lesson very carefully I had never played as badly, despite the fact that the Sonatina is a supposedly 'easy' piano piece . . . Neither technical problems, nor even lack of preparation were the cause for this, but simple 'fear'. Instead of being absorbed in the music, I could not stop thinking of my getting through the piece, and the professor then, without a word, putting the score into my hands, turning and leaving the No. 14 teaching room. He had already sometimes reacted in this way if someone was poorly prepared. Perhaps he would remain inside and just send me out . . .

It ended up just the same as at other times, as if a Bartók work were not even involved. He stood up from the writing desk, placed the score on the second Bösendorfer, and, without making a single comment, played the three movements of the Sonatina through from start to finish. The only difference I could note was that while he played Beethoven sonatas and Kodály's works from memory, he read his own Sonatina from the music, even putting on his glasses so that he could see it better, and I had to turn the pages. Only after he had finished the third movement did that which I had so dreaded actually happen: he gave the music back to me and left the room. But, since before doing this he had himself played the piece, my distress disappeared . . .

Bartók tanár úr, rev. ed., Budapest (Kozmosz), 1978, pp. 44–5, 49–51, 56, 59–60, 62, 67–9, 75, 77, 80–1, 82–4, 86–8

LAJOS HERNÁDI

(1906–81)

Hernádi recounts his similar experiences as one of Bartók's students during the mid-1920s.

He was never late for a lesson; he never stopped before it was time. When one pupil was unable to come, another pupil got a longer lesson. (On one occasion, I remember, he gave me a two-and-a-half-hour lesson.) He never tired of playing excerpts to his students. When necessary, he played a phrase 8 or 10 times. He often took ten minutes to clear up one single bar. His teaching was *par excellence* musical: although he never made light of the importance of technical details, fingering, variants, ways to practise, etc. he thought the purely musical aspects more important. He believed that at an advanced level the technical details must on the whole be worked out by the students themselves.

And here, to be fair – I have to say something else. I think it is clear by now how compelling and overwhelming Bartók's style as a pianist was. No one who heard him play could escape his magnetic influence. Well, this influence was, if possible, even greater when one heard him speak; when one saw the firm, blazing light in his eyes at arm's length. Bartók himself never wanted to impose his personality on his students, but close proximity to him made it impossible to avoid it. To adopt his essential greatness was impossible: that was *his* only. But many of us adopted what was external to his playing. By using the word 'external' let no one think of Bartók as a *poseur*. There was no other person more remote from tricks of any kind. By the external qualities of his playing I mean his characteristic carriage when sitting at the piano, the fixed, almost stiffened state into which his creative efforts forced him. This was mostly due to his physique; he was a light, small, muscular but very bony person. He could exploit his small weight in a masterly fashion when he played, but all in all his playing was characteristically striking. His wrists and arms were all fixed. That is why he sounded, as I said, as if he had carved each piece in stone. It was combined with an unmatched clearness and plasticity of sound, a sound that was convincing from him alone. No one with a personality different from

Bartók could make use of this sound convincingly – it was too specific, too unique to create a 'school,' like the schools of Leschetitzky, Philipp or the Hungarians Thomán and Szendy. These notable teachers, though far from Bartók's status as composers, could, precisely because their approach to the piano was not so extremely individual as his, create a school with their neutral (I use the word in its best sense) handling of the piano. Their 'neutrality' could exert a fertile influence on the most diverse talents.

'Bartók – Pianist and Teacher', *New Hungarian Quarterly*, no. 30 (Summer 1968), pp. 198–9

GEORG SOLTI

(b. 1912)

Georg Solti studied piano with Arnold Székely and composition with Albert Siklós at the Budapest Academy of Music, before embarking on a long career as a conductor. Since the 1930s he has been accorded leading positions with opera houses and symphony orchestras in Hungary, Austria, West Germany, France, Britain and the United States, where he has been Music Director of the Chicago Symphony Orchestra for over twenty years. In the absence of his usual piano teacher during a short period in the mid-1920s Solti was reassigned to study with Bartók.

I was about 14 years old. He was a teacher of piano in the Budapest Liszt Academy: he never taught composition, strangely enough – always only taught piano. I was not his pupil but my teacher got pneumonia and was away for six weeks. At that point there was no penicillin so pneumonia could not be cured more quickly.

So we in the class were assigned to Bartók to our terrible fright, because I cannot explain what it was like to go on the Monday afternoon – eight of us appeared in that classroom – and he came in. He never raised his voice in the six weeks that we saw him; he always spoke softly and slowly. He had unforgettably big eyes which looked at one in a most piercing way. Of course I worshipped him together with the whole of the younger generation; we knew that one of the living geniuses of the twentieth century was in that classroom. We knew that very well; but this was not a very well-known fact either in Hungary or the outside world at that point.

So we started the lesson, which was more or less a normal academic lesson. One played the piece and he then made criticism. Not much – most of the time he sat down at the other piano in the classroom and played, making some corrections. Then he said 'bring it again' or 'do that'. What was interesting was that, before my teacher became ill, I played his very famous piece called Allegro Barbaro and I very proudly wanted to play that for him. He didn't want to hear it. He thought, rightly, that it was not good that this young boy wanted to play that piece. What he really wanted was to emphasize Bach, Mozart, not much Beethoven, and then an interesting jump came. We played everything – we played also Schubert and Brahms and Chopin but what he really loved was Scarlatti and Debussy, strangely enough, which at that point we played a great deal. As the six weeks passed, only the fright got less but I must tell you that the presence of that wonderfully evocative face, which I knew from seeing in the corridors – because we were involved in the same school – that was absolutely a miracle.

From the transcript of a talk at a Bartók seminar organized by The Women's Association of the Chicago Symphony Orchestra, Chicago, 5 February 1988

GYÖRGY SÁNDOR
(b. 1912)

Having completed his studies at the Budapest Academy of Music under Bartók (piano) and Kodály (composition), Sándor performed extensively in Western Europe before moving to the United States in 1939. There, he kept in contact with Bartók right up to the composer's death. In 1945 Sándor gave the first public performance of the piano version of Bartók's Dance Suite, and in February of the following year he premièred the Third Piano Concerto under the direction of Eugene Ormandy. Among his many awards Sándor includes special commendations for his recordings of Bartók's and Prokofiev's piano works. He continues to teach at the Juilliard School in New York.

It would be difficult to describe the piano teaching method of Bartók, because he had none. He was very active as a pedagogue, has written a number of 'study' pieces (they all turned out to be masterpieces, too), has edited the entire W.T.C. [48 Preludes and Fugues] by Bach, the Mozart Sonatas, a number of Beethoven Sonatas, etc., but as far as piano technique goes, he recommended 'practicing'. How? That was up to you. Just as well, since his own mechanical equipment was so much 'sui generis', that he developed a technique that suited *him*. Needless to say that most of his pupils (and he had many, during the 28 or so years he was professor of piano at the Liszt Conservatory) had mimiqued knowingly or unknowingly his technique, but this usually turned out to be more or less a caricature of some of his mannerisms. This happens most of the time when people are under the influence of a strong individual, that Bartók certainly was.

Difficult passages had to be 'practiced', that was all. However, he played [al]most everything and showed *his* way, how he would play the piece . . . His only concern was the music itself. And there, of course, he had a lot to say. To use a crude analogy, I remember distinctly that listening to his interpretations of Bach, Beethoven, Mozart, Schumann, Liszt, Debussy et al, I had the feeling as if the wrappings, the covering of the works had been eliminated – one heard, sensed the piece as it ought to be, not the way one knew it before. The inner meaning, the structure and above all, the creative drives were everpresent, the music was fermenting. Nothing was stereotyped, according to formula, but individually shaped, molded in a most convincing manner. By the way, his technique was simply spectacular . . .

In his polite, reserved manner, whenever I played a piece for him, he inevitably said 'This is fine, Mr Sándor', then sat down, played it through – and changed practically every note of the performance, for the better, of course . . . Only very seldom did he stop at the first statement.

Letter to Reginald R. Gerig, 1 March 1970, in Reginald R. Gerig, *Famous Pianists & Their Technique*, Washington (Robert B. Luce), 1974, p. 484

Bartók in about 1929

STORM BULL
(b. 1913)

Storm Bull studied music in Chicago before venturing to Paris
and Budapest for further training as a pianist. From 1932 to
1935 he studied with Bartók at the composer's home on the Buda
foothills. Among the works they studied together was Bartók's
recently completed Second Piano Concerto, of which Bull gave
the American première with the Chicago Symphony Orchestra in
March 1939. On occasion, Bull also helped Bartók refine English
translations of his writings. In 1947 Bull was appointed to the
University of Colorado, of which he is now an emeritus
professor.

Three years as a pupil of Béla Bartók have not lessened the difficulty of
deciphering him as a pianist and teacher, though possibly I have had a
better opportunity than most to study him in this capacity. The last year
of my apprenticeship was at a time when Mr. Bartók was intensively
engaged in folk song research and composition, and therefore would
accept but two students, of whom I was one. His greatest asset as a
teacher – his ability to make one figure things out for oneself – has
complicated the task of separating his methods of procedure from my
own.

Béla Bartók is a firm believer in a technical equipment so complete
that physical difficulties cannot in any way hinder a facile expression of
musical thought. The mind must be free to devote all its energies to the
task of giving life to music. Any slight uneasiness of the performer who
is uncertain of his memory encroaches upon the ability of the mind to
concentrate on interpretation. Realizing this fact, Mr. Bartók has the
printed page before him when playing in public, even though his
memory is quite capable of performance without it. While playing, he
gives voice to a belief that the primary purpose of music is to stimulate
the conscious mind – that all development, thematic or otherwise, must
be used to present music as completely and thoughtfully, as possible.
Music must be conceived in its entirety and all details must build
toward a common, predetermined goal. The adage 'take care of each
little thing as it comes along and the big things will take care of
themselves' is not always in tune with this objective.

Before implementing the beliefs expressed above as an outline or guide in analysing Bartók's method of teaching, one must understand that although he is precise in his basic attitude toward music and its interpretation, he urges that, within this basic musical concept, each pupil give as wide a latitude as possible to individual expression. He presupposes that students of piano coming to him for instruction have a technical foundation and a knowledge of how the foundation was acquired, so that their own procedures may be applied to new problems as they arise. It is also assumed that no serious student of piano can be without knowledge of, and experience in, theory, composition, etc.

The new pupil, dreaming of an easy future after the first meeting with Mr. Bartók may be pardoned, because Mr. Bartók states in a very convincing manner that four or five hours of practice each day should enable one to accomplish the necessary results. I was not alone in finding nine or ten hours of daily work a prerequisite for any achievement approaching required results. Although I have never discussed the subject with him, I believe the discrepancy in the number of work hours needed was intentional on his part. Surely no student can object to a reasonable amount of work, especially a modest five hours of daily practice. Thus, the student, wedged between his pride and four or five hours of daily work, usually worked nine or ten hours with no complaint other than a silent self-recrimination for being 'slow'.

A selection from Clementi's *Gradus ad Parnassum* edited by Árpád Szendy is, to my knowledge, the only collection of piano studies used by Mr. Bartók. This collection consists of some of the more difficult studies, with phrasing and expression marks added. Technical problems are to be solved with a view to playing the studies as music for the concert hall rather than as exercises, for whatever the music demands, the technique must provide without undue exertion. Mr. Bartók suggests that anything demanding unusual stamina be practiced until the passage can be played twice through without pause. Fortissimo in chord passages must be equaled by fortissimo in passage work, with especial emphasis laid on tonal balance and the control of dynamics – as in the *Andante molto* of the Brahms F minor Sonata where five different levels of tonal volume can be used simultaneously. Difficulties that do not respond to direct attack are to be solved by the composing and practicing of pertinent exercises. Mr. Bartók offers to solve through personal illustration only enigmatic problems which seem to admit of no circumvention. For example, constant practice of finger trill is likely to achieve no result other than increased speed. Mr. Bartók shows how, in a pianissimo trill, an exaggerated roll of the hand and wrist supplementing slight finger action obviates unevenness.

Physical difficulties must be lessened through the ingenuity of the performer as well as through practice, in order that more of the mind may be devoted to the musical aspects of the performance. The student is expected to rearrange any phrase or section, through division of hands, etc., where such technical revision permits greater freedom of expression. Few composers are good pianists and a passage of years often brings with it a simplified approach that the composer might have used, had he thought of it. Even in Béla Bartók's own compositions, the composer does not always indicate the hand distribution which he uses, preferring to write the music as it should sound, since he believes that the performer capable of playing the music has the intelligence to make any technical revision needed for ease of performance.

Mr. Bartók teaches interpretation mainly by asking apposite questions which are supposed to nudge the student along the right track. Music brought to the lesson is played without pause while Mr. Bartók, using a type of musical shorthand, indicates corrections and possible points for discussion. Whatever interpretation the student may use is acceptable, providing a complete line of reasoning that elucidates each step is given. The student may be asked how some of the stereotyped means, used by musicians the world over to convey musical thought, accomplish their purpose. More often than not the student has unthinkingly used these clichés so long that an answer is far from easy. The purpose is to make the pupil conscious of a design which guides musical feeling, in order that a foundation for future musical expansion will be sound. When Mr. Bartók illustrates how he thinks a phrase should be played, you are not asked to imitate, but you are asked why he played as he did.

Teaching of this type requires long lessons. The average lesson, during my final year of study with Mr. Bartók, lasted between two and three hours. In short, I should say that Mr. Bartók's teaching, apart from other musical objectives, is to insure a thorough reasoning to confirm the student's musical convictions, so as to guarantee a full and many-sided development of talent throughout the years to come.

'Bartók, the Teacher', *Musical Facts*, vol. 2/3 (March 1941), p. 7

The ethnomusicologist
BERNARD VAN DIEREN
(1884–1936)

In 1909 the Dutch composer Bernard van Dieren settled in
London, where he came to know of Bartók's music through his
association with the British composer–critics Cecil Gray and
Philip Heseltine. His own compositional output was mainly in
the area of chamber music and he respected some of Bartók's
earlier compositions in that field. He was less charitable about
Bartók's ethnomusicological endeavours, which he considered a
thorough waste of time for a man of such talent. This opinion is
elaborated in the following excerpts from van Dieren's review of
Bartók's volume *Hungarian Folk Music*, which was published by
Oxford University Press in 1931.

Of all artistic childishness, that of composers – although sometimes
disarming – is usually the most exasperating. Their posturing is as
irritating as a forward child's play-acting. Strauss's affectation of
profundity or terribleness, for instance, may make one smile, but not
for long with patience. Now his particular form of romanticism is
despised by the composers who adopt the up-to-date pose. Yesterday's
terrible boy registered devilry, with a red cloak, a rapier, and a
mocking laugh. The one of to-day presents the rationalizing expert.
His 'props' are the dictaphone and the card-index . . . A positively
painful demonstration of the inadequacy of the newest faith is supplied
by Béla Bartók's 'Hungarian Folk Music'.

A first-rate composer here shows himself so bewitched by the
glamour of supposed 'scientific research' that he expends his valuable
time on work that any efficient clerk might in a couple of years be
trained to do. He aspires to rank with the palaeontologist with his
stones and bones, or the biologist with his microscope, diatoma, and
protozoa.

But a scientist does not publish his observations unless they are of a
startling or original nature. He would, at least if he were a scientist of
any standing, present raw material only as an introduction to a new
working method. Or his gathered facts would be given for reference,
with deductions leading to a system or theory from which he could

claim personal credit. Thus would he justify a plodding occupation with minutiae. Failing this, he could delegate the hack-work to the mechanics of whom there are enough in the lower ranks of the army of scientific research workers who can compile statistics with equal skill and patience. Such unimaginative, elementary labour is not performed by the creative spirits among scientists. There are scientific navvies for that. What Bartók has done in this work would in the real world of science be unacceptable even as a student's first tentative academic thesis. Conceivably a Haldane or Almroth Wright might delight in playing the nightingale gurgle in a toy orchestra. They would hardly imagine that thereby they qualified for citizenship in the State of Music of which Bartók is one of the notables. They might do it for a joke. But Bartók's excursion into the scientist's domain is by no means made in that spirit. He is portentously solemn about it . . .

It might with equal reason be called 'scientific research' if Bartók and his friends had been roaming the Hungarian countryside counting the hairs of horses' tails, informing the world subsequently that a five-year-old at Felsoeboldogfalva had by Bartók's own count a tail composed of 475,982 hairs (sub-class 5cIII. α), while Mrs. Kodály ran to earth a filly in Magyargyeroemonostor with a grandsire from Szentegyhazasfalu which with 475,999 tail-hairs on September 5, 1910, triumphantly entered Class II.3, sub c. β. There are all these classes and just such facts – not to mention the names! – in this book. I need only refer to page 62, where I find under 'II., No. 1(α) strophes isorhythmic': 'Only one rhythm schema is known (two tunes); (β) strophes heterorhythmic: only one tune known.' With due respect, this is bunkum and by no chance anything else. Science is no more in the habit of dealing with classes of 'two' and sub-classes of 'one', than are armies with brigades of two men and battalions of one soldier each, unless it is in some of the South American Republics where then the single soldier is a General – for which reason these armies are sniggered at just as Bartók may be sniggered at for his South-American-Republic-Army Science with its comic divisions and nursery organization.

Bartók as a comic-opera scientist is not one whit less burlesque than a beplumed and bemedalled General who, in his capacity of Dictator–President, has bestowed all his Orders on himself . . .

The prose of the book abounds with such flowers of style as: 'Generally speaking, it may be posited that the more truly rural the song the less exclusively any one text is associated with any one tune . . .' The 'science' is obviously on the same plane as that of the police surgeons who are desperately seeking a sound definition of alcoholic intoxication. One is naturally moved to unfavourable reflections by the similarity in terminology and the capricious classification of both pursuits.

Conceivably folk-music research may in time become a recognized branch of authentic science. But at this stage one regrets to see a man of Bartók's attainments wastefully occupying himself with the crudest ordering of doubtful material. At the same time, it is significant that these modest, groping, early efforts are carried on in the limelight of publication in several languages. Apparently the name alone of the musician Bartók makes such an undertaking commercially acceptable. For that very reason it is the more regrettable to see him availing himself of the chance.

Bartók has not as a composer developed in a promising direction in recent years. Still, we may expect much from him when we remember his earlier musical achievements. But to see a man so feebly tottering while he proudly thinks he is blazing a trail makes one sorry for him. Whatever there is to be done in the way of musical research by the examination of racial popular idiom, Bartók shows in his book that he is not the man to do it. He certainly should not try again, since what he attempts can be done by others, while he can use his energies for work that others could not do.

'Musical Microtomy', *Monthly Musical Record*, vol. 61 (1931), pp. 330–1, 333

A. ADNAN SAYGUN
(b. 1907)

Born in Izmir, Adnan Saygun first trained as a school music teacher. In 1928 he left Turkey to further his studies with Borrel and d'Indy in Paris, and on returning to Turkey in 1931 pursued a wide range of musical interests, holding successively various senior positions as pedagogue, conductor, composer, ethnomusicologist and bureaucrat. Saygun met Bartók in 1936 when the Hungarian visited Turkey to study Anatolian folk music, advise on aspects of Turkish music education, and give concerts and lectures. He was one of the three Turkish musicologists who accompanied Bartók on his field trip. Although only lasting ten days, this expedition resulted in a valuable collection of sixty-six tunes which was finally published in 1976.

At Ankara, where he had given three lectures on folk music (interestingly enough, the first in French, the second in German, and the third in Hungarian) and three concerts, we had been able to collect some songs. Perhaps it might be well to say a few words about his manner of working which, in my opinion, deserves to be known by folklorists. Bartók had assigned to me the phonetic transcription of the text; I took down this text only during the singing. For his part, he tried to write down as exactly as possible the melody itself. If I happened to finish with the text before he had completed his notation of the melody, I was to set to work writing down the melody also, for later comparison with his version. Of course, I jotted down on my piece of paper the necessary data about the singer, the place where the song was collected, etc.

Using a metronome, moreover, we would indicate the tempo at the beginning of each song; and with a pitch-pipe we would verify and note the register of the voice. In the course of the repetition of the melody, we constantly tried to indicate the variants that presented themselves and I was to pay special attention to the changes that might occur in the course of the repetition of the text.

Obviously, it was not easy to write all this down at one time. But after this first part of the work had been completed, there remained for us only the task of turning on the old Edison recording machine, to get the song down on the wax cylinder. I was not at all pleased with this piece of apparatus, which had many inconvenient features. It could not, for example, record clearly both the voice and the accompanying instruments at the same time. Truly it was also annoying to Bartók. But he preferred it to the other machines, which needed either to be plugged into an electric system or to be accompanied by heavy storage batteries . . .

In a neighboring village [near Adana] we had the good fortune of finding two musicians, one of whom played the *zurna*, a kind of rustic oboe with piercing tone, and the other the *davul*, a species of primitive big drum. This was the first time Bartók had seen these instruments.

Bartók and A. Adnan Saygun on a folk music collecting expedition in Turkey, 1936

That evening, we set up our equipment in a schoolroom, full of country people, our inquisitive spectators. Seven oil lamps spread a pale and wavering light in the room. As usual, before recording we were to write down the melody of the *zurna* and the rhythm of the *davul*. The musicians began to play, and – something strange resulted: the blows that the old fellow gave to his instrument made the whole building shake. The panes of glass in the windows never stopped making their extraordinarily droll answers to the powerful drum-beats. The piercing cry of the *zurna* made the air of the room most vibrant, producing a deafening and bizarre roar. And to crown the situation, as each blow of the percussion instrument jarred both the oil and the wicks, the light of the seven lamps dimmed in cadence, almost going out, and then in a moment coming back on again most brilliantly, so that there was a peculiar and constant alternation of light and darkness in the room. I can still see Bartók, with a start, dropping his pencil and paper, signalling me to continue, and putting his hands to his ears. He remained thus, his ears tensely stopped, to the end of the performance. This posture that he assumed greatly amused the country people, who did not cease laughing. Truly it amused us too.

Bartók had set to work for some time studying the Turkish language. The words common to the two languages repeatedly became the subject of our conversation. Having encountered considerable difficulties in convincing not only the women to sing but also the men, whether young or old (for they had a vague apprehension before a stranger who did not speak their language), I proposed to the Master that we make up a sentence that would be almost the same in Hungarian and Turkish. Then whenever we again met some people who were intimidated by the presence of a stranger, I would take over and give them a little talk about the history of the two peoples, in which I would say that the Hungarians were only Turks who had settled somewhere else, that they always had spoken Turkish, but that evidently in the course of the centuries their accent had become more or less different. After that I would ask the composer to repeat the sentence we concocted. Bartók would repeat it readily with an anxious smile barely visible on his lips. Of course, everyone understood it, and after several disquisitions on this subject we quietly set to work. Here is the sentence:

In Hungarian: *Pamut tarlón sok árpa, alma, teve, sátor, balta, csizma, kicsi kecske van.*

In Turkish: *Pamuk tarlasinda çok arpa, alma, deve, çadir, balta, çizme, küçük keçi var.*

(Translation: In the cotton field are much barley and many apples, camels, tents, axes, boots, and young goats.)

'Bartók in Turkey', *Musical Quarterly*, vol. 37 (1951), pp. 6–7, 8–9. © 1951, *The Musical Quarterly*. Reprinted by permission.

PÁL GERGELY
(1902–82)

Pál Gergely worked in the office of the Secretary-General of the Hungarian Academy of Sciences during the 1930s, and later in the Academy's Library. He had frequent dealings with Bartók from 1934, when Bartók left his teaching position at the Academy of Music and came to direct the folk music section of the Academy of Sciences.

I met Bartók for the first time one hot August afternoon in 1933, in the General-Secretariat of the Academy, where I worked. He was wearing a light-coloured linen suit when he came into my room on the 1st floor (this is now the Library's large manuscript reading room), and, taking off his dark glasses, announced that he wanted to speak with the Secretary-General, Mr Jenő Balogh, for whom I was working as an assistant at that time.

Introducing myself to Bartók, I immediately addressed him with the proper title of 'Master'. He was amazed: from where did I know him? I replied that it would be shameful for me not to recognize an artist who was heard so often on the platform and was our greatest living composer . . .

From this time [mid-1934] Bartók regularly came to the Academy's Horseshoe Room every second day, and he frequently worked there from morning until late in the evening, with his back to the Danube and the Fishermen's Bastion. There, he pored over his phonograph and music sheets. His first associates were the composer György Kerényi and the singing teacher Ilona Rácz, who both participated in ordering the material, playing back the phonograph cylinders and revising the transcriptions. But from the summer of 1934 they were already also thinking of further collecting, and many hundreds of new cylinders were bought for that purpose – from that year on, always being covered by their Academy allowance. We were able to spend 4,000–5,000 pengős annually from the folk music subcommittee's account. Their first collectors were Vilmos Seemayer, Péter Balla and Gábor Lükő. Seemayer gained an allowance from the Academy for making several hundred phonograph recordings in Murakeresztúr, while Balla and Lükő gained travelling allowances for collecting Csangó–Székely folksongs in Moldavia and Bukovina. Pál Péter Domokos, whose Csangó [Hungarian-speaking Moldavian] collection of 1928–30 was well known to Bartók, had carried out the pioneering work in this field.

From the summer of 1934 they began to listen again to the cylinder material from previous collecting expeditions, and to copy out and correct the earlier notations, at the cost of 30 fillérs per small-sized music sheet. In the payment registers of the day we find the names of Sebestyén Pécsi, Gyula Dávid and Zoltán Pongrácz in the list of newer associates. Bartók had the pianist Jenő Deutsch, Kerényi, and Ilona Rácz revise most of the cylinders. When Bartók handed over to me the

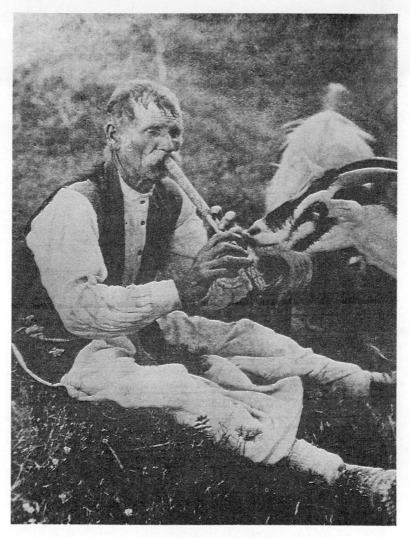

Shepherd playing furulya

work sheet of his pupil Jenő Deutsch for payment, he noted: 'This fellow has one of the best ears of us all.'

It was typical of Bartók's willingness to help and thoroughness that in the spring of 1935, when the Secretary-General asked him for a *brief opinion* of the Chanson Populaire volume published in Paris for the Academy's Committee for Intellectual Cooperation, Bartók wrote an entire little treatise, listing on *ten full pages* the errors and omissions of the French publication.

Many times we borrowed books and journals for Bartók from the University Library or the Library of the National Museum: in the summer of 1935 I myself brought across from the National Museum the Kenesei manuscript on folk music.

In the spring of 1935 Bartók was proposed for membership of the Academy . . . At the congress on 16 May 1935, by an almost unanimous vote, Bartók was elected a corresponding member, along with a number of eminent medical scientists: the Nobel Prize winner Albert Szentgyörgyi, Baron Sándor Korányi and Ágoston Zimmermann. In a beautiful letter Bartók expressed gratitude at his election. His letter to Secretary-General Balogh is one of the leading exhibits in the Manuscript Archive's display room. According to the constitution new members had to give their inaugural lectures within two years, but Bartók did not wait even a year, as in February 1936 he delivered the lecture entitled 'Ferenc Liszt and Hungarian Music' . . .

Bartók and Kodály planned to set up an East European Folk Music Institute, with the support of the Academy. He talked with me, too, about this, stressing the affinity which existed between the music of Cheremiss and other Finno-Ugrian peoples, and Hungarian folk music. He also talked about his imminent research trip to Turkey, which received various kinds of recommendation from our General-Secretariat. On the basis of the invitation received from the Turkish government, the librarian László Rásonyi wrote out, at Bartók's request, a detailed itinerary in Turkish, and together with him we drafted a recommendation from the President of the Academy to the two Foreign Ministers, and also to the Hungarian customs authorities. Because of previous bad experiences, Bartók feared for the safety of his photo and cylinder materials if, out of curiosity, the customs authorities investigated them for duty.

Returning home from his Anatolian trip, he prepared a long, updated report for an international folklore symposium in which he detailed the Hungarian researches to that time and our collections of data. In this he enumerated – besides the 1,500 + 900 cylinders in the Ethnographic Museum – just how many cylinders and transcriptions could be found, and with whom. He provided a first-rate summary of numerous transcriptions or cylinders in private hands and still to be worked with, in addition to the collection of 4,000 Hungarian and 3,000 foreign folksong materials in the Museum. There were also by then 121 cylinders from new collections in the Academy's holdings. In 1937, together with Zoltán Kodály, he appraised the transcriptions to see how much of the material which had already been revised definitively could be prepared for printing: according to this appraisal the big Hungarian folksong collection would have run to about four thousand printed pages. They wanted to publish this collection in a series of booklets, and therefore applied to the Ministry of Education for state assistance, as it would not have been possible to cover the horribly large costs of publication from the Academy's multifaceted budget (on which so many other disciplines had to rely). If the world war had not intervened there was every likelihood that these booklets would have been published. The Academy's General-Secretariat meanwhile secured fine-quality printing paper with funds from the Vigyázó Estate. For more than twenty thousand pengős we bought one truck-load of quality art paper, but during the bombing raids of December 1944 this pile of paper (which had been stored in the Franklin printery) was destroyed, along with the printing equipment.

From 1937 Bartók began to supplement the number of his copyists: Sándor Veress was attached to the Academy as an associate. Amid these copyists and others revising the cylinders, we saw Endre Szervánszky and Ferenc Ottó ever more frequently in the Academy's corridors, as they brought their material to Bartók. Bartók also requested the appointment of Dénes Tóth, which occurred at the end of 1939.

The work of collection and classification did not stop when Bartók went away to America in the autumn of 1940. The members of the folk music subcommittee continued to work under the guidance of Kodály. Led by György Kerényi they set about classifying the material, still according to the system enunciated by Bartók. Nonetheless, the wartime economies and, from 1943, the ever greater frequency of air-raid warnings made all our work harder or even impossible.

'Bartók Béla hét éve a Magyar Tudományos Akadémián', in Ferenc Bónis, ed., *Magyar zenetörténeti tanulmányok: Mosonyi Mihály és Bartók Béla emlékére*, Budapest (Zeneműkiadó), 1973, pp. 307–11

SÁNDOR VERESS

(b. 1907)

During the 1920s and early 1930s Sándor Veress studied piano with Bartók and composition with Kodály. From 1927, however, he also started to work with folk music, firstly in connection with László Lajtha at Budapest's Ethnographic Museum, and later, in the 1930s, as an assistant to Bartók at the Academy of Sciences. Parallel with this work he was gaining an international reputation as a composer, and was eventually appointed a composition teacher at the Budapest Academy of Music in 1943. In 1950 he gained a teaching position in Berne, where he still lives. Veress has published many studies of Bartók's music.

I remember some thirty years ago, when working at the Folk Music Department of the Hungarian Academy of Sciences in Budapest, I asked Bartók, whose assistant [at] that time I was, something about Bulgarian folk music. In those days Bartók, besides preparing the complete edition of the Hungarian folk music collection, was also doing research on Bulgarian folk melodies, being interested especially in their intricate rhythmical structures. When he heard my question he looked up from his notations with the ear-phones of the phonograph still on his head and in his soft, slightly nasal voice answered: 'I am sorry to be unable to give you precise information about your question but up to now I have looked through only about five thousand Bulgarian folk songs and I have to collect more data before deciding about this matter.' This answer was very typical of Bartók. He conducted his folk music research with utmost scientific conscientiousness and he would never conclude a postulate before having proved it from every available source.

However I also remember another occasion which is connected with Bartók's own music. It happened in 1936 when a Hungarian composer and writer on music, Sándor Jemnitz, published a thorough analysis of Bartók's 5th String Quartet, after this magnificent work had been played by the New Hungarian Quartet for the first time at a private circle in Budapest. Jemnitz sent his analysis to Bartók for approval and later, when he visited him to discuss his writing, Bartók revealed that he was surprised by reading about motivic, formal and harmonic connections Jemnitz discovered in the Quartet and of which he was quite unaware.

These two events, seemingly contradictory in their nature, are most characteristic because they reveal essential constituents of Bartók's genius. For it was this complete integration of intellectual power for investigation of scientific data with his intuitive creative fantasy coupled with an unusually strong potential of visionary insight into the very nature of musical logic, which created this balance between his different approaches to scientific and artistic thought. The two main fields of his activity, his research in musical folk-lore and his creative work, complemented each other in the same way. His music was nourished by his folkloristic studies while the scientist profited by the musician's experience in both theoretical and practical issues. Viewing it from this angle Bartók was a very rare combination of scientist and artist. Although art always has a part which touches the realm of science, the latter is not necessarily connected at every instance with art. We know about many great musicians, painters and sculptors who were also erudite scholars and even creators of new theoretical systems in their respective fields of art. But Bartók's life-long ardent devotion to folk music was something quite different; indeed it became a genuine scientific department with its own specialized methodical rules of research which occupied the greater part of Bartók's life. And Bartók himself considered his folk music research as entirely equal in importance to his creative activity as a composer.

'Some Notes on Béla Bartók', *The Peabody Notes* (Spring 1966), pp. 3–4

ILONA RÁCZ

(1897–1985)

Bartók's former piano student Ilona Rácz worked with him during his final years at the Academy of Sciences.

In the autumn of 1938 I came to the Hungarian Academy of Sciences, where I worked as an assistant to Bartók until the autumn of 1940, that is, right up to the time that he went into voluntary exile in America. It is possible to say that we worked together until the last minute of his time here, as he was still at the Academy on the days just before his departure . . .

Bartók worked in the so-called Horseshoe Room. It gained this name because a big horseshoe-shaped table ran around the room, with its opening towards the small room. This room was actually the Kisfaludy Society's session room. At the end beside the entrance door stood Bartók's phonograph, and this was Bartók's permanent place. There he sat on a seat built up with a book and a pillow which he had brought from home. He wrapped the headphone around with a white handkerchief, and bound it in a knot at the top of his head, so that – at an initial glance – he looked like someone with a headache or toothache. I believe he enjoyed this image, as he had a sense of humour for things like that.

Working beside Bartók, I could observe two typical features of his character: his incredible capacity for work, and his great concern for accuracy. This concern for accuracy was evident in even the most trivial matters. Bartók's working schedule was like this: from 2 o'clock to 7 o'clock he worked at the Academy. Until 4 o'clock he listened to the phonographic cylinders, revising his Romanian collection. At 4 o'clock he took a break, got up from his place, [and] took out from his coat pocket a little bottle, in which was some white coffee, and a small slice of bread as well. This was his afternoon tea. He never ate anything else. (For example, I can't think of him having ever eaten fruit.) During this break he would lean against the window or the table facing the window – and this was his time of relaxation. On one such occasion, as he was standing there by the window and looking out on the stormy Danube, he suddenly began to speak in an unusually tender voice, saying: 'Look, it has fled here away from the storm!' A little butterfly had fluttered between the two windows. Bartók loved animals such a lot, even the smallest insects. During afternoon tea, in his free time, I would go to him and ask him one thing or another about the ordering of material. After that it was only in a cigarette break – if he lit up – that I could speak with him. I collected together all my questions for that time. I remember that once he wearily put down his headphone and said with a sigh: 'It will only be possible to notate these songs exactly when we have a machine to measure the sounds.' Towards evening he left off making his revisions and joined me in ordering the songs. He arranged the A category; he left it to me to arrange the

B category. When he was engaged with the song classification, too, I left off my own work and went across to assist him. I selected songs and prepared the individual groups of songs for him. So, we became absorbed in the work and often did not notice the time until it was already after 8 o'clock.

'Bartók Béla utolsó évei a Magyar Tudományos Akadémián', *Magyar Tudomány*, 1961, pp. 383–5

IV
America:
in exile
(1940–1945)

Bartók was acutely distressed by the advances of Nazism in Central Europe during the 1930s. In 1938 he started to send his most precious manuscripts out of Hungary, but only after the death of his mother in the following year did he personally become convinced of the necessity of emigration. During a concert tour of the United States in April–May 1940 he assessed the viability of settling there, which he and his wife did – in New York – late in October. Performing opportunities were initially satisfactory, and he was offered a research fellowship at Columbia University working on Serbo-Croatian folk materials, but by 1942 his life had reached a low-point: he was grieving at the ever-growing world conflagration, was receiving little work as a pianist, felt disinclined to compose, and was suffering from the first stages of an illness which eventually developed into leukaemia. The remaining years until his death in 1945 were remarkably productive owing to generous medical supervision, the support of family and friends, and the resilience of his own character. Bartók completed his studies of Turkish and Serbo-Croatian folk musics and thoroughly revised his Romanian collections. The Concerto for Orchestra and Sonata for Solo Violin were also written in these final years, while his Third Piano Concerto and Viola Concerto were sufficiently advanced for his friend Tibor Serly to complete them after his death.

HARRIET COHEN

(1895–1967)

Harriet Cohen studied piano in London at the Royal Academy of Music and the Matthay School, and became a leading British exponent of contemporary music during the inter-war years. Among works dedicated to her were Vaughan Williams's Piano Concerto (1933) and the 'Six Dances in Bulgarian Rhythm' which conclude Bartók's *Mikrokosmos* series of piano pieces. During April 1940 both Bartók and Harriet Cohen were touring the United States, and met up at a 'surprise dinner' in New York to celebrate the publication of the final volume of the *Mikrokosmos*.

At the end of the month Ralph Hawkes telephoned that he wanted me to dine with him at the *Pavilion*, the superb French restaurant. Béla Bartók was to be the only other guest. They were already awaiting me at our table, armed with cocktails, as I arrived on time and they seemed in most excellent mood practically dancing around the table on which lay, with some gardenias, a volume of music. It was the day of the publication of volume VI of the *Mikrokosmos*. 'Blow me down,' I said to myself, 'an autographed copy' and opened it to find a neat inscription in Bartók's handwriting. I was overjoyed and showed it in my thanks. But Béla and Ralph continued to dance about, getting more and more excited and waving their glasses. 'Too many cocktails,' I was thinking, when Ralph stammered: 'Turn to page 35,' and I did so, reading to my utter amazement:

SIX DANCES IN BULGARIAN RHYTHM
Dedicated to Miss Harriet Cohen

I nearly fainted. 'The only dedication in the six volumes,' said Ralph Hawkes, hugging me. 'And these pieces are the final, the most difficult for your tiny hand,' added Bartók, kissing it. We ate enormously, drank enormously and then repaired to a small circular hall, in the Frick Museum or some similar place where Bartók was to give a recital. Ralph and I sat in the front row whilst Bartók played wonderfully well considering all the wine he had imbibed. He then addressed the audience and told them of the dedication and of his

Aboard ship on the way to America, 1940

feeling for my playing, before giving the first performance of the
Bulgarian Dances.

A Bundle of Time, London (Faber and Faber), 1969, pp. 296–7

AGATHA FASSETT

Now (1990) in her late seventies, Hungarian-born Agatha Fassett (Ágota Illés) gained fame in the 1950s for her factually based novel, *The Naked Face of Genius*, which depicted the life of Béla and Ditta Bartók in America. She assisted the Bartóks during their first couple of years there, and all three family members – Béla, Ditta and Péter – stayed at her vacation home in Vermont at various times during 1941–2.

I never knew anyone who was so completely without wastefulness. The tiniest bits of pencil, an eraser too small to hold, a rusty old paper clip – all were carefully saved in the hope that somehow, sometime, they might grow back into usefulness again. The same meticulous care was given to his clothes. His tweed country outfit with its knickerbockers was twenty years old if a day, he informed me, when I asked him if it had just been purchased for his Vermont trip. 'Buy new clothes!' The very idea irritated him. 'I have enough to last me a lifetime even if I live to be ninety.'

He could simply not understand when Ditta suggested one day that the next time they went to town she would buy a pair of shorts for him, so that sunshine could have a chance to brown his pale legs.

'I have plenty of shorts,' he said, dismissing the suggestion.

'But Béla,' Ditta explained, laughing and blushing at the same time, 'I don't mean the kind of shorts one wears underneath, I mean the other kind that are worn on the outside.'

'I don't see any difference between the two,' Bartók insisted.

Ditta tried again. 'The shorts you are talking about are worn underneath the shorts I am talking about.'

'Oh, is that all!' Bartók said with relief. 'Next time I set out for a walk, I shall put on two of my own shorts. That should prove satisfactory, I hope, to all concerned.'

RANDALL THOMPSON
(1899–1984)

The American composer and teacher Randall Thompson was Director of the Curtis Institute of Music in Philadelphia from 1939 to 1941, during which time he offered Bartók a senior position on the Institute's composition staff. In subsequent years he held positions at Virginia, Princeton and Harvard universities, gaining an increasing reputation as a composer of choral music. Among his more famous pupils or assistants were Samuel Barber and Leonard Bernstein.

[Bartók] listened . . . like a child and then in that gentle, almost Franciscan manner, he declined categorically, saying that he could not and never wanted to teach composition. He said that to *teach* composition was to imperil his own composing: it was as though he wanted to keep that side of his nature unspoiled by any burden of pedagogy.

In Halsey Stevens, *The Life and Music of Béla Bartók*, New York (Oxford University Press), 1953, p. 38

JENŐ ANTAL
(b. 1900)

Nearly a decade after working with Bartók at the Mondsee summer music school Jenő Antal met up with Bartók again, in America, where the two performed together at a concert in 1941. By this time the Róth Quartet had disbanded and Antal was Head of Strings at Westminster College in Pennsylvania.

I met up with Bartók in America, too. In January 1941 the head of Princeton University's Music Faculty, Mr Welch, announced that Bartók had been contracted for a solo recital. Knowing that I lived there, Bartók had requested that, if possible, I take part in the programme. And so I called upon the Bartóks in their New York apartment to discuss the programme.

Bartók recommended that we put the Romanian Dances and the 2nd Rhapsody on the programme, because the 1st Rhapsody was better known, easier and more often played. Even at that time I had not played either of the rhapsodies, but I was happy to tackle it as I had the whole of the summer to learn it. He advised me that, since I had a copy of the Universal score, I should contact Szigeti and ask him for the photocopy on which the cuts were marked. I did this and, if my memory serves me correctly, we performed both works in one of the university's concert halls at the beginning of the 1941–42 concert season. In the concert Bartók also performed some of his own compositions and some piano pieces by Kodály . . .

Turning back to my first meeting [in New York] with the Bartóks: after our business discussion, when I enquired about their state of affairs, it turned out that they were then wearing clothes loaned by friends and acquaintances, and were in other regards also in a bad way – both materially and in spirit – because they had received no news of their lost luggage. (As is known from Bartók's letters, it only arrived on 11 February.) When I asked about concert possibilities and plans for teaching he just gestured despondently and said that there were just no prospects at all.

I was so appalled at this situation that the following morning I called on Carl Engel, the president of Schirmer publishers – with whom I had maintained a good friendship since the Quartet's very first appearances in America – and told him just how poor the Bartóks' situation really was. He grasped the situation, although he remarked that he had met Bartók not long before, when he had been awarded his honorary doctorate by Columbia University, and Bartók had replied 'Well, thank you' to questions about his state of affairs. Engel wanted to plead in excuse that this was the real reason why the leaders of the musical community had not had the chance to learn of the Bartóks' straitened circumstances. I was not surprised at this, naturally, since Bartók had never complained.

Well, continuing with the story: Mr Engel sent me to see Mr Douglas Moor[e], the head of the Music Faculty at Columbia University, so that I could tell everything which I had related about the Bartóks to him as well. About half an hour later, when I reached Mr Moor[e], he received me with the news that Mr Engel had already phoned him and they had already even arranged for Bartók to receive a one-year bursary from the University's 'Ditson' Fund, on the top pay scale allowed under the fund's regulations. He was not to be required to do any teaching in return. As far as I am aware the bursary was extended.

In Lili Veszprémi, 'Bartók és a Róth-kvartett', *Muzsika*, vol. 14/3 (March 1971), p.20

FRIEDE F. ROTHE

During the war Friede F. Rothe worked for the Publicity
Department of Boosey & Hawkes' fledgling Artists Bureau in
New York. She consequently met with Bartók many times during
the early 1940s, and was able to elicit from him some valuable,
candid comments about his own music and his development as a
composer.

On meeting Bartók, you were first startled by the very determined,
quiet, and self-contained appearance of the man, and by the very small
slender form, the chiselled, transparent features, the blue eyes, large
and fearless. You knew instantly, without being able to explain it, that
here stood no ordinary man. You may not have been familiar with his
most significant scores, nor have even heard a single note of his music,
but the mere physical impact was enough to give you the feeling of the
strength and dynamism which emanated from that seemingly frail
exterior. And who, having come to know his music, has not been
moved by the rhythmic vortex which compels him and by the
tremendous individual direction of his thought and expression?

With Bartók all this was immediately felt on coming face to face with
him. The personality was forthwith made clear. With all its complex-
ities and depths it was made clear because of the essential honesty of the
man. One looked at him and knew that he would not abide compromise, untruth, or pretence. His blue eyes seemed to look through you,
remote and disdainful; the warm human side of him may even have
been lacking altogether, you think, yet his personality compelled you
with something akin to awe. This was no more movingly demonstrated
than at the concert and reception tendered by the League of Composers
on his arrival here [New York] in the fall of 1940; the whole large
audience stood up as one man to greet him. This was repeated again at
several other concerts, so spontaneous was the reaction of even his most
unconcerned listeners.

Coming to know Bartók more closely, you realized that his shyness
was no outward defence, but rather the expression of a great gentleness
and an inward preoccupation. And as is often the case with uncommon
minds, that gentleness of his was paved with firm convictions and hard
thinking, coming from a complete surety of direction. There is nothing

that Bartók hated so much as to discuss his own music, particularly if you asked such fool questions as what he had in mind when he wrote this or that, or whether he believed that his music spells the end of a period or the beginning of a new. To all such questions, he would give you a blank, incredulous look. But ask him purposeful questions, of historical, aesthetic, or material import, and he would be at your disposal. Then the logic of his thought was delightfully informative and instructive and the flow keen and jestful. The reticent Bartók was gone and the true Bartók was to the fore – a Bartók who was charming, frank, searching, and gracious.

This was made especially clear to me when, after the third or fourth meeting with him, I went to visit him at Columbia University, where he had a research fellowship. Spending a good part of his working week in the transcription of a fine collection of Yugoslavian folk-tunes gathered by the late Harvard professor, Milman Parry, who was an authority on the subject, I found Bartók one late afternoon amid his studies. The first thing he did was to show me a little bit of his manner of working; how he listened to the recorded folk-song over and over again, and how it finally looked after he had got it down on paper. Examining the music, with its melodic line of complicated details expressing the original as closely as is possible on paper, one got a measure of the man, of the painstaking work that must go into it and of the imagination and knowledge it requires. All this which Bartók has so admirably shown in his own researches in the folk-music of Hungary, Rumania, Turkey, Arabia, and other sections reflects in Bartók the composer. The logic and thought of his music are like the logic and thought of his folk-song research, and the organic form and meaning of his music are like the articulate force of the anonymous folk expression with which he has such deep kinship.

Thus warmed up in talking about something he loved, Bartók turned the more easily to the question of his own music, for the two – folk-song research and the creative realization – were at one with him through an inner affinity and intuition. In this happy mood, Bartók even accepted questions he would ordinarily not countenance. Smoking one cigarette after another (he was practically a chain-smoker), he answered with great patience, quiet humour, and deep thought. And once started, the talking became free, and inspired. The blue eyes sparkled, the small delicate face was alert and alive. Sitting quietly in his chair, or occasionally jumping up to make a point clearer, the hours rolled by, so much was there to hear and so much to say. And though the evening was late, Bartók excused himself, for he had to return to work. One left with a feeling of pleasure and gratefulness at the time so profitably spent.

GEORGE HERZOG
(1901–83)

George Herzog received his musical training at the Budapest Academy of Music (1917–19) and the Hochschule für Musik in Berlin (1920–22). In the mid-1920s he migrated to the United States, where he studied, and later taught, anthropology at Columbia University in New York. There, he pioneered some of the earliest American courses in ethnomusicology and comparative musicology. Herzog influenced the decision to appoint Bartók to a research position at Columbia in 1941, and later wrote the introduction to the volume which presented the outcome of Bartók's work at Columbia, *Serbo-Croatian Folk Songs*. In his later years Herzog held a senior professorship at Indiana University.

A combination of creative musical genius of the very first rank with persevering and detailed scientific creativity is rare. Bartók looked upon the tasks and responsibilities of the collector and of the composer as entirely distinct. Those of the collector, he felt, were to gather and present the material exactly and faithfully, without any patronizing emendations or collated versions of the sort which were current in Europe and are still popular in this country. In his settings of folk melodies he often submitted also the notations of the tunes as they were recorded from the folk singers, so that the reader could compare the two and see the material in its pristine form. Characteristically, perhaps, he gave no opus numbers to those compositions which were based chiefly on folk tunes. At the same time Mr. Bartók manifested some of the same traits both as composer and as scholar: integrity of purpose, a complete lack of capacity for compromise, subordination of the subjective element to what he felt were the dictates of his material, and a careful workmanship with regard to details which, no matter how large the framework, was so exacting as to result almost in self-negation. He made it his task to acquire an intimate familiarity with the general folklore of the national group in which he worked and sufficient knowledge of the language for the arduous task of recording and studying thousands of song texts.

It is, perhaps, characteristic of his mode of workmanship that in order to provide the general observations in this book of seventy-odd melodies with a broader basis, Mr. Bartók made a systematic analysis and a melodic index of thousands of Yugoslav melodies, practically all that have appeared in print so far. Also, in his introductory essay he has presented a unique and searching discussion of the difficult problems of notation, classification, and analysis in the study of folk music . . . the details of this ornamentation and of the plastic fluctuations of time and of intonation were caught and notated by the author, as in his other transcriptions of folk melodies, with an exactitude practically photographic. This was possible only for a musician with an unusually discriminating and well-trained ear.

Foreword to Béla Bartók and Albert B. Lord, *Serbo-Croatian Folk Songs*, New York (Columbia University Press), 1951, pp. xi–xii; republished as Volume 1 of Béla Bartók, *Yugoslav Folk Music*, Albany (State University of New York Press), 1978

HANS W. HEINSHEIMER
(b. 1900)

Of all who had dealings with Bartók during his final years, Hans Heinsheimer was one of the best placed to observe his personal characteristics and day-to-day reactions. Having only recently left Bartók's Viennese publisher, Heinsheimer found that his new work in the New York office of Boosey & Hawkes required him to act as concert agent to the Bartóks and also as one of Bartók's principal contacts with the publishing wing of the firm. Over these years Heinsheimer received a good number of querulous letters, telephone calls and visits from the frustrated pianist and ailing composer.

. . . there was never, in the years of his exile, either doubt or regret. His determination, as always, was absolute. After he had put the ocean between himself and the enemies of everything he had been living for, he even refused to speak or to write German. He spoke, instead, a very selected, highly cultivated English, slightly stilted, choosing his words slowly, striving perceptibly always to find the right expression. His speech retained a quite undefinable foreign flavor. It was highly civilized, rich, and often amazing in its variety of vocabulary and the elegance of its grammar. Even when we were alone and when the conversation might have been easier and much less of a strain on both of us if conducted in German, he would never use the language of the enemy.

His letters, too, ever since he had come to America, were always written in English, composed by the hand of a master and just as dense in their texture as they had been in the old days. Only once in a while he would question with a (?) his own proper use of a word or a phrase, sensing infallibly the slightest error or foreignism in a language he had spoken for only a short time.

Bartók's letters were always written by hand, in a small, clear script that looked as if every word had been put down slowly and deliberately. Every thought, it seemed, had been completed in his mind before it was put on paper, just as if the words were musical notes, the result of an intense process of formulation. There were no unnecessary phrases in these letters, and, wherever possible, he used postcards, filling them to the edge. Neither time nor space was ever wasted on courtesies, on how-do-you-dos, on anything personal that had no connection with the subject of his message. When, after his death, we went through his letters to help provide 'human interest' material for a man who wanted to write Bartók's biography, we found almost nothing that would shed light on his character or his life.

The letters covered the paper from top to bottom. Even the margin was usually used for a postscript or two. If the letter did not fill the page, he would tear off what wasn't used, mailing only a closely covered scrap of paper. His room was always overflowing with little paper strips and torn-off pieces of printed matter, every one of them covered with notes, figures, symbols, and a special musical shorthand understandable only to him. All these notes, clippings, letters, books, manuscript paper, music, were scattered throughout the room, overflowing from the piano to the floor, covering chairs and tables – an appalling accumulation. Seemingly aimlessly scattered throughout the room, they were in reality exciting witness to a mind that never rested and was occupied, simultaneously, with many problems and ideas. Every one of them was always present and ready to be consulted whenever he would have need of them.

New York was the powerful, unconquerable enemy. Traffic frightened him deeply. He would never walk against a light, and even when he crossed with a green light he was tense and disturbed, hurrying across the street in short, hasty steps, like an animal that has left his protecting woods, and faces, wide-eyed, the roaring uncertainties of the metropolis. The climate, New York heat and New York cold alike, was a constant source of preoccupation. Noise, and particularly any emanation of music penetrating his privacy, caused him physical suffering. The vicinity of a radio meant painful disruption of his creative work.

Sometimes he seemed to delight, in a strange and almost self-destructive way, in the difficulties and setbacks he experienced; he used to relate them in great detail, an ironical 'I told you so' in his voice. At the same time, he would discard any good news we had for him with a deep-rooted disbelief that his fortunes would ever take a decisive and permanent turn for the better. The difficulties of finding an apartment where he and his wife would be allowed to practice were at first insurmountable. When, finally, friends located a place in Forest Hills where practicing pianists were not regarded as breachers of the peace, he only shrugged his shoulders – there would be other difficulties, he asserted. And he was right. After the Bartóks had moved in and the two pianos had been delivered by an obliging manufacturer, it was discovered that they could not be placed in one room. Triumphantly Bartók reported that they had to practice in two different rooms, separated by a corridor, unable to see each other, with co-ordination established only by ear . . .

During the first year or two after his arrival, Bartók appeared as soloist with a few symphony orchestras, but dates were few and scattered. The joint recitals he gave with his wife were not too successful. The programs he chose reflected, again, his uncompromising mind. Not too many organizations were prepared to forgo the commercial appeal of other two-piano teams for the unbending austerity of the Bartóks. The fact that they never performed from memory proved an added handicap. Their appearance on the stage in the company of two page-turners seemed old-fashioned and was easily misinterpreted as a lack of preparation or courtesy by audiences that had been treated to flashier displays of virtuosity.

And Béla Bartók's bows were certainly a concert manager's nightmare: stern, professorial, unsmiling to the extent of chilliness – of a great, very moving dignity, but bare of everything the public had been trained to expect from a performer. Nothing, of course, that anyone would ever dare to suggest to him would change his attitude toward his programs and their presentation, and his hopes to earn a livelihood on the concert stage were sadly disappointed. Later, as his illness progressed, even the few concert appearances and lecture recitals we had been able to book for him had to be cancelled.

Fanfare for 2 Pigeons, New York (Doubleday), 1952, pp. 109–13

DOROTHY DOMONKOS
(b. 1912)

Dorothy Domonkos (née Parrish) went to Hungary in 1934 as an exchange student of the Institute of International Education, and for the academic year 1936-7 took private piano lessons with Bartók. On returning to the United States she initiated a correspondence with her teacher which was maintained until the last few weeks of his life. During Bartók's years in America the two occasionally met, either in Huntingdon, Pennsylvania, where Domonkos lived, or in New York. This recollection dates from the 1950s.

At first our relationship was rather formal. Bartók was loved and revered by his students, for whom he was an heroic figure not quite of this earth. And Bartók himself always kept a certain distance between himself and his students. When he came to America this relationship changed a great degree. The distance between Bartók and his young students dissolved: he was very human and approachable as far as I was concerned. His brilliant personality far surpassed the average, not only in music, but in general knowledge. I can only say he was a phenomenon with whom I can't even begin to compare anyone else. The privilege of knowing one such man is, I believe, a miraculous gift of providence.

His own musical life absorbed him so, that when he worked he was quite oblivious to what happened around him; he wouldn't care whether he hurt any feelings or not . . .

I met him from time to time in America during the last years of his life, and on two occasions when there was talk of Communists and communism, his sharp reaction left no doubt that he considered them no better than the Nazis.

When the Second World War ended and the Russians took over Bartók's homeland in place of the Germans, he said: 'Scarcely is one bad situation over, but we are in another.' He was very depressed, literally miserable because of this, but thought it would be quite hopeless, under the circumstances, to initiate anything to the end that the United States intervene to free his homeland from the latest oppression. He was broken up by the fact that there seemed to be no way out either for him or for his nation.

Small things often annoyed and hurt him a great deal; still, he must have had an unusually strong nervous system to be able to retain his balance despite so many upheavals and the attendant suffering.

After Bartók came to the United States I continued my studies with him, though sometimes there were long intervals between lessons. I should mention one such occasion. Bartók then lived at the Hotel Woodrow. When I arrived, Ditta was there too. I told them I was expecting a child. They were very happy, and Bartók showed great interest. Ditta remarked that she would be glad to be in the same situation. After my little girl was born, I paid them a visit with the baby. I was surprised to see Bartók play with her so long and with such absorption: till then I could never have imagined that he'd know what to do with an infant. We named her Ditta, after Mrs Bartók . . .

His American compositions, I feel, showed a sort of equilibrium after his revolutionary career. In these latter works he attains heights beyond mere originality and independence, heights which in my opinion he achieved only in certain portions of his earlier works.

As Interviewee G. in Vilmos Juhász, ed., *Bartók's Years in America*, Washington DC (Occidental), 1981, pp. 74–7

GYULA HOLLÓ

(1890–1973)

Gyula Holló was the Bartóks' family doctor in Budapest during the 1920s. In 1931 he emigrated to the United States, where in the 1940s he was again consulted by the family, and saw them socially from time to time. After the war he continued to practise in the United States.

His relation to people was the same here in America as back home. His illness caused little change in this. Naturally, it affected his moods, but he was able to avoid the posture of a 'sick man' through incomparable self-discipline. In small companies here, too, he was gracious, often humorously derisive. There was a certain sly mischief in his smile. I could characterize him by saying that the finest qualities of the folk manifested themselves in the fashion in which he handled others. In the peasant attitude there always has been a certain elegance and this characterized Bartók on a higher artistic plane. He hated all things artificial . . .

His whole spirit recoiled from any endeavor to play the 'great man'. As a rule, he created with utmost ease. On his own compositions he spent but a small fraction of [the] time he devoted to research and to folk music collecting. He would scribble his musical thoughts on scraps of paper, and by the time he transposed these to the actual manuscript, the composition was in final form – he almost never made corrections. He was intensely concerned with questions of form, and also interested in jazz, seeing in it the possibility of new forms.

Among his favorite composers were Beethoven, Bach, Liszt, Debussy; but we shouldn't forget Schubert. He loved the purity of Schubert's mode of musical expression and of his whole outlook as a man. 'If I didn't detest the word so, I'd say he wrote very charming music,' said Bartók to me.

He did not compose at the piano. Music lived in him full-blown – he had no need of intermediaries. He practiced only before a performance. When for a time the Baldwin Company took away the piano it had placed at his disposal – because of cutbacks – he missed it only on his wife's account, because now they couldn't practice two-piano pieces together. Somehow, whatever he was concerned with lived

within him as though the work of creation require[d] no contact with
the outer world. Characteristically, he always learned languages alone.
He never went to plays or movies, and even attended concerts but
rarely. He loved to walk in open country and, if possible, to climb
mountains. He often visited New York's zoos.

Perhaps his most characteristic quality was his unspoiled taste.
Everything cheap and fashionable repelled him. Music was a religion
for him. He so abhorred things mechanical that he didn't listen to the
radio or even to records. More than once he noted the lack of artistic
comprehension on the part of those who expected the art to amuse them
or 'make their lives pleasant'. His severest judgment on a composer
was: 'He speaks much more than he has to say.'

As Interviewee B. in Vilmos Juhász, ed., *Bartók's Years in America*,
Washington DC (Occidental), 1981, pp. 51–3

CLAIRE R. REIS

(1888–1978)

Educated in France, Germany and the United States, Claire R.
Reis embarked upon a career as a concert organizer and adminis-
trator in New York. She was an important figure in the formation
of the League of Composers in the United States in 1923, and its
executive director for twenty-five years. During those decades she
came in contact with Bartók on several occasions.

When Dr. Koussevitzky suggested in 1925 that Béla Bartók might
write a new work for the League which he would like to conduct in a
world *première* in Town Hall, Bartók had very quickly sent us a new
work for chamber orchestra and vocal quartet, called 'Village Scenes'.
This was in the early days of the League, before we had found the
means of raising money to pay for commissioned works. Bartók
undertook this labour out of his respect for Dr. Koussevitzky, and as a
generous gesture toward his unknown colleagues in the League of
Composers across the ocean.

At the time [February 1927] very little of his music had been played
in this country. Dr. Koussevitzky even repeated 'Village Scenes' at the
close of the program; it was a delight to see that almost the entire

audience was sufficiently interested to stay, vigorously applauding the repetition. It gave me a feeling of confidence that evening – there was a public eager to know the work of a great man. Then for some years we were out of touch with Bartók. When he left Hungary in 1940, a voluntary exile, we immediately planned an evening in his honor at the Museum of Modern Art. Two great Hungarian artists – a Metropolitan Opera singer, Enid Szantho, and the great violinist Joseph Szigeti – were delighted to help us and happy to interpret Bartók's chamber music. Both of them revered this great master.

Szigeti played the Rhapsodie No. One which, interestingly enough, Bartók had dedicated to him. Miss Szantho sang a group of his famed arrangements of Hungarian folk songs. The program concluded with the composer playing selections from *Mikrokosmos*, a *première* performance in the United States. The evening proved a great success and a letter from Bartók later showed his deep feeling.

In 1942 we invited Bartók to join the League's National Committee of Composers. He was having difficulties at the time in becoming an American citizen. In May he wrote,

I wanted to be in a position to give you a clear picture of the prospects of becoming a citizen or not . . . It appears that there are some difficulties for me as a Hungarian citizen, in going to Canada, because of a declaration of war by Canada on Hungary . . . There are negotiations with the American Consul in Montreal . . . but again a postponement . . . I applied for reexamination of my case in Washington. Apparently they are still examining the case. As you see, I am still very far even from the 'first paper'. This probably constitutes an obstacle to becoming a member of your National Composers Committee.

We assured him immediately that Europeans domiciled in this country, even if their citizenship was not established, were eligible to this committee. He seemed relieved and pleased, and joined the group.

A short time thereafter Minna Lederman invited Bartók, André Schulhof, and me to the Café Lafayette. As always Bartók was very cordial in manner, yet extremely quiet, a man of few words, shy and simple. There was an ascetic quality about him which even seemed to intervene in his choice of the famous Lafayette food.

One felt about Bartók that at all times he was deeply involved in his creative life, completely dedicated to his composition, not a man to promote himself in any circumstances at any time. Yet, notwithstanding his aloofness, one could feel very warmly toward him because of a great sincerity and an innate cordiality.

In 1946, a few months after he died, we gave another evening of his compositions, for the benefit of the Bartók Fund. This time the Budapest String Quartet, Andor Földes, Arthur Balsam, Tossy Spivakovsky, and – again – Enid Szantho, all volunteered their services to honor his memory.

Bartók's life contained many elements of tragedy. Only once in his lifetime was the famous piece, Music for Strings, Percussion and Celesta played [by the League]. Ironically it was played five times in the three years following his death! This was only one of many unfortunate situations.

Composers, Conductors and Critics, New York (Oxford University Press), 1955, pp. 189–91

YEHUDI MENUHIN
(b. 1916)

Over the last sixty years Sir Yehudi Menuhin has juggled the varied roles of violinist, teacher and philanthropist. In 1943–5, while still in his late twenties, Menuhin came to know Bartók well. A personal as well as musical empathy clearly existed between the two. Bartók wrote his Sonata for Solo Violin (1944) to a commission from Menuhin; Menuhin gave numerous performances of Bartók's violin works, including both the première of 'his' sonata and the British première of the Second Violin Concerto in 1944. Only ill health prevented the Bartóks from spending some weeks of the summer of 1945 with Menuhin in California.

So, at Doráti's urging, I came to love above any other contemporary works the compositions of Bartók, and more particularly the Second Violin Concerto and the First Sonata for Piano and Violin (Bartók's own instrument was the piano, but like all Hungarians, he understood the violin). I decided to include both works in the 1943 season, playing the Concerto at Minneapolis with Mitropoulos – he conducted not only

the performance but the rehearsals from memory, an unbelievable feat
that he repeated each week with a new program – and the Sonata with
[Adolph] Baller a few days later at Carnegie Hall. Between the two
concerts, in November 1943, I met Bartók. Before my first performance of the Sonata I wanted Bartók's comments on my handling of it,
and wrote to ask him if he would hear me. My old friend 'Aunt Kitty'
Perera – a violinist herself and a friend of Toscanini, a charming lady,
full of warmth and good works and zest for living – readily agreed that
Bartók, Baller and I should meet at her apartment on Park Avenue.
When Baller and I arrived toward the end of a wintry afternoon,
Bartók was already there, seated in an armchair placed uncompromis-
ingly straight on to the piano, with a score laid open before him and
pencil in his hand: an attitude both chilling and, in my experience,
characteristically Hungarian: Bartók, like Kodály, was pitilessly severe
with his students. There were no civilities. Baller went to the piano, I
found a low table, put my violin case on it, unpacked, tuned. We
started to play. At the end of the first movement Bartók got up – the
first slackening of his rigid concentration – and said, 'I did not think
music could be played like that until long after the composer was dead.'
If I were truly modest I would not record this tribute; I do so because it
was an unforgettably glad experience to know one had penetrated to the
very heart of a composer through his music, and that he, the living
man, who had given his all, knew that it was understood. It broke the
ice completely, of course. Without idle words we made each other's
acquaintance. Baller and I played the remaining movements.

Knowing that I had just performed his great Concerto, Bartók
probed to see how well I had grasped it, asking particularly my opinion
of a passage in the first movement. 'It's rather chromatic,' I offered.
'Yes, it's chromatic,' he said, but then, nudging me toward the point he
was making: 'You see that it comes very often?' – which it does, some
thirty-two times, never exactly the same. 'Well, I wanted to show
Schoenberg that one can use all twelve tones and still remain tonal.'
Here was one of Bartók's barbs: any one of these repeated sequences
would supply a dodecaphonist with material for a whole opera, but
Bartók pours them out with a lavishness of invention which the
twelve-toner, working away with his slide rule, will never know. His
was that kind of profligate exuberance which throws away something,
never to be used again.

Except for the extraordinary precision of his speech and manner, reduced to a diamondlike sharpness and brilliance which concentrated meaning and rejected superfluous expression, Bartók's presence in the last two years of his life, when I knew him, belied the fire of his character. The contained surface gave no evidence of the barbaric grandeur and mystic vision within. If I had known him in his youthful, exuberant mountain-climbing days, my impression might have been less awed, and his impatience with conversational exchange less total – although I doubt that he was ever socially loquacious. A creator's life being in a sense secondary to his creation, Bartók's genius was permitted to devour him, leaving him exposed. Words were no longer necessary, even life was hardly necessary alongside the expression his music gave to life, to his own life and his convictions. Thus, exile made of him unaccommodated man, solitary, intense, requiring for material support only a bed, a table to write at and – but this might be considered a luxury – absolute quiet in which his inner concentration might bear fruit. These wants provided, he poured out the riches of his spirit, needing apparently neither critical acclaim nor the affection of the public.

What he did need, and missed in the streets of New York, was contact with the natural. Among the gasoline fumes one day he stopped in his tracks, sniffed the air, and exclaimed, 'I smell a horse!' – he had the keenest sense imaginable. Sure enough, following his nose, he came upon a little stable which hired out mounts for riders in Central Park, and filled his lungs with its nostalgic fragrance. Animals would come to him with extraordinary confidence in his sympathy, and this sympathy was one and the same as his feeling for human beings who were rooted in their land. The longing he felt for such natural societies is demonstrated, I believe, in the greater simplicity of his last works, written in his race with death in the unfriendly urban environment of New York. Despite what must have struck him as the inhumanity of the streets, Bartók closed his ears to the roar of traffic, but opened them with interest to the rhythms and tunes of that American–African–European synthesis which is jazz; moreover, he incorporated some of what he heard into his Concerto for Orchestra.

I knew he was in financial straits, that he was too proud to accept handouts, that he was the greatest of living composers. Unwilling to waste a moment, I asked him on the afternoon of our first meeting if I might commission him to compose a work for me. It didn't have to be anything large-scale, I urged; I was not hoping for a third concerto, just a work for violin alone. Little did I foresee that he would write me one of the masterpieces of all time. But when I saw it, in March 1944, I admit I was shaken. It seemed to me almost unplayable.

The first hasty impression was ill-judged: the Solo Sonata is eminently playable, beautifully composed for the violin, one of the most dramatic and fulfilling works that I know of, the most important composition for violin alone since Bach.

Unfinished Journey, London (Futura), 1978, pp. 219–22

ANTAL DORÁTI
(1906–88)

During the Second World War Antal Doráti worked as an opera and ballet conductor in New York. There, he occasionally met up with his old piano teacher.

Once when we were alone, Bartók asked me 'Do you know what the interruption in the [Concerto for Orchestra's] "intermezzo interrotto" is?'

'Of course I do, Professor'.

'Well?'

'It is a quote from *The Merry Widow*'.

'And who is that?'

Momentarily nonplussed, I then established that he did, after all, know who Lehár was, and had heard of *The Merry Widow*. But because the music was quite unfamiliar to him, and had no conceivable bearing on what he had been thinking of, he had not grasped what I was referring to.

So, evidently, it was not a quote from there. What was it then? Having extracted my solemn promise that I would not tell anyone while he was still alive – oh, that the secret could have been kept far longer! – he confided that he was caricaturing a tune from Shostakovich's Seventh Symphony, the *Leningrad*, which was then enjoying great popularity in America, and, in Bartók's view, more than it merited. 'So I gave vent to my anger', he said.

His verbal description of that Interrupted Intermezzo is very touching and should be remembered:

The melody goes on its own quiet way when it's suddenly interrupted by a brutal band-music, which is derided, ridiculed by the orchestra. After the band had gone away, the melody resumes its waltz – only a little bit more sadly than before.

On 25 March 1945, I went to see Bartók on his birthday, with some books as a small present. He was alone, and not quite ready. He asked me to wait in the living-room. There I spotted a yellow Eulenburg pocket-score. To my surprise, it was Grieg's Piano Concerto. I must have looked very amused about that, because when Bartók came in he said: 'Why are you grinning so broadly?'

I explained that I found this sudden interest in Grieg's Concerto, which he must have heard many times, somewhat comical. 'You're wrong', he replied: 'I did not know this piece, although I heard much about it, good and bad. So I wanted to find out for myself'.

'And what is your verdict, Professor?'

'Oh – a little "insafolato" (boxed in) but otherwise very good, fresh in invention and very sincere. Altogether one has to take Grieg very seriously. He was a very important composer'.

'??'

'Don't you know that he was one of the first of us who threw away the German yoke and turned to the music of his own people?'

It was as if the circle had closed there.

'Bartókiana (some recollections)', *Tempo*, no. 136 (March 1981), pp. 12–13

ERNŐ BALOGH

(b. 1897)

Balogh staunchly supported his former teacher through many of his troubles in America. In 1943 he led the petition for the American Society of Composers, Authors and Publishers (ASCAP) to take over Bartók's medical treatment.

During the second period of his last years, which started from May

1943, when the efforts of ASCAP restored his health as far as was humanly possible, he got much more attention from the musical world, which resulted in more commissions than he could fulfil and performances of his works, causing him great joy.

The last time I saw him was when I bid him farewell in New York in June 1945 before he went to the country with his wife. He looked well and was in best spirits. His wife remarked as they both took me to the elevator, 'Now there is really no reason for Béla to complain; his health is good, he has composing to do in a place he loves and where he can work undisturbed.' Bartók smilingly added, 'Yes, I think everything is all right now. But how will my health be in the future?' The elevator arrived, we wished each other a pleasant summer and looked forward to seeing each other in September. I never saw him again.

Bartók knew the nature of his illness, but whereas his wife was told six months before he died that his case was fatal, he was never aware of this. The day he was taken to hospital he planned to continue his composing.

During that last summer he worked in the only way he knew how: from sunrise to sunset. And he loved it. Under these conditions his 3rd Piano Concerto and Viola Concerto were created. This way of working, without interruption, was characteristic of the man, and his *Concerto for Orchestra*, written in Summer 1943, was done in the same continuous way.

During Bartók's life he did not enjoy in America such wide popularity and recognition as, for instance, the also foreign born (but American citizen) Ernest Bloch. Bartók's recognition was limited to the advance guard of the professionals. Nevertheless, two of the richest Conservatories of this country, Julliard and Curtis, offered him highly-paid positions as Professor of Composition, as did also the University of Seattle (State of Washington). Bartók, who was not a man to compromise, refused these because he had never taught composition and did not care to start to work out courses in that field. Since practically all his life he had taught piano he preferred to continue that. But his reputation in the musical world and particularly in the United States was as a composer, not a pianist. Whereas the schools I mentioned had no vacancies at all, they would gladly have created an additional Chair of Composition for him. They had no place for him as a pianist.

It was part of the 'Bartók Tragedy' that not until immediately after his death did his popularity spread to every part of the world. On the other hand fate did smile at Bartók in his last two years. He enjoyed, finally, the applause of the widest public and not only of the selected audiences of the various small societies for contemporary music. He had the pleasure of being wanted and commissioned by such outstanding artists of his time as Koussevitzky, Primrose, Bartlett and Robertson, Menuhin, Goodman and Szigeti.

'Bartók's Last Years', *Tempo*, no. 36 (Summer 1955), pp. 15–16

WILLIAM PRIMROSE
(1904–82)

The Scottish-born viola player William Primrose spent his early years as a chamber and orchestral player, but then from the late 1930s established a reputation as the world's leading soloist on the instrument. As well as the Viola Concerto which he commissioned from Bartók, Primrose elicited important works from such composers as Britten, Milhaud, Rubbra and Rochberg. During the early 1960s he gained fame as a performing associate of the violinist Heifetz and cellist Piatigorsky. A heart attack in 1963 made further intensive performing inadvisable, and he devoted the remaining years of his life to teaching in Indiana, Japan and, finally, Utah.

I had known Bartók no more than casually since the twenties. I met him when he visited London, and occasionally after that. I didn't know much about his music, but then nobody did. (I reflect on the fact, for instance, that although I was a member for a number of years of the London String Quartet, which along with the Flonzaley was recognized as the outstanding quartet of the period, we never ventured a Bartók string quartet. It was unheard of for anybody to play a Bartók string quartet except, perhaps, the Kolisch Quartet. But they were almost run out of town for doing it.)

[In January 1945] I sought an interview with Bartók in his New York apartment, and told him what I was after. He was quite reluctant, because he felt he didn't know enough about the possibilities of the viola as a solo instrument. I admired his integrity because at that time he sorely needed the money. I told him not to make a decision until he had heard the Walton concerto, which I was playing a couple of weeks later in New York with the late Sir Malcolm Sargent. He planned to come to the concert, which was on a Sunday afternoon, but it so happened that that was one of the days when he felt particularly ill, and he couldn't come. He did hear the broadcast, however, and was struck with the concerto and the way that Walton used the viola. He told me that he would definitely accept the commission and write a viola concerto. Afterwards, in the summer of 1945, I went on a tour of South America, and I returned with the hope of enjoying the cool and early fall of New England. It was my intention to stop on my way north from Philadelphia to see Bartók in New York City. I had received in Philadelphia a letter from him in which he said that the concerto was finished in draft, and all that remained to be done was the orchestration, which was routine work. But he wanted to see me and discuss it for certain reasons that he outlined. It was raining heavily on that day in New York, and parking became a problem. I thought that I would drive on to my destination and see him on the way back. (It was a situation, which we all encounter, where we put off until tomorrow . . .) On a beautiful day about two weeks later, on the way back, I stopped outside New York for lunch, picked up the [New York] Times and read that Bartók had died the day before.

In an interview (1970), reproduced in David Dalton, 'The Genesis of Bartók's Viola Concerto', *Music and Letters*, vol. 57 (1976), pp. 127-8

TIBOR SERLY

(1901–78)

Although Hungarian by birth, Serly spent much of his youth in the United States before returning to Hungary in 1922 to study music in Budapest. There, he learnt violin with Hubay and composition with Kodály, and became casually acquainted with Bartók. When Bartók visited the United States in 1927–8 Serly spent much time with him, often in the role of translator. The friendship was deepened during Serly's subsequent visits to Hungary and Bartók's wartime residence in New York. Serly

BELA BARTOK DIES IN HOSPITAL HERE

Noted Hungarian Composer, Specialist in Music Folklore, Played Own Works at 10

BELA BARTOK
The New York Times, 1940

Béla Bartók, Hungarian composer, died yesterday morning at the West Side Hospital after a long illness at the age of 64. One of the most important composers of modern music, he was also an outstanding specialist in musical folklore and a teacher of wide repute. He was a leading spirit of the "revolutionary" generation of musicians born in the early Eighties and ranked as the chief and most representative Hungarian composer of his epoch.

Bartók was born March 25, 1881, at Nagyszentmiklós, in the Hungarian district of Torontal, now in Yugoslavia. His father was director of the school of agriculture in that community and his mother a schoolteacher. When his father died, Bartók, who was 8 at the time, already had begun to compose. His mother gave him his first piano lessons and his progress was so rapid that at 10 he made his initial public appearance as composer-pianist. From 1893 to 1899 he was in Pressburg, where he studied piano and composition with Lázlo-Erkel and Janós Batkai and wrote a number of unpublished works influenced by Brahms.

In 1899 Bartók entered the Royal Academy of Music in Budapest, remaining there until 1903 as a pupil of János Koessler in composition and István Thomán in piano. While at the academy he came under the spell of the music of Liszt, Wagner and Richard Strauss, but his "Kossuth" symphony, written the year he left the school, was Hungarian in essence.

Collected Folk Music

Bartók, in cooperation with Zoltán Kodály, began collecting Hungarian folk music soon after he left the academy. Their first joint publication, "Hungarian Folk Songs for Voice and Piano," appearing in 1906, being followed by Bartók's own "Twenty Songs" and "Székely Ballads." His researches were extended to the folk music of Slovakian, Rumanian and Turk-

string quartets and several unpublished works. He also composed a large amount of piano music and wrote a large number of songs, many based on Hungarian folk melodies, and choral works. Some 450 songs from his collections were published, as well as his two books.

From 1940 until his death Bartók lived in New York. He added several extensive works to his long list of compositions, including a violin sonata composed last winter for Yehudi Menuhin and not yet played. Bartók made his last appearance before the public Jan. 21 and 22, 1943, when he and his wife were the soloists in a new orchestral arrangement of the "Music for Two Pianos and Percussion" as a concerto.

According to As Ember, New York Hungarian newspaper, the American Control Commission in Hungary recently notified the Foreign Minister that it had given permission to Bartok to return to Budapest. Bartók recently was elected a member of the Hungarian Parliament.

Besides his widow, he leaves two sons, Béla and Peter. A funeral service will be held tomorrow at 2 P. M. at Universal Chapel, Lexington Avenue and Fifty-second Street. Burial will be in Ferncliff Cemetery, Hartsdale, N. Y.

New York Times, 27 September 1945, portion of Bartók's obituary

transcribed some of the *Mikrokosmos* pieces for chamber
ensembles, to Bartók's satisfaction, and after Bartók's death was
entrusted with the task of completing the Viola Concerto. A
debate still continues over how much Bartók and how much Serly
really contributed to the work.

While he lived in New York, we often played scores together. We
played Bach chorales and organ works, four-hand, and discussed them.
But, of course, that was more – if I may be permitted to say so – as
colleagues than as student and professor.

. . . during the last years especially, Bartók worked in such a
remarkably tight fashion, that, as you can see – we have here a replica
of the manuscript of the Viola Concerto in front of us consisting of
thirteen pages – no bar or space was spared or wasted. He used the
method of writing immediately in ink, no pencil. All corrections were
made exactly as they were a hundred or so years ago, before such a
thing as an eraser existed. Composers simply scratched out incorrect
bars, or added their corrections in ink. That is what makes working on
such a manuscript so difficult. There is a scratch here and a scratch
there in the manuscript, then Bartók would go to some other spot and
make marks. But the work was done so tightly that the sketches were
put down [on] between two to four staves, and in rare instances, even
overlapping four or five staves. Therefore, very few pages were
used . . .

Bartók never worked in a reduced score, or a piano reduction. He
did not like to make piano reductions; he always refused to do that.
Bartók was one of those rare composers who thought orchestrally. He
tried to put down the orchestration as best he could so that it would be
visible and possibly playable. He did not think in terms of just writing
down the harmonic content, then the melody, and then going on from
there. This manuscript is not a reduced sketch in any sense of the term.
Where it was completed, every single instrumental part, every single
particle has been put in. However, he did not mark the instruments; he
made very few designations. If you could once decipher those parts, the
orchestration was complete as it is. I had to clearly decipher the sketches
so that everything went into place: skipped bars, additions, and other
alterations. Now there are a few little places, for instance in the slow
movement, where he knew exactly what he wanted to do, but put in
only touches of the orchestration. There are other parts, as in the last

movement, where only the melodic line comes up, but he knew what was going on there; he had just not put it in.

In an interview (1969), reproduced in David Dalton, 'The Genesis of Bartók's Viola Concerto', *Music and Letters*, vol. 57 (1976), pp. 120–2

ISRAEL RAPPAPORT/ERNŐ BALOGH

Israel Rappaport trained as a doctor in Hungary and practised there for some years during the 1910s. About 1920 he emigrated to the United States, settling in New York. He first examined Bartók in 1943, at the instigation of ASCAP, and continued to supervise Bartók's treatment to the end. In this Budapest newspaper article his views are reported by Ernő Balogh.

BÉLA BARTÓK – FIRST CIVILIAN PATIENT TO RECEIVE PENICILLIN

Endre Ady's doctor treated Béla Bartók in New York
The eminent American–Hungarian composer, Ernő Balogh, who was a close friend of the musical genius Bartók, has written an article in an American newspaper about Béla Bartók's illness and the circumstances of his death.

— People in Hungary too would like to know the details about this — writes Ernő Balogh – and so I went to see the doctor who treated Bartók from May 1943 right up to the day of his death, 26 September 1945. His name is Dr Israel Rappaport. He was born in Pest. He graduated from the medical university in Pest and it fell to his lot to treat not only the greatest Hungarian musician, but also the great Hungarian poet Endre Ady – during one winter (in 1917) at the Városmajor sanatorium.

Chronic fever
Dr Rappaport has lived in New York for 26 years and is one of the city's most famous internal specialists. In May 1943, when Bartók's state of health and financial position had both reached crisis point, Ernő Balogh went to the American composers' society. Bartók was not a member of the society and not even an American citizen, but immediately the society took up Bartók's case.

— When I informed them — continued Balogh — that Bartók's

lungs had given him trouble when he was a youth and his present constant state of fever was perhaps indicative of a return of this lung problem, they sent the city's foremost lung specialist, Dr Edgar Mayer, to check Bartók's condition. Mayer immediately put him in hospital, under the constant supervision of Dr Rappaport. According to Dr Rappaport the following specialists examined Bartók during the final two and a half years of his life: Dr Nathan Rosenthal, a professor of haematology; Dr Pfeinnan, a specialist in the illness of leukaemia. Bartók suffered from this disease, and it was the cause of his death. But they disguised the fact from him right up until his death. They also called in Emanuel Friedmann as a consultant neurologist.

— As there was some slight problem with Bartók's eyes, as well, they sent for Professor Elwyn, a renowned ophthalmologist, and because of other symptoms, they consulted Dr Frederic Reiss, a Hungarian-born dermatologist.

Penicillin

— Bartók was one of the first civilian patients, perhaps the very first, to receive penicillin. At the start of the war it had been reserved for military use only. Bartók's doctors and the composers' society had to go to Washington to receive special permission to use it. But the doctors and the union spared neither trouble nor cost. Bartók always received the nicest private room in the best hospital. The American Society of Composers, Authors and Publishers spent 16,000 dollars on medical diagnoses, X-rays and other expenses, thereby saving Bartók's life, or at least prolonging it.

Blood transfusion

— In the spring of 1944 the symptoms of leukaemia were first observed. But initially they were able to fight the disease with drugs and blood transfusions. Later, however, its pace began to quicken and it started to become painful. Whereas in 1944 6,000–8,000 white blood cells were detected in Bartók's blood, in 1945 100,000 were found, and in September 1945 250,000 – which heralded his end. Dr Rappaport saw Bartók daily in the final weeks of his life, sometimes even visiting him 5–6 times in a day. Bartók spent his last days in hospital, in a painful, semi-conscious state. Later, he became completely unconscious and died in that condition. Day by day he lost weight, became exhausted, was consumed by the illness, and passed away. ASCAP buried him in a metal coffin, so that if the Hungarian nation wants to transport his body away, then this can be done.

— Hungary will be forever grateful to the American Society of Composers — concluded Ernő Balogh's article — since it prolonged Bartók's life by two and a half years, during which time he created the four final great masterworks of his life.

Hungarian newspaper report, mid-late 1940s, reproduced in Károly Kristóf, *Beszélgetések Bartók Bélával*, Budapest (Zeneműkiadó), 1957, pp. 185–7

MRS BÉLA BARTÓK (née Ditta Pásztory)

(1903–82)

Ditta (Edith) Pásztory studied in Bartók's piano class at the Budapest Academy of Music for the academic year 1922/3. In the summer of 1923 she became the composer's second wife, following his sudden divorce from his first wife, Márta. During the 1920s and 1930s she studied piano privately with her husband, as family demands and her own uncertain health allowed. The Bartóks began to perform publicly as a piano duo in January 1938, making their début in Basle with the world première of the Sonata for Two Pianos and Percussion. Their final public performance together took place in New York in January 1943, when they performed in the orchestrated version of this same sonata. In 1946, one year after her husband's death, Ditta Bartók returned to Budapest, where she lived in seclusion for many years. During the 1960s, however, she began to perform again, even recording, in collaboration with Tibor Serly, the composition which Bartók had written for her in his final year, the Third Piano Concerto.

Towards the end of June [1945] he sought to take a vacation, as his doctors advised and he himself wished. We travelled to Saranac Lake, where we stayed in a small cottage. The owner of this little house lived next door in a bigger dwelling. Béla found peace and quiet here and worked simultaneously on the Third Piano Concerto and the Viola Concerto. I do not remember when he began these works — unless he himself noted such a thing down it was quite difficult to find it out, as he did not talk about things like that. He once told Péter that he was writing the piano concerto for me, and wanted to present it to me for

Bartók and his second wife, Ditta, 1938

my birthday on 31 October. He did not hurry with this work; he rested
a lot, read many newspapers – as always – and books, too, especially
ones in English which he had brought with him from New York. He
always had several dictionaries to hand, because he wanted to know the
exact meaning of every word. Occasionally he played passages from his
new composition on an upright piano that we had there. I remember
that I had to turn the pages a number of times, as he played from the
sketches. Since the composition appeared to be finished and the sheets
followed one another in order, I thought that these were sections of a
piano concerto, although he did not talk about it. At Saranac Lake he
also went walking a little, but he looked after himself as much as
possible and took care not to tire himself out.

After about 10 August the situation began to deteriorate: he felt
unwell and started running a temperature. It disturbed him greatly that
his fever would not go away, and though we had planned on staying at
Saranac Lake until the end of September we returned to our flat in New
York on the last day of August. Immediately we called Dr Israel
Rappaport, who was treating him. Béla felt very depressed at the state
of his health. He no longer wanted to be alone, and loved it if one came

and chatted with him. He was very patient; during the day he lay fully dressed on his bed for hours, walked around a little in the flat, and worked, too, at his desk. But it did not last long. After 15 September the situation suddenly deteriorated to such an extent that the doctor had him taken to the West Side Hospital, where he passed away on the sixth day.

Péter and I visited him every day in the hospital – Péter had come to join us in Saranac Lake in August, after being demobilized as a marine, and for just a short time at the start stayed in our flat in New York – [in hospital] Béla did not work any more, and did not even read. He practically never said anything, as he was always sleepy or sleeping. He had already been like this for a couple of days before he was taken by the Red Cross ambulance to the hospital. I remember that on one occasion he woke up, asked for a glass of water, drank from it and went straight back to sleep again. During the few moments that he was able to talk with me, he complained that he had shoulder pains, could not eat, and felt no appetite any more. Although he slept a lot, he was restless by day and by night; but he had already been like this at home. Péter and I were told nothing of his condition; they wanted to spare us the pain. Then, during one of the last nights the Kecskemétis, at whose place I was spending the night, received a call from the hospital. They reassured me that it was nothing serious. Even though I knew that Béla was very ill I could not believe that the situation was actually beyond hope. I think that Béla did not receive visits in hospital from anyone else, and even if he did, they certainly could not have spoken with him any more. I do remember seeing Dr Bátor there once, but Béla did not speak with him.

On the evening before he died I went to the hospital, after I had had dinner with Péter, because I felt agitated. I spent the night sitting up in an armchair in his room. A nurse sat constantly by his bed, and watched over him while I slept. In the morning, as I awoke, Dr Rappaport came in and gave Béla an injection. He exchanged a few words with the nurse, and left. During the late morning Péter arrived with Pál Kecskeméti and his wife. They knew about the worsening situation. The Kecskemétis stood at the foot of the bed, but left the room when they realized that the end was near. Béla had spent all the morning half asleep. Around midday the nurse covered his face – I don't know why – but when he began to breathe heavily she took the cloth away again. Béla then looked smilingly towards the armchair in which I had spent the night, but did not say a word. Péter took his right hand; I took the left. After a little while his breathing became weaker, he became quite still, and quietly passed away with a soft, smiling expression on his face. Péter and I then went into the next room, where the Kecskemétis and Dr Gyula Holló and his wife were waiting for us. Mrs Holló took me to her apartment, and later took me home.

On the day before the funeral Péter and I were in the room where Béla was laid out, and we stayed there for a while; that was the last time that we saw him. For the funeral on the 28th, Péter, Dr Holló, Dr Bátor and I travelled together in a car. The hearse went in front of us. Péter and I were not present during the service in the Unitarian chapel. I asked the minister for this, and Péter stayed with me in a small adjoining room. Afterwards we accompanied the coffin to the grave, but I do not remember now who went with us. I only remember that the minister gave a short sermon at the graveside.

After Béla's death Mrs Kecskeméti really looked after me and helped me in every way. My health had further deteriorated; I felt so ill that for a while a nurse came to visit me every day, until I went to a sanatorium. In the summer of 1946 I went back again to Saranac Lake, where I stayed in a private guest house. Péter came with me and immediately began to arrange for my return to Hungary. The journey home, for which Béla had so yearned, I had to make alone.

'26. September 1945: Zum 20. Todestag von Béla Bartók', *Oesterreichische Musikzeitschrift*, vol. 20 (1965), pp. 446–9

GYÖRGY SÁNDOR

(b. 1912)

György Sándor was one of the small number of Bartók's friends who were close at hand during his final weeks. This radio interview from Budapest dates from 1947. (Some minor corrections, made by Sándor in 1989, have been incorporated into this text.)

Reporter: I would like to hear something about Béla Bartók's last days.

György Sándor in conversation with Bartók, January 1945

Sándor: In early September 1945, when I had returned from one of my concert tours, I telephoned Bartók. Ditta Pásztory, Béla Bartók's wife and an excellent pianist, picked up the receiver. Her voice was barely audible and she told me that the Master could not come to the phone, and that he was unwell. The whole matter was so mysterious. Immediately I dashed up to his flat. Béla Bartók was already seriously ill by this time. On arriving at his home on 57th Street the ambulance was already there, and they took Bartók to the West Side Hospital. While they were busy getting everything ready, I asked Bartók – whom I hardly recognized as he was so thin, his face was haggard, and he was listless – whether he felt very poorly. Softly Bartók replied 'I'm very sick . . .' Then he continued a little more loudly: 'Tell me, Sándor, do you have some spare time at the moment?' I didn't know why he asked this. I answered that I did. 'Then I'll ask a favour from you,' he went on. 'Here are the second proofs of my Concerto for Orchestra. I have begun to correct the mistakes. I have no strength; I can't work . . .' I took hold of the proofs and promised that I would make the necessary corrections quickly. Bartók was then taken off to hospital.

Reporter: What did you have to correct in the music? Wrong notes? Faulty engraving?

Sándor: Bartók had completed a good part of the work and had supplied notes in the margins of the corrected parts. Some of the marginal comments were unusual. Some were of a political nature. There was an incorrect capital letter in one of the Italian terms which they had set. Beside it Bartók had written the following sentence: 'It is so typically German to set this word in such a way'. He was strongly anti-German in all his activities, except his musical work. Bartók loathed Nazi Germany.

Reporter: When did you see Bartók for the last time?

Sándor: In September 1945, after he had been taken to hospital, I visited him several times. The doctors had determined that he was suffering from leukaemia. He was growing a beard, as he couldn't shave. On the hospital bed I saw only the broken shell of a man. After having finished the proof reading of the Concerto for Orchestra, on the day before his death, I again hastened to the hospital. The sister said that I could not go in to him because they were carrying out a blood transfusion, as Bartók needed fresh blood. I thought that I would wait since I still wanted to see him for a moment. The sister and a doctor said that it would not be possible to go in to him later. If he should have some strength then he would dictate his will. On the following day, 26 September, he died. The *New York Times* paid homage to our famous musician, now departed, with a big article and the other papers also praised the art of Béla Bartók in a very appreciative tone.

Reporter: Were you there also at the funeral?

Sándor: Yes. They laid Béla Bartók out in an undertaker's funeral parlour. This is the custom in America. The American composers' and librettists' union, ASCAP, covered Bartók's medical costs, hospital fees, and funeral expenses as well. Several hundred people were present at the undertaker's. I need to state that really famous people were, unfortunately, absent. Toscanini was not there, nor were the other famous musicians. Then a few of us accompanied Béla Bartók's earthly remains to the cemetery. We went in two small cars. Apart from Mrs Bartók and her son Péter there were only eight of us. The cembalo player Erzsébet Láng – Mrs Pál Kecskeméti – and her husband, who lived in the same apartment block as Bartók, came out to the cemetery with me, as well as a few other close friends: Mr and Mrs Tibor Serly,

Professor Láng, Mr Bátor (his trustee) and Mrs Bátor. Immediately after his death all the orchestras and soloists began to stick Bartók's works into their programmes. In January 1946, a few months after Bartók's death, I gave the world première of his last work, the Third Piano Concerto, with Eugene Ormandy and the Philadelphia Orchestra. Since then I have presented it in Europe, Australia, South America and the Far East.

In Károly Kristóf, *Beszélgetések Bartók Bélával*, Budapest (Zeneműkiadó), 1957, pp. 155–7

HANS W. HEINSHEIMER

(b. 1900)

Heinsheimer also attended Bartók's funeral service.

When I saw him a few months later, he rested, at last. The little funeral parlor on Lexington Avenue in Manhattan was filled with a hushed, deeply stirred crowd. There were no representatives of organizations, no honorary pall bearers, nobody who had come because he wanted to be sure his name would be in the register. I don't believe there was a register. No reporters were there, no pictures were taken as the mourners, stunned, filed out. But there were many people who had known him and who suddenly felt that they must come to pay their respects. Suddenly, this very day, he had become great. As I took the last look before they closed the coffin I felt again, stronger than ever before, that this tiny face, so beautiful, so great in the peace of death, drawn even now by suffering and still reflecting an unending struggle, was not only the unforgettable face of a great musician. It was the shining example of bravery, faith, and an indomitable spirit that will live on, long after the frame that carried them has been taken back, forever, by the dust.

Fanfare for 2 Pigeons, New York (Doubleday), 1952, p. 123

Hans W. Heinsheimer during the 1940s

V

Obituaries and testimonials

ERNST KRENEK

(b. 1900)

The composer Ernst Krenek emigrated to the United States from his native Austria in 1938. His works reveal a great diversity of styles, reflecting the successive influences of many of his contemporaries: Bartók in the early 1920s, as in the First String Quartet and First Symphony; Stravinsky in the neo-Classical works of the mid-1920s; the Second Viennese School in his compositions of the late 1920s and 1930s. Some of his later compositions involved aleatoric techniques. Krenek was shocked at the death of Bartók in 1945, writing soon after a substantial essay, 'Conversation past midnight', from which the extract below is drawn.

A column and a half about *La Bamba* and a column on the rise of Robert Todd Duncan (under the title 'Porgy to Pagliacci') – that comprises the music section of *Time Magazine* of October 8, 1945. The musician, who, during this week learned some very sad news (not through the newspapers, incidentally, but by word of mouth) is surprised to find no trace of it in the magazine that takes pride in gathering, editing, interpreting and publishing all the important events of the week. But he finds it after all a few pages further on in the column called 'Milestones', which summarises all the facts of life (and death) considered worthy of inclusion in a weekly survey:

Died: Béla Bartók, 64, prolific Hungarian composer of piquant, sometimes cacophonous orchestral and chamber music; long-time student of Magyar and Jugoslav folk music; after long illness; in Manhattan, his home since 1940. A radical modernist, Bartók in 1938 wrote Rhapsody for Clarinet and Violin especially for his friend Joseph Szigeti's violin and Benny Goodman's rippling clarinet.

For the musician these seven lines are almost as shattering as the news they report. It seems to him that the catastrophe which dried up for ever one mighty stream of living music should have been included among the musical news rather than in the personal column. In his agitation he gives way to the temptation to subject the dialectic of the term 'news' to a critical analysis. Obviously the mere death of a composer is not musical news, since it does not represent a musical event such as the launching of a new dance at Ciro's in Mexico City or the assumption of a particular role by a Negro singer. It might have been different if the composer had died after dedicating a new work to Frank Sinatra or at least while bringing out a new piece of cacophony. If we understand it rightly, the final and irrevocable loss of his power to bring out any more new pieces is not news only for the reason that in the act of dying he did not use that power. Since, however, he had used it on occasions in the past, his death is noted, albeit in a different context. There is reason to believe that Bartók owed this passing mention only to the fact that one of his works could be coupled with Benny Goodman's 'rippling clarinet'. For though the Hungarian master is dubbed prolific, no other individual work of his is named, and the one thus singled out is accorded three of the whole seven lines of the obituary . . .

The case of Béla Bartók upset me so, you understand, because I am convinced that he is a part of immortality, whatever that may be, and in his own time that has gone largely unrecognised. If immortality, however far we push the idea into symbolic regions, means anything at all, then surely it must have something to do with eternity. What is exercising me is the question of how this participation in eternity can be recognised in the earthly existence of the immortals.

Exploring Music: Essays by Ernst Krenek, tr. Margaret Shenfield and Geoffrey Skelton, London (Calder & Boyars), 1966, pp. 231–2, 238

OTTO GOMBOSI
(1902–55)

Born in Budapest, Otto Gombosi studied piano at the Academy of Music there. Studies in musicology followed with Curt Sachs and Erich Hornbostel in Berlin. During the late 1920s and 1930s he pursued a career as free-lance journalist, lecturer and musicologist in various European countries. In 1939 he settled in the United States, where he taught successively in Seattle, Chicago, and at Harvard, and was in occasional contact with Bartók. At the time of his death he was writing a book about Bartók, who was godfather to one of his children.

On the 26th day of September, in his sixty-fifth year, Béla Bartók found the final solution of all earthly problems. Attacked by an obstinate and mysterious malady, he had been wasting away for several years. Physical misery and financial worries increased the mental anguish of voluntary exile from his native land. A living symbol of the universal human substance of his folk, Béla Bartók was utterly uprooted.

Yet the tragic conflict of his personal life left no imprint on his *oeuvre*. No break in his creative work is apparent. To an almost Mozartean degree, his art was detached from his outer life. Autobiographical facets will hardly tempt or bother the future student of his musical output. In a very un-Mozartean way, however, Bartók let himself be affected by emotion and pathos; he did not have the poise and patience of the 18th-century composer, who could embrace an already existing idiom and adapt it to his own uses. By intellectual bent a seeker after hidden truth, by temperament an explorer of unheard sounds, by sheer strength of character a champion of honesty, Bartók became one of the great reformers of music. His position in history will be similar to that of a Monteverdi . . .

At sixty-four, man has left behind him the threshold of old age. The comparison with Bach, who lived to be not quite a year older than Bartók, is tempting. To our mind Bach, at sixty-five, was an old man. For the last ten years of his life he labored on a final recapitulation of his work. All the forms and techniques of his earlier years pass through his hands anew, to be molded into absolute perfection. The last creative period starts with the Italian Concerto and the French Ouverture and ends, after the *Goldberg Variations*, the last cantatas, chorale-variations, Preludes and Fugues, and the *Musical Offering*, with the most grandiose artistic testament of all times, the *Art of the Fugue*. Death came just a few days too early; the great work remained unfinished. Except for these few days, Bach's life came to a perfect crowning. The last ten years are rightly called his 'old age'.

There is no such perfection and acquiescence in Bartók's passing away. He did not plan a musical testament, he did not take stock, he did not look back. At sixty-four Bartók was not old. Torn and tormented, he was still an *avant-gardiste* – in a way the only one of our time. Knowing his destination, hardly susceptible to success, and untouched by official or public awareness of his genius, he pursued his course with unerring self-reliance.

A solitary soul, he was not easy to approach. But his friendships were built on rock. He lived the simple life of a scholar, a busy, secluded, almost monotonous life that only occasionally became interspersed with rather quixotic fighting against stupidity, chauvinism, and dilettantism in his field of scholarship. He did not understand the little amenities of sociability or the innocent half-lies of daily life and rejected them with a child-like, brusque, perturbed amazement. His character was hard and clear, like a glowing crystal radiating its inner heat without getting warm and soft on the surface. His words were few and to the point; his interests, intense and critical. His judgment was uncompromising in the rejection of all moral, mental, or artistic dishonesty. To his mind, the good was good and the evil, evil; he could not forgive or forget.

Adversities, bitter experiences, or happiness could not change his character. This explains, in the last analysis, the inner logic of his artistic history, the rare consistency of his new and individual style, the unromantic intensity and universality of his emotions. The portrait of the man and his work consists of diametrically opposed features: frailness and energy, critical mind and naiveté, modesty and self-reliance, icy aloofness and fiery humanity, accuracy in minutiae and generosity in matters of importance, virgin purity and elemental sensuality, the cool concentration of research and the ravishing fever of creation.

Bartók is gone where all is one and nothing matters, and everything melts into the great *coincidentia oppositorum*. Our Janus-like century has lost one of the giants who shaped its better face.

'Béla Bartók (1881–1945)', *Musical Quarterly*, vol. 32 (1946), pp. 1, 8–9. © 1946, *The Musical Quarterly*. Reprinted by permission.

PAUL HENRY LANG
(b. 1901)

Paul Henry Lang (Pál Láng) graduated from the Budapest
Academy of Music in 1922 after studies with Zoltán Kodály and
Leó Weiner. Further studies in musicology and literature followed at Heidelberg, the Sorbonne and Cornell. From 1933 to
1969 he taught at Columbia University in New York, and was
editor of *The Musical Quarterly* between 1945 and 1973. Lang
had considerable dealings with Bartók during 1940–5 and was
one of the ten people present at his burial. In 1942 Bartók and
Lang became the leaders of the short-lived 'Független Magyar-
országért' movement, which sought American support for an
'independent, free, democratic Hungary'.

It sometimes appears that one of the worst scourges of mankind – war
and its daughter, revolution – is not an accidental catastrophe coming
from without, but a tragedy conceived in ourselves and measured to
each one of us individually; a tragedy that completes our own little
destinies. There are figures, situations, lives, around which the theater
of the great debacle ranges itself with the inexorability of fate.

Such a situation can be seen in the fate of Béla Bartók, whom we have
just buried. This victim of our modern civilization was a strong soul in
a frail body; a man with penetrating bright eyes, lively gestures,
precise and ready words, always alert and always courageous, as if the
whole man were the blade of intelligence drawn from its sheath. Can
we picture him, in good health, supported by national pride, the
recognized master of a national art and of an international discipline,
receiving his due, wholly engaged in his dual work of composer and
scholar, and living in peace with ignorance and indifference, producing quartets, symphonies, and operas, and restoring the song of the
people, finding it unnecessary to expend his powers on the daily
struggle for existence? It was this sort of life for which his situation,
birth, and the natural course of events had singled him out. When his
health failed, his illness was not such as proper care and rest,
environment and climate, money and everything that peace could have
provided could not have alleviated.

There is one thing that even his admirers often overlook although they appreciate his labors as a collector: Bartók was one of the greatest scholars in the field of comparative musicology, a musical enthnologist of the first order whose vast erudition was unexampled. There is no other instance in the history of music, with the exception of Rameau, where creative force and scholarly patience have been so harmoniously wedded, but even the old French master could not avoid a fundamental conflict between his two natures and died a disillusioned man, whereas Bartók's legacy contains several large compositions, some barely lacking the finishing touches, together with an awe-inspiring treatise on Serbo-Croatian folksong to be published in the near future. There is nowhere a conflict of the scholar and the artist; they inspired each other. Because his intelligence was freer, his judgement less biased than those of his contemporaries, his creative activity uncompromising and absolutely beyond the pale of expediency, his scholarly work is unassailable . . .

In the end Bartók succumbed, the soul was vanquished by the frail organism that kept it soaring, for the world which showers its gratitude on the fashionable idols of the day does not understand artistic and moral integrity of so uncompromising a nature. Succeeding generations will tell moral stories about society's lack of responsibility towards its great, and Bartók will join the ranks of the consecrated martyrs – Mozart, Schubert, Chopin, Bizet, and all the others – whose cruel fate is described to children with such touching compassion while their elders say a sanctimonious *mea culpa* on behalf of their ancestors who permitted genius to perish. But Bartók's death is our fault, our bitter responsibility, for 'we know better', and cannot divest ourselves of this responsibility by saying that we are powerless against the traditional inertia of public, press, and the business of music, that the public wants bread and circuses and not saints and philosophers, that fate wills that the great of mind shall perish because they outdistance ordinary mortals. Like the others Bartók perished, but like the marble torsos of the heroes of antiquity his hardness and harmony, even though broken, are stronger than fate.

Editorial, *Musical Quarterly*, vol. 32 (1946), pp. 131–2, 135–6. © 1946, *The Musical Quarterly*. Reprinted by permission.

DENIJS DILLE

(b. 1904)

The Belgian music historian Denijs Dille studied theology, philosophy and music in Mechelen and Antwerp, before taking a position in a teacher training college in Antwerp. He came to know Bartók personally in the 1930s and published his first book about the composer in 1939. In 1961 Dille was invited to become the founding director of the Budapest Bartók Archive, a position which he held until 1971.

Bartók's life might, taken as a whole, be regarded as a failure, and in the purely worldly sense perhaps it was. Yet against that, his work represents a series of triumphs . . . What must strike everybody most is the fact that he lived a life of self-denial and complete dedication to his work, yet did nothing to push that work or direct the limelight on to it. He did, however, speak of the work of other composers; his admiration for Strawinsky, for instance, is well known; equally, in his recitals, he went to more trouble to defend Debussy, Ravel, Strawinsky and Schönberg than he did on behalf of his own compositions. Of these he once said to me that they would have to fight for themselves and that they were strong enough to do so. This is a generous attitude, but it is rare in our time. To maintain it through all the confusions and misfortunes that fell to his lot demanded fanatical courage and conviction, a self confidence illuminated by clear intelligence and sure instinct. I have never known anybody who was so modest, for all the greatness of his genius, who was so uncompromising and upright, yet at the same time so natural and simple, and who never shrank from even the hardest consequences.

These qualities made mighty conflicts for him. The scrupulous conscientiousness he brought to his scientific work (compare, for instance, his last, unpublished transcriptions of folk songs with the same that he had scored twenty years earlier) and the exaction of his rehearsals, were legendary. There was about him a fanatical passion for detail that some people might interpret as a mania. I maintain myself that it was the complete devotion of a man of genius to the task which life had set him: the creation of music, the performance of music, the study of music.

From a distance he would appear unsympathetic, because in the
presence of people who did not know him he was by no means
approachable. But whoever saw and understood him could not but feel
a deep affection, and spontaneously an approach was found. This
modest, aloof figure, sparing of words, only interested in measured,
thoughtful conversation, and whom one had the utmost difficulty in
getting to talk about himself and his work, could be as cordial and
could laugh as heartily among his intimate friends as any one of us.
This small, slight, grey-haired man, who seemed always absorbed in
music, was innocent of any kind of pose, above all at the piano, which
he played with remarkable ease, as if meditatively and for himself
alone. His features were fine and ascetic, and his dreamy, always
pensive eyes, that revealed nothing of his inmost feelings, could
illuminate his whole expression with the slightest smile, if a performance were a success, or could stare at you dazzlingly when he wanted to
express his will or his conviction; and then, for a few moments, one
received an astonishing flow of words.

I could go on indefinitely describing his character, his way of life,
his working methods. But it would take too long. I want only still to
point out that the extent of Bartók's activity is staggering, when one
considers that his composition and his scientific work alone could have
filled a lifetime, quite apart from his professorship, to which he
devoted a great deal of attention. It is my belief that, because of his
many-sidedness, he was the most complete musician of our time, taking
first place in every sphere of music except conducting. And as a man he
was as wonderful and rare as the work to which he put his name.

'The Life of Béla Bartók', in *Béla Bartók: A Memorial Review*, New York
(Boosey & Hawkes), 1950, pp. 10–11. This extract is included by permission
of Boosey & Hawkes Music Publishers Ltd.

CECIL GRAY

(1895–1951)

In his volume of memoirs, *Musical Chairs*, which appeared in 1948, Gray looked back on his association with Bartók, producing this paradoxical assessment of his character.

Béla Bartók, of all the great men I have known, was at once the simplest and most elusive, the easiest and the most difficult to describe. He was, to a greater extent than anyone since Mozart, the complete musician, to the exclusion of every other interest in life. He had no feeling for literature, painting, or other form of art whatever. I remember well an occasion . . . when he visited me at my place in London where I had a studio, the walls of which were lined with several thousand books. He looked at them in helpless, child-like amazement and said: 'You are a musician, and yet you seem to have nothing but books, books, books!' – He could not understand it. He was married at least twice, to my knowledge, and possibly oftener, but even if he had been married a hundred times I should never be able to believe that he was interested in women as such, or in any aspect of sex. He was, moreover, completely indifferent to the pleasures of the table, whether of food or wine. He was, in fact, a complete ascetic, but with the important distinction that, whereas ascetics are generally tormented by desire for the things which they deny themselves, Bartók was indifferent to all joys save one alone – music: nothing else existed for him. I should say that the only real human relationship in his life consisted in his friendship for Zoltán Kodály, to whom he was devoted; but even this, I suspect, on his side at least, was rather the comradeship of fellow-artists and fellow-workers than of warm human feeling.

Béla Bartók, in short, was completely inhuman. He hardly existed as a personality, but his impersonality was tremendous – he was the living incarnation and embodiment of the spirit of music. He was pure spirit, in fact, and his frail, intense and delicate physique gave the impression of something ethereal and disembodied, like a flame burning in oxygen. No need to inquire, no need to know, the cause of his death: he consumed himself, burnt himself away in the fire of his genius and of his selfless devotion to his art.

Musical Chairs, London (Home and van Thal), 1948, pp. 180–1

HANS W. HEINSHEIMER

(b. 1900)

In his volume of recollections published in 1952, Heinsheimer
elaborated on the uncompromising purity which he saw at the root
of Bartók's character.

. . . one could never think of him as a Hungarian, or, for that matter,
as belonging to any nation, group, or race. He was a human being,
pure, strict, of an almost abstract, sidereal quality, governed only by
the laws of decency, integrity, and faith, which he applied uncompro-
misingly to his own conduct and whose breach by others he never
forgave.

His angelic righteousness made him unfit for a world where
everything has become a give-and-take, where every hand washed
every other hand, and where there was an angle to everything. He
neither knew of nor tolerated angles. In his music as well as in his life
the very thought that he would ever compromise, accommodate himself
to the demands of the day, to practical considerations, to any detour
from what he felt to be right, was unthinkable. He would never take
the easy way, always the hard one.

How it all comes back to me now as I look at the picture here, on the
wall. The penetrating, clear, oh so serious eyes staring at me again,
demanding, quiet, uncompromising. The beautiful, wise face: calm,
stern, seldom ruffled by a short, rapidly subsiding wave of bitter,
puckish laughter.

He was shy, very quiet-spoken, constantly on the alert, suspicious of
everyone and everything. Never did I hear him raise his voice. When
others would shout he would clam up, retire silently, his face even
more drawn, into an icy sphere of disapproval that was much more
difficult to take and to dispel again than any temperamental outburst
would have been. He was small, almost tiny, terribly frail. His thin
body, the sharply pointed nose, the noble forehead with the soft, silken
hair, the transparent, childlike hands, the slow, swinging walk (as if he
walked on clouds) – his was the appearance of an ascetic, a thinker, a
brooder, a ponderer, never at ease, relentlessly driven by an inner
flame that eventually consumed him in the very sense of the word.

The first impression that struck me when I saw him again here in

America was how little he had changed. His hair had become white, but his face, his eyes, his body seemed never to change in all the years I knew him. He seemed quite ageless – he had never looked really young, and even through the years of his sickness he changed little outwardly.

Fanfare for 2 Pigeons, New York (Doubleday), 1952, pp. 107–8

ZOLTÁN KODÁLY

(1882–1967)

'I am very much alone here apart from my one friend, Kodály', wrote Bartók to Frederick Delius in 1910. From early in the century until 1940 Kodály was the only one with whom Bartók felt he could openly air his worries and enthusiasms, and upon whom he could rely in times of adversity. Kodály's career bore many parallels with Bartók's. He studied composition with the same teacher, Hans (János) Koessler. In 1906 he was awarded a doctorate for a thesis about Hungarian folk music; the following year he was appointed a professor at the Academy of Music, and taught there almost continuously until his retirement in 1956. Compositionally his style was more conservative than Bartók's and its folk influence was more strictly Hungarian in origin. He did not always agree with Bartók's methods of classifying folk music, and this was one of the reasons for a cooling of relations between the two at the time that Bartók moved to America. From the mid-1920s Kodály became increasingly interested in reforming music education in Hungary and he lived to see many fruits of his efforts in the years after the Second World War. Shortly after Bartók's death his 'one friend' made the following comments about his character.

Possibly, precise people are not content with the impressionistic pictures offered by poets and they crave, first of all, for the positive facts of science. Let us see what we should write about him on the basis of the group divisions of Kretschmer's characterology. None of the *cyclothyme* traits refer to him. There are, however, features of the other, the *schizothyme* group, that fit him: fragile, fine, sensitive, cool, severe, withdrawn, cold, dull, indolent. (Grades from the uppermost extreme to the lowest.) Up to the attribute cold, all fitted him. The categories of psychic tension (beginning from the bottom): fanatical, pedantic, unyielding, persevering, systematic. Only the upper extremes – capricious and confused – do not fit him, whilst the rest hit the nail right on the head. The agility aspect, speed in reactions to stimuli: inadequate, that is to say, reactions to stimuli quicker than customary. The subtitles of this heading are: restless, precipitate, hesitating, awkward, aristocratic, contrived, angular, rigid. With the exception of this last, all the rest more or less fit him. With respect to social relations: self-contained, reserved. Grades: idealist, reformer, revolutionary, systematic, organiser, self-willed, crotchety, dissatisfied, restrained, mistrustful, lonely, unsociable, misanthropical, brutal, anti-social. With the exception of the last three there is none that could not have been attributed to him with more or less reason. The categories of psychic tension: ingenious, lively, susceptible, energetic, inhibited. He could have been a typical example of the schizothyme mental form.

If we consider the more detailed characterisations we can distinguish three groups in each of the principal types as regards the differences in the degree of these qualities: an intermediate, a so-called average degree, then one showing a more intensive agility and finally a duller one below the first. The average is cold, energetic, systematic, consistent, calm and aristocratic. The more agile: fragile, inwardly sensitive, nervous, idealistic. All these qualities fit him. Only the attributes of the level below the average: rigid, nervous, strange, crotchety – do not correspond, although there were occasionally times when many people considered him eccentric and strange – and not without reason.

This is what characterology says of him. It sounds fairly precise, though here, too, the conditions of life are such that science cannot catch up with life. For even if it is true that these qualities emerged at times, man is not so simple a phenomenon that his eternal secret can be solved by a label with a few lines on it.

'Béla Bartók the Man' (1946) in *The Selected Writings of Zoltán Kodály*, tr. Lili Halápy and Fred Macnicol, London (Boosey & Hawkes), 1974, pp. 97–8. This extract is included by permission of Boosey & Hawkes Music Publishers Ltd.

In 1913 he learned Arabic because of his Arabian collecting. And in 1938 [*sic*; 1936], on account of his collecting trip at the invitation of the Turkish government, he studied enough Turkish to be able to write down his recordings himself. Alongside such knowledge of languages and such exceptional musical ability, only the collector's passion was necessary to make a large-scale folklorist out of anyone. And that, too, was there: from early childhood Bartók loved to collect insects and butterflies (later bringing home such specimens from Africa). He often spent the summer in the Swiss Alps. On such occasions he conscientiously collected and pressed the mountain flowers and read the various plant identifications. Besides this he collected folk embroidery, carvings, jugs, and plates, and studied their literature. Such widely diverging interests would have dissipated any other person's energy. It was Bartók's achievement that his various activities instead of obstructing each other, helped each other.

His creative and performing work was accomplished with the precision and fastidious care of the scientist. His scientific work, apart from the necessary precision and thoroughness, is brought to life by artistic intuition. The folklorist offered the artist knowledge of a rich musical life from outside the ramparts of art music. On the other hand, the folklorist received from the artist superior musical knowledge and perception. Apart from the two being an inseparable unit, in his work he was nevertheless able to separate them, unlike the majority of art-dabbling folklorists or artists who dip into ethnology. For he went all the way in both.

For the roots of science and of art are the same. Each, in its own way, reflects the world. The basic conditions: sharp powers of observation, precise expression of the life observed, and raising it to a higher synthesis. And the foundation of scientific and artistic greatness is also the same: just man, *vir justus*. And Bartók, who left Europe because he was unable to bear the injustice raging here any longer, followed Rousseau's slogan: *vitam impendere vero* (stake one's life on justice).

Thus it was possible, without any university studies, without scientific training, for someone who started out as a great artist to become a great scientist.

The man of justice can be recognised by the extraordinary sense of responsibility in his life and work. This was present in Bartók from the very beginning and merely increased in the whole course of his development.

In the works of his youth he sought an outlet from the ups and downs of life in the verbose, animated, though somewhat loose forms. Later his ever increasing concentration thrust out every superfluity, everything inessential.

Constantly he observed and studied; to the works of his contemporaries few active composers devoted so much attention. But he spent no less time on the earlier composers. Everywhere he sought his ancestors, his spiritual brothers.

He was stimulated by the knowledge of the loose and romantically incomplete composition training of his youth. In the end, having browsed through a borrowed copy of Jeppesen's counterpoint book one summer, he finally bought it in 1938. At the same time an occasional Palestrina volume came into view among the piles of music which covered his piano. He realised that here we can admire what is not to be experienced elsewhere – the highest level of responsibility. Who knows what he might have written once these later influences had matured in him, if cruel fate had not snatched the pen out of his hand so early?

'Bartók the Folklorist' (1950), *ibid.*, pp. 105–7. This extract is included by permission of Boosey & Hawkes Music Publishers Ltd.

VI
Bartók in brief

ALBAN BERG

I consider Bartók has a very original and powerful character, although his character is far distant from me, personally.

Statement of 1920, reproduced in János Breuer, 'Alban Berg Bartókról', *Muzsika*, vol. 23/9 (September 1980), p. 4

ENDRE ADY

Yes, Bartók . . . somehow I imagined he was bigger.

Reported in Denijs Dille, 'Bartók et Ady', *Studia Musicologica*, vol. 23 (1981), p. 126

BENJAMIN BRITTEN

I am always more interested in the man who writes the music than in the form and technique he applies in his writing . . . Shostakovich, Bartók and Kodály are much more exciting and interesting to me than the avantgarde composers.

Statement from the mid-1960s, reproduced in Előd Juhász, 'Britten in Hungary', *New Hungarian Quarterly*, no. 66 (Summer 1977), p. 201

IGOR STRAVINSKY

I never liked his music anyway.

Statement of 27 September 1945, as reported in Vera Stravinsky and Robert Craft, *Stravinsky in Pictures and Documents*, New York (Simon and Schuster), 1978, p. 648

AARON COPLAND

By now I have met many hundreds of composers, but I should not think that one of them has been able to approach Bartók in sensitivity and musical sincerity. In his presence one felt inescapably that here was an extraordinary personality. I feel that the American public is now fully aware of the unrivalled legacy which Bartók left to the development of contemporary music.

'In memoriam 1945. szeptember 26.', *Muzsika*, vol. 13/9 (September 1970), p. 7

LÁSZLÓ LAJTHA

Above all, Bartók was Hungarian, and he served his country with a great sense of duty. He worked so much, hardly without a break. How often I had to wonder that that delicate, fragile body of his could endure such enormous, ceaseless activity. It could stand up to it, however, because of the sense of conscience, responsibility and duty which invisibly drove him.

'Megemlékezés Bartók Béláról', *Muzsika*, vol. 8/10 (October 1965), p. 3

FERNANDO LOPES GRAÇA

But even if his body was so slight and delicate, one could immediately sense the unusual breadth of his spirit just from a single look from him. What a look! Bartók's deep black eyes looked straight out and radiated some kind of flame or fluid which pierced to the very core of one's being, and left you as if in a trance. In his countenance – ever tinged with sadness – they acted like an abyss, like a fiery focus, where the most refined passion and the most penetrating intellect burned in equilibrium.

'Évocation de Béla Bartók', *La Revue musicale*, no. 224 (1955), p. 114

MICHAEL TIPPETT

I never met him and saw him only once. He came with his second wife to England just before the last war and played with her, for the BBC, the Sonata for 2 Pianos and Percussion. After the concert he was dawdling by the piano and our eyes accidentally met as I watched him from among the seats. I remember the sense of being for a second the object of an acute spiritual vision, which seemed to look at once right inside me from right inside himself. I am certain he had no consciousness of the extreme subjective impression this moment made on me, and which I can recall to this day with eidetic accuracy. But I am also certain I saw something of the real Bartók, if only by intimation.

Preface to *Béla Bartók Letters*, ed. János Demény, London (Faber and Faber), 1971, p. 9

EDITH GERSON-KIWI

His great legacy to the younger generation of composers is to have conveyed to them the definite possibility of a new alphabet, grammar and syntax for modern music, not contrived in a vacuum of speculation like the dodecaphonic system, but built up on the pre-alphabetical elements of a living folk language in song and dance.

'Béla Bartók – Scholar in Folk Music', *Music and Letters*, vol. 38 (1957), p. 153

BÉLA BARTÓK

I never created new theories in advance, I hated such ideas. I had, of course, a very definite feeling about certain directions to take, but at the time of the work I did not care about the designations which would apply to those directions or to their sources. This attitude does not mean that I composed without . . . set plans and without sufficient control. The plans were concerned with the spirit of the new work and with technical problems (for instance, formal structure involved by the spirit of the work), all more or less instinctively felt, but I never was concerned with general theories to be applied to the works I was going to write. Now that the greatest part of my work has already been written, certain general tendencies appear – general formulas from which theories can be deduced. But even now I would prefer to try new ways and means instead of deducing theories.

'Harvard Lectures' (1943), in *Béla Bartók Essays*, ed. Benjamin Suchoff, London (Faber and Faber), 1976, p. 376

Select bibliography

Readers may find the following selection of English-language volumes useful
in deepening their understanding of Bartók's life and works.

1 *Writings of Bartók*
Béla Bartók Letters, ed. János Demény, London (Faber and Faber), 1971
Béla Bartók Essays, ed. Benjamin Suchoff, London (Faber and Faber), 1976
Rumanian Folk Music, ed. Benjamin Suchoff, The Hague (Martinus Nijhoff),
    1967–75. 5 vols.
Turkish Folk Music from Asia Minor, ed. Benjamin Suchoff, Princeton
    (Princeton University Press), 1976
A. Adnan Saygun: *Béla Bartók's Folk Music Research in Turkey*, ed. László
    Vikár, Budapest (Akadémiai Kiadó), 1976, pp. 9–188
Yugoslav Folk Music, ed. Benjamin Suchoff, Albany (State University of New
    York Press), 1978. 4 vols., including, as its first volume, Béla Bartók and
    Albert B. Lord, *Serbo-Croatian Folk Songs*, New York (Columbia
    University Press), 1951
The Hungarian Folk Song, ed. Benjamin Suchoff, Albany (State University of
    New York Press), 1981; originally issued as *Hungarian Folk Music*,
    London (Oxford University Press), 1931

2 *Writings of others about Bartók, his music, and Bartók studies*
Antokoletz, Elliott: *The Music of Béla Bartók*, Berkeley (University of
    California Press), 1984
Antokoletz, Elliott: *Béla Bartók: A Guide to Research*, New York (Garland),
    1988
Bónis, Ferenc: *Béla Bartók: His Life in Pictures and Documents*, 2nd edition,
    Budapest (Corvina), 1981
Crow, Todd ed.: *Bartók Studies*, Detroit (Information Coordinators), 1976
Gillies, Malcolm: *Bartók in Britain: A Guided Tour*, Oxford (Clarendon),
    1989
Griffiths, Paul: *Bartók*, London (Dent), 1984
Kárpáti, János: *Bartók's String Quartets*, Budapest (Corvina), 1975
Kroó, György: *A Guide to Bartók*, Budapest (Corvina), 1974
Lampert, Vera and Somfai, László: 'Béla Bartók' in *The New Grove: Modern
    Masters*, London (Macmillan), 1984, pp. 1–101
Lendvai, Ernő: *The Workshop of Bartók and Kodály*, Budapest (Editio
    Musica), 1983

Lesznai, Lajos: *Bartók*, London (Dent), 1973

McCabe, John: *Bartók's Orchestral Music*, London (BBC), 1974

Ránki, György ed.: *Bartók and Kodály Revisited*, Budapest (Akadémiai Kiadó), 1987

Stevens, Halsey: *The Life and Music of Béla Bartók*, 2nd edition, New York (Oxford University Press), 1964

Suchoff, Benjamin: *Guide to Bartók's Mikrokosmos*, 2nd edition reprint, New York (Da Capo), 1983

Tallián, Tibor: *Béla Bartók: The Man and His Work*, Budapest (Corvina), 1988

Ujfalussy, József: *Béla Bartók*, Budapest (Corvina), 1971

Walsh, Stephen: *Bartók Chamber Music*, London (BBC), 1982

3 *Specialist journals* (articles in various languages)
Documenta Bartókiana
Studia Musicologica

4 *Facsimile editions of Bartók's compositions*
Dille, Denijs ed.: *Béla Bartók – Zoltán Kodály: Hungarian Folksongs*, London (Boosey & Hawkes), 1970

Somfai, László ed.: *Béla Bartók: Sonata*, Budapest (Editio Musica), 1980

Somfai, László ed.: *Béla Bartók: Black Pocket-book*, Budapest (Editio Musica), 1987

5 *Writings about Hungarian history and culture*
Berend, I.T. and Ránki, G.: *Hungary: A Century of Economic Development*, Newton Abbot (David & Charles), 1974

Czigány, Lóránt: *The Oxford History of Hungarian Literature*, Oxford (Clarendon), 1984

János, Andrew C.: *The Politics of Backwardness in Hungary*, Princeton (Princeton University Press), 1982

Macartney, C.A.: *Hungary: A Short History*, Edinburgh (Edinburgh University Press), 1962

Szabolcsi, Bence: *A Concise History of Hungarian Music*, London (Barrie & Rockliff), 1964

Index